FOR WOMEN ONLY

The Fine Art of Being a Woman

Edited by
Evelyn R. Petersen
and J. Allan Petersen

TYNDALE
House Publishers, Inc.
Wheaton, Illinois

Coverdale House Publishers, Ltd.
London, England

*Library of Congress
Catalog Card Number
73-93968
ISBN 8423-0895-4 cloth;
8423-0896-2 paper*

*Copyright © 1974 by
Tyndale House Publishers, Inc.,
Wheaton, Illinois.
All rights reserved.*

*First printing,
February 1974.*

*Printed in the
United States of America*

CONTENTS

FOREWORD
by Ruth Bell Graham

I can think of no more rewarding job than that of wife and mother. Exhilarating and exhausting, inspiring and demanding, hard and happy.

And perhaps no institution in our country has come under attack more than marriage and the home.

It is time for Christians to rethink their position on marriage and the family in the light of the Bible. It is time for the Christian woman particularly, in the light of the new emphasis on women's liberation, to reevaluate her role.

This book will help her do just that.

PREFACE

Evelyn R. Petersen, Omaha, Nebraska

I'm so glad God made me a woman! I love it! Even as a little girl, I enjoyed all that goes along with femininity. In fact, I thoroughly enjoy living!

Life has been very good to me. My wonderful parents loved me and showed it in so many ways. They provided us eight children with a warm Christian atmosphere, and followed the old Dutch custom of Bible reading and prayer at every meal, three times a day. The summer months, spent together as a family in our mountain cabin, were sheer delight. Then my marriage to an evangelist was an exact answer to my girlhood prayers. Ultimately, God gave me a speaking and counseling ministry to other women, and the privilege of traveling at home and overseas.

But I entered marriage with great idealism, not expecting difficulties, but knowing if they did come, they would be few and easily handled. But life just isn't that simple. I was hardly ready to face the inevitable disappointment that came from having my girlish dreams thwarted. The responsibility was really more than I had bargained for, and I came head on into the problems that overwhelm many a woman.

At one time, I was completely enveloped in loneliness and self-pity. After our third boy was born I felt trapped and utterly alone, with my evangelist husband traveling most of the time. Why would God lead me to marry a man, only to have him gone more than he was home? Something seemed to be dying inside of me. When he'd leave for another crusade, I would cry and accuse him of not caring about me. I became bitter and resentful.

Of course, rearing the children alone only added fuel to the fire. How could I possibly cope with three lively boys when their father was gone so much? How could I find wisdom and strength to face all the childhood diseases and disasters? And there were plenty of them. And what would I do when they became teen-agers — with driving, dating, and multiplied temptations?

I began to doubt. Did God really care about me personally? Was he a loving Father, as I had been taught? Would a real Christian always be struggling with sin, and be constantly defeated? Would God keep on forgiving?

I slipped into deep depression. A thick, black cloud seemed to smother my soul, and for months paralyzing fear and utter hopelessness gripped me. I lived in a daze of unbelief and confusion, often despairing of life.

I had to learn so much. My knowledge and understanding had to be increased, if I was ever to rise above my difficulties. So I began diligently reading the Bible every day, saturating myself with the Word of God. Also, I sought out other books relating to my present need, and devoured them. As I read, I prayed for wisdom, and God graciously gave me direction through these circumstances, above all I could ask or think.

Today I am a free woman, relaxed in spirit and filled with peace and joy. God has been teaching me how to take advantage of every problem and turn it to good. What I have learned from counseling others has confirmed my own experience — women have special needs that must be met if we are to find fulfillment and be used by God. We must have practical and spiritual understanding.

This book helps provide these. Each chapter was chosen for its insights into an important phase of a woman's life. You will find in these pages insights into what you are and what you can be.

ACKNOWLEDGMENTS

"Do You Like Yourself?" by Eugenia Price, taken from *A Woman's Choice* copyright © 1962 Zondervan Publishing House, Grand Rapids, Mich. Used by permission.

"A Worm in the Apple," by Gladys Hunt, taken from *Ms Means Myself,* copyright © 1972 Gladys Hunt. Used by permission of Zondervan Publishing House.

"Everybody's Lonesome," by Inez Spence, condensed from Chapter 6 of *When The Heart Is Lonely,* copyright © 1970 Baker Book House, Grand Rapids, Mich. Reprinted by permission.

"That Certain Something," by Arlene Francis, from *That Certain Something,* copyright © 1960 Arlene Francis. Reprinted by permission of Julian Messner, division of Simon & Schuster, Inc.

"How Big Is Your World?" by Charlene Johnson (Char J. Crawford), from *Beautiful Homemaking,* copyright © 1961. Reprinted by permission of Fortress Press, Philadelphia, Pa.

"The Three R's of Business," by Wilbert Scheer, from *From Nine to Five.* Reprinted by permission of The Dartnell Corporation, Chicago, Ill.

"Moonlighting Mother," by Martha Nelson, from May 1972 *Home Life*, copyright © 1972 The Sunday School Board of the Southern Baptist Convention. All rights reserved. Used by permission.

"The Truth About Consequences," by Evelyn Shafner, from *When Mothers Work*. Reprinted with permission of Pacific Press, Santa Barbara, Ca.

"Twentieth-Century Lydia," by Leslie Parrott, condensed from Chapter 13 of *Easy To Live With,* copyright © 1970 Baker Book House, Grand Rapids, Mich. Reprinted by permission.

"You and Other Women," by

Eileen Guder, taken from *We're Never Alone,* copyright © 1965 Zondervan Publishing House, Grand Rapids, Mich. Used by permission.

"Live Alone and Love It," reprinted by permission from April 1973 *Coronet.*

"A Few Kind Words for Femininity," by Mrs. Norman Vincent Peale, from *The Adventure of Being A Wife,* copyright © 1971 Ruth S. Peale and Arthur Gordon. Published by Prentice-Hall, Inc., Englewood Cliffs, N.J. Used by permission.

"Nine Steps to a Longer Life," by Blake Clark, reprinted with permission from October 1970 *Reader's Digest,* copyright © 1970 The Reader's Digest Association, Inc.

"Take Time for Yourself," by T. Leo Brannon, reprinted with permission from March 1965 *The Christian Home,* copyright © 1965 Graded Press.

"Don't Worry!" by John Edmund Haggai, taken from *How To Win Over Worry,* copyright © 1959 John Edmund Haggai. Used by permission of Zondervan Publishing House.

"What to Do About Premenstrual Tension," by William A. Nolen, M.D., copyright © 1972 by the author. Reprinted by permission of Lurton Blassingame.

"Inside Insomnia," by Jean E. Laird, from March 1973 *Marriage,* copyright © 1973 Marriage, St. Meinrad, Ind. Used by permission.

"Menopause—Something to Look Forward To?" by Sally Olds, condensed and reprinted from May 1970 *Today's Health,* published by the American Medical Association. Used by permission of the author.

"What Does a Man Really Want in a Wife?" by Robert

H. Schuller, from *Power Ideas for a Happy Family,* Fleming H. Revell, Old Tappan, N.J. Used by permission.

"Love You?—I Am You!" by Arthur A. Rouner, Jr., condensed from Chapter 7 of *Marrying Sam Speaks Out.* Reprinted by permission of Baker Book House, Grand Rapids, Mich.

"Sensitivity and Your Sexuality," by Sandra S. Chandler, from *The Sensitive Woman,* copyright © 1972 Compass Press, Pasadena, Ca. Used by permission.

"How Not to Be the Girl He Left Behind," by Dorothy Carnegie, from *How to Help Your Husband Get Ahead.* Reprinted by permission of Hawthorn Books, Inc., New York, N.Y.

"Win Him to Christ," by Jill Renich, taken from *To Have And To Hold,* copyright © 1972 The Zondervan Corporation. Used by permission.

"Fill the Vacuum," by Patricia Young, from March 1970 *Marriage,* copyright © Marriage, St. Meinrad, Ind. Used by permission.

"Wife or Mother?" by Henry E. White, Jr., from August 1972 *Home Life,* copyright © 1972 The Sunday School Board of the Southern Baptist Convention. All rights reserved. Used by permission.

"Does Your Daughter Have A Mini-Mother?" by Abigail Van Buren, from "Are You A Mini-Mother?" from March 1969 *Family Circle.* Used by permission.

"Let Your Son Grow Up," by Carlyle Marney, from *Dangerous Fathers, Problem Mothers, and Terrible Teens,* copyright © 1958 Abingdon Press, Nashville, Tenn. Used by permission.

"Discipline for Life," by Dr. Fitzhugh Dodson, from *How To Parent,* copyright © 1970

Fitzhugh Dodson. Reprinted by permission of Nash Publishing Corporation, Los Angeles, Ca.

"Lift Your Receiver," by David and Virginia Edens, from *Why God Gave Children Parents* (Nashville: Broadman Press, copyright © 1966). Used by permission.

"Build Their Self-Image," by Elizabeth Peterson, from August 1972 *Covenant Companion*. Reprinted by permission of author.

"Show Them Courtesy," Mildred Martin, from August 1968 *Home Life,* copyright © 1968 The Sunday School Board of the Southern Baptist Convention. All rights reserved. Used by permission.

"Say I'm Sorry," by Ruth Hayward. Reprinted by permission of Bill Hayward.

"Mrs. Billy Graham Answers Your Questions," by Ruth Graham and Joan Gage, from *Ladies Home Journal.* Used by permission.

"Make God Real," by Robert H. Lauer, from July 1968 *Home Life,* copyright © 1968 The Sunday School Board of the Southern Baptist Convention. All rights reserved. Used by permission.

"Give Children Spiritual Direction," by Patricia Hershey, from Summer 1966 *Today's Christian Mother.* Reprinted by permission of Standard Publishing Co., Cincinnati, Ohio.

"Are You a 'Trapped' Housewife?" by Norman M. Lobsenz and Clark W. Blackburn, from *How To Stay Married,* published by the Cowles Book Company, a subsidiary of Henry Regnery Company, Chicago, Ill. Copyright © 1968, 1969 by Family Service Association of America. Used by permission.

"Have a Master Plan," by Marguerite and Willard Beecher, from *Parents on the Run,* New York: Julian Press, copyright © 1955; A & W Promotional Book Corp., 1973. Used by permission.

"Does Anybody Like Housework?" by Wilda Fancher, from *The Christian Woman in the Christian Home* (Nashville: Broadman Press, copyright © 1972). Used by permission.

"Enjoy Your Family," by Marion Leach Jacobsen, taken from *How to Keep Your Family Together and Still Have Fun,* copyright © 1969, 1972 Zondervan Publishing House, Grand Rapids, Mich. Used by permission.

"The Secret of Hospitality," by Irene Burk Harrell, condensed from *Security Blankets — Family Size,* copyright © 1973 Word, Inc. Reprinted by permission of publisher.

"Get Along with Your In-laws," by Edith M. Stern, from April 1964 *Parents' Magazine.* Reprinted through the courtesy of *Parents' Magazine,* New York, N.Y.

"Her Need for Security," by Pat Hare, reprinted by permission from March 1967 *His,* student magazine of Inter-Varsity Christian Fellowship, copyright © 1967 IVCF.

"Her Need for Liberation," by Joyce Landorf, condensed and reprinted by permission from *To Lib Or Not To Lib,* published by Victor Books, copyright © 1972 Scripture Press Publications, Inc.

"Dare to Trust God," by Catherine Marshall, from *Beyond Ourselves,* copyright © 1961 Catherine Marshall. Used with permission of McGraw-Hill Book Company.

"Prayer Is Conversation," by Rosalind Rinker, taken from *Prayer: Conversing with God,* copyright © 1959 Zondervan

Publishing House. Used by permission.

"Me? Grow Up?" by Mary Lou Lacy, from *A Woman Wants God*, copyright © 1959 by C. D. Deans. Used by permission of John Knox Press.

"Unforgiveness Is Unforgivable," by David W. Augsburger, from *The Freedom of Forgiveness*, copyright © 1970 Moody Press and Moody Bible Institute of Chicago. Used by permission.

"The Way Up Is Down," by Mabel Francis, taken from *One Shall Chase A Thousand* and used by permission of Christian Publications, Inc., Harrisburg, Pa.

"Find Your Place in the Church," by Lois Bartel, condensed by permission from *A Farthing in Her Hand*, edited by Helen Alderfer, copyright © 1964 Herald Press, Scottdale, Pa.

"Put On Your Coffee Pot," by Helen Kooiman, taken from *Share Your Faith*, edited by Russell T. Hitt, copyright © 1970 Zondervan Publishing House. Used by permission.

"Don't Limit God," by Frances Gardner Hunter, from *Go, Man, Go*, copyright © 1969 Warner Press, Anderson, Ind. Reprinted by permission.

"Finding Peace in Dark Hours," by Elizabeth Strachan, reprinted by permission from *Eternity*, copyright © 1969 The Evangelical Foundation, Philadelphia, Pa.

THE FOLLOWING SHORT FEATURES are reprinted with the permission of the copyright owners:

"Father, please don't let me . . ." by Marjorie Holmes, from *Who Am I, God?*, copyright © 1970, 1971 Marjorie Holmes Mighell. Reprinted by permission of Doubleday & Company, Inc., New York, N.Y.

"I have often thought it would be . . ." by Helen Keller, condensed from "Three Days to See," from *The Atlantic Monthly* and used by permission.

"There is nothing unusual . . ." by Inez Spence, from *When the Heart Is Lonely*, copyright © 1970 Baker Book House, Grand Rapids, Mich. Used by permission.

"This business of being self-appointed . . ." by Marjorie Frost, from Chapter 1 of *Charming You*, copyright © 1968 Zondervan Publishing House, Grand Rapids, Mich. Used by permission.

"Short Course in Human Relations," reprinted from April-May 1973 *The Christian Reader*. Used by permission.

"I wished for home and husband . . ." by Geraldine Everett Gohn, from January 1970 *Home Life*, copyright © 1969 The Sunday School Board of the Southern Baptist Convention. All rights reserved. Used by permission.

"The idea of a maternity 'sabbatical' . . ." by Joyce Kissock Lubold, from *This Half of The Apple Is Mine*, copyright © 1965 by the author. Reprinted by permission of Doubleday & Company, Inc., New York, N.Y.

"Some studies show . . .", from the radio broadcast "Pause for Good News." Used by permission.

"If, from all the thousands . . ." is reprinted with permission of the Nightingale-Conant Corporation, Chicago, copyright © 1971, producers of the Earl Nightingale radio program, "Our Changing World."

"Faith is . . . cooperating with God . . .", by Pamela Reeve, from *Faith Is . . .*, copyright © 1970 Multnomah Press, Portland, Ore. Used by permission.

"Instead of withdrawing . . ." by Paul E. Little, from *How To*

1 THE WOMAN AND HERSELF

DO YOU LIKE YOURSELF?

by Eugenia Price

Among Christians, the expression *self-love* has unfortunately come to mean something to be avoided at any cost. This is far from a helpful concept.

Jesus said we were to love our neighbor in the same way we love ourselves. If he had meant we weren't to love ourselves, he would never have used this analogy. On the other hand, he also said we were to deny ourselves. Is this a contradiction? If we face the real issues involved in the concept of love as Jesus taught and demonstrated it, no.

Undoubtedly we are to deny or refuse the kind of destructive self-love that propels us into the grabbing behavior in which Mother Eve indulged herself. But there is a *right* and *creative* self-love that is affirmed by Jesus' instruction to love our neighbors with the kind of concern we have for ourselves.

Concern is the key word to this puzzling concept of self-love. You and I must have genuine, God-directed concern for ourselves. If you drink all the coffee you want, just because you want it, it can be destructive. There is no concern here for your real self, only a desire gratified at the moment your nerves are screaming for more caffeine. If you really care about yourself you'll drink only a cup or two, and stop.

There is nothing destructive in real self-love. In fact, if we don't love ourselves, we belittle the God who cared enough about us to create us in the first place. More than that, we hamper our own growth. Here we must make a distinction between hampering and pampering: The right kind of self-love never *hampers,* but the wrong kind of self-love always *pampers*.

I have just returned from a short but exhausting speaking engagement. The first two days I was home, I slept as long as I wanted to in the mornings. This was not *pampering*. Had I forced myself to get up before I was properly rested, I would have been *hampering.* My knowledge of myself, and my limitations when I have not had enough sleep, clears the issue here. Some people seem able to go on working day after day, with night after night of short sleep. I cannot. This I know and accept about myself, and act accordingly.

Too much to eat at bedtime, lack of sleep and adequate exercise, irregular functional habits, a sagging mattress, or incorrect glasses can cloud the windows of our souls. To mistreat our bodies means we don't love ourselves in the right way. The wrong kind of self-love is in reality self-hatred. Here is an example:

"My parents slaved and scrimped to put me through college. I am a school teacher and I despise it! For six years I have strained every effort to adjust to my profession. I try with every ounce of energy to love the children and to have real interest in them. At the end of every day of these six years, I have hated myself for failing miserably. I feel so ungrateful toward my parents and so ashamed before my students. I just don't understand myself at all."

She certainly didn't understand herself. Six years is long enough to try anything for "inner size." This woman finally began to respect herself enough to face the real issues. A good teacher is a *called* one. She reexamined her abilities, applied for a position in personnel work, and is now making a good adjustment.

"I hate housework! I hate being tied to the responsibility of three meals a day and four children. In fact, I dodge my responsibilities every chance I get. I got into this mess when I was too young to know my own mind and now I know I should have been a writer. I almost hate *you*, because you're not in prison as I am and can write for a living!"

The teacher could change jobs. What about this woman? Should she divorce her husband and desert her children? Obviously not. The key lies in the different *tone* of the two letters. The school teacher felt a failure. Her attitude was one of wanting to make a "go" of a wrong choice. The woman who hates her domestic life seems only resentful and sorry for herself. Many women find themselves in this "prison." Many find themselves in the wrong job, as did the teacher.

But the key to *living through* the problem lies, I believe, in first taking stock of our true feelings about ourselves. Utmost honesty is required. If we simply feel mistreated and a victim of circumstances, as this housewife so obviously did, we cannot do more than endure.

Understanding and loving ourselves does not imply the right to self-pity and resentment. Can you imagine Jesus urging us to love ourselves in that destructive way? There is a right kind of self-love, and there is a wrong kind.

It seems equally difficult to discover the truth about both. Most of us have both, and then comes the problem of distinguishing. Which is to be dealt with? Which is to be cultivated?

When we find our "love" causing strain of any kind for the other person, we can know at once that it is destructive self-love.

"My heart is broken over my daughter. My son is so good to me. He visits me every day, sees that I have plenty of groceries, and never misses calling me at night before he and his wife go to bed.

"But my daughter is just the opposite. Ever since my husband died I have been so lonely, but do you think my daughter cares? Oh, she calls me two or three times a week, and drops in now and then. But I don't dare ask her to do me a favor. When I do, she grumbles and tells me it will do me good to get out and run the errand myself! I haven't wanted to go out at all since their father died. I'm much happier just to stay in the house. My son understands me, but my daughter doesn't."

Obviously the daughter understands this woman and the son does not. No wonder she doesn't visit her mother more often (although once or twice a week should be enough). This mother loves herself more than either child, and because she does, she puts her children in a strain over her. When a woman just sits at home and waits for attention, those outside begin to dread her. It becomes a duty to "go by Mother's house." It should and can be a delight. I love my own mother more now than before my father died.

She has left me free to love her. Our friendship is one of my big joys.

Self-love of the possessive, self-centered variety shackles the hearts and spirits and minds of those we "love." Are you tying someone in knots because you love yourself wrongly? If so, you are not only binding that person, you are binding yourself as well. And your *self* is meant to be free.

"If the Son shall make you free, you shall be free indeed." Jesus meant this for everyone. This is why he longs for us to love ourselves enough, and in the right way, so we will want to be free.

Since my father has been gone, I have written at least a funny card to my mother almost every day. I don't do it because she expects it. I do it because I love her and think about her that often. If several days go by with no word from me, she doesn't feel neglected. She simply knows I'm busy and is glad. If anything were wrong, she would be notified. She knows I'm happiest when I'm busy, and because she loves *me* and wants the best for me, she doesn't sink into self-pity when I happen not to write to her for a while. We are free to love each other *and* ourselves in our relation-ship. If I felt guilty and tied to this kind of regular correspondence, I would soon resent having to do it.

Real love *liberates*. And in the climate of liberty, love can grow.

A middle-aged couple had been going together for five years, with the idea of getting married. Then the gentleman involved began to back down. The woman almost lost her mind. "I love him, I love him!" she wailed. "He's my whole life. I want to take care of him and know that he's all right, and after all this time of being so close I don't see how he can suddenly grow cold toward me."

She had smothered him with possessive love and the wise gentleman acted in time to prevent a lifetime of misery for them both. If she had been willing to see her wrongly directed love, perhaps they could have gone on with their marriage plans after a while. She couldn't see or she wouldn't see that her "love" was entirely self-directed. She loved him because of the way

she felt when she was with him. Her concern when
he asked to postpone their marriage was not for him
to find himself and be sure. It was for her *self*.
She couldn't live without taking care of him. Three years
have gone by and she is still trying to find someone
to listen to her pathetic story.

If you aren't, first of all, concerned for the welfare
and freedom of the person you think you love, then you
are mistaken in your idea of real love. If you are
constantly being hurt and slighted by someone, it isn't
because you love that person so much. It is because
you love *you* in a self-protecting, egocentric way.
You will suffer, if this is true, but perhaps not as much
as those who really love you and hate the destructiveness
of your misplaced self-love.

To love ourselves rightly, we must leave ourselves free
to be whole persons in the midst of anything life can
hand us. When we love and respect ourselves this way,
we will have tapped the Source of love and will find
ourselves able to give constructive, creative devotion to
those whom God has given us to love.

To love ourselves rightly, we must love ourselves
in God. We must respect ourselves as God's creation,
and love ourselves as redeemed daughters of the King.

Father, please don't let me be so impatient with myself.
I fret, I scold, I deplore my many shortcomings.
Why am I so messy? Why do I get myself into such
complicated situations? Now why did I say that?
Won't I ever learn?

My mind carries on an idiot monologue of self-
reproach. Or I lie awake bewailing the day's mistakes.
I wince before them. I call myself names I would never
call other people. I am stung and tormented by these
self-lacerations.

I know all this is useless. The more I berate myself
the worse I seem to become. And it gets between us.
It is unworthy of the trust I should have in You who
made me as I am, and who loves me despite my faults.

I know that You want me to be aware of them and to improve as best I can. But help me to forgive myself a little more quickly, to be a little kinder to myself.

Marjorie Holmes

A WORM IN THE APPLE

by Gladys Hunt

Life for the single woman has never looked better. Professionally she can enter almost any field her abilities and inner drives might inspire. The career girl is definitely a positive concept in today's world. She often owns her own car, has her own apartment, and has the freedom to order her life without having to take others into account. An aura, a mystique hovers over the career woman.

But that's only half the story. The single woman must still battle the instinct of her heart and body, the injustice of discrimination, and in today's world a feminist raid on her value system. If she is restless, there is irony in her discontent. Clearly there aren't enough men to go around: 109 women to every 100 men. And some of the women who have the men seem strangely unhappy with the idea of belonging to them. They complain of having lost their identity, while it may seem to the unmarried women that society is structured to give identity only to the married. There's a worm in the apple no matter where you bite!

Many single women have to wrestle repeatedly with the longing to be married. Loneliness is real. It is hardly an issue one settles once for all. Handling this inner longing presents a problem to the single woman. She may often feel frustrated and even angry at God for her spinsterhood. She may feel deprived of sex and motherhood. But she has to feign contentment. If she allows her disappointment at being unmarried to show, she is the brunt of jokes and ridicule.

Somewhere along the line women ought to catch on that marriage does not automatically equal happiness. We have to stop letting society — and the news media's interpretation of male thinking — tell us who we are. Every woman should have the chance to be her unique self without the trappings and trimmings of psychological hang-ups or society's pressures. She not only has the right to be an individual; she has the obligation to be one.

She cannot make any useful contribution to life unless she does. After all, the purpose of life is to live it eagerly and without fear.

Women are exploited emotionally about physical beauty. Badgered by Madison Avenue's manipulation of their natural desire to be attractive, women go through painful anxieties over their appearance. And that's not all bad. Every woman ought to look as good as she can. Sloppiness is no virtue. Neither is a head of hair that needs a good styling job. Perfume smells better than body odor. Too many rolls of fat are neither healthy nor pretty, and a scrubbed-looking face is more pleasant than an overly painted one. Looking our best makes us stand taller and gives us more confidence. Our mistake comes when we derive our value from our physical appearance. If we believe that an unattractive nose makes an unattractive person we've lost the battle at the first pass. Don't be found hating thick ankles more than an ugly soul!

All women are potentially selfish simply because they are human. The hazards for single women to become rigid and self-centered are greater. The married woman will have her selfishness contested by both her husband and children. If she doesn't outgrow it, she leaves a scar on more than one life. The disaster for the single person comes when she retreats from interpersonal relationships and increasingly grows inflexible, opinionated, set in her ways, and miserably self-centered.

Some women are neurotic; they may need to change either their job or their outside interests. Others have sharp, shrill voices; they need to relax inside and learn how to laugh and play. Some women come into any friend's life like a two-ton Mack truck; they need to examine what dominance-need makes them act this way. Some women have trouble loving, and need to learn the freedom love brings.

But many single women grow older with quiet good humor and rich lives. They spread love and light and joy around because they have a large supply of it inside. They enter the lives of others with an easy grace. They are interesting, loving human beings who aren't obsessed with their singleness. Men like them; so do women. Usually they have a high calling and are doing what they enjoy.

These women have not let marriage define life for them. They are confident of their personal worth, and live with a wholesome awareness and aliveness to the world that belies the stereotyped image of the spinster. No one pities them, because their life is wide and full and rich.

In fact, the kind of single women I am thinking about could rightly be called sensuous. *Sensuous* is a word that needs to be rescued from purely sexual connotations. To be sensuous means to be present in every moment of life — feeling life, enjoying it, learning, exploring, appreciating the world God made and the people in it. It is simply to be alive in one's senses.

Many of these women have given themselves to large purposes in life. They may feel called by God not to marry to fulfill the task, to use the gift, to finish the job. In short, they are caught up in an adventure larger than their own life, and in the end this is what makes life significant and fulfilling for anyone.

In particular, women have done an incredible job in the mission of the church with an enthusiasm and dedication that puts men to shame. Women counselors, teachers, doctors, nurses, translation specialists, writers — the list of noble achievements is known only to God. The important factor for us to observe is that these women have linked their lives up with God and the ultimate meaning of the universe. Anyone who looks at such a woman and bemoans, "What a pity she didn't marry!" has a small view of what living is all about. From my point of view, I'd rather ask a question about the judgment of the men who passed up these noble women to choose an often shallow, self-centered woman instead. But I am content to let God be the Sovereign who calls such women into adventure with himself.

It is true to say that the single woman has a difficult task. She must adjust to hope. She must be prepared for marriage if it comes and for singleness if it remains. Some women decide that they do not want to marry, and therefore settle into a single life. They do not live with either the joy or the sorrow of expectancy. Others take matters into their own hands and maneuver for marriage, sometimes with a panic that lacks the dignity of personhood. Whichever the case, women can cut themselves off from the surprises of God. The "resigned" woman, whether married or single, lacks the vibrancy that expectation brings. And if a woman knows a creative God she may be in for all sorts of surprises.

"Why do you want to marry?" is an important question. Marrying for the wrong reasons has brought all the miseries the single girl can't avoid noticing. Grabbing at marriage to fill inner emptiness soon reveals that marriage is a false god. Marriage does not change one's essential character or nature. Nor is it a happiness button. A second question: "Are you becoming the person the kind of man you want would marry?" We keep wanting to conjugate the verbs *to find, to want, to do,* forgetting the important verb is *to be.* What you are becoming is vitally important.

Reasons for marriage usually fall in the category labeled *human* or *emotional* or *physical.* Safety, protection, companionship, provision, sex, status — the list could go on. But the list is valid for a Christian only when the larger spiritual factor is taken into consideration: Is this marriage the will of God? And the will of God lines up with the principles of marriage found in the Scripture.

Which brings us to the point of the goodness of God. God's will is never second best; his will is always first best. The first step to real life is always hooked up to our relationship with God. If we do not believe we are loved by him we can go on an endless search for love. It is not idle, easy talk to say that our most profound contentment is found in Christ.

If she fails to believe in the goodness and love of God, strange things can happen to a woman. She grows brittle inside. Blaming external circumstance for lack of fulfillment or frustration, she uses the cutting edge of sarcasm to make her way through life. Or she becomes uptight, a kind of pseudo-woman, domineering and brusque. Harboring resentments, making mountains out of molehills, she throws her failures on someone else. She begins to live against the world. It's the dread disease of dissatisfied womanhood.

Every woman has to work through her own barriers. She cannot do this as long as she refuses to face reality. A woman's challenge is to make a success either of her celibacy or her marriage. Both require effort, commitment, and development of inner resources. If a woman spends her time dreaming only of what could be or living in an unreal existence, she ceases to live in the *now*. And no one is attracted to an empty shell. You don't start living when a man comes into your life; you have to live *now*. You have to be someone worth knowing whether married or single, if life is to be rich.

Never be content with trivia. You can squeeze your heart dry over nothing. The attitude of faith is the only truly human one because it gets us beyond ourselves and focuses our attention on the purpose in the universe. We can be conscious of doubts, but we need to be more conscious of God. We need to get our approval, our sense of being loved and worthwhile from him, not from the response of those around us.

In the final analysis, whether a woman is married or single, she has two choices: either to live her life reluctantly or with conviction. If she lives it with conviction she will find an outlet in life, a way to use her energy, love, gifts, mind — her totality — in a way that will bring fulfillment. A single woman who thinks marriage is the only worthwhile adventure is going to have a shriveled life. She needs to like what she is doing now. And with all the choices in the world and given a creative God, it is likely that a person can find a niche in life that already has her name on it. It may be a growing niche, but she won't find it if she lives like a butterfly, flitting from place to place, unwilling to commit herself to the discipline of self-discovery.

For some this will be working in partnership or assisting a worthy man, making a contribution to his work, enjoying his friendship and the camaraderie of work. For others it will be soaring out to new heights on her own. Since femininity is enhanced by masculinity, the intellectual and social exchange with men is a desirable part of life, and it falls in the realm of meaningful

friendships which enhance our lives. I think single
women can realistically pray for these kinds of male
friendships. The quickest way not to realize them
is to communicate that you have more in mind
than friendship.

God has in mind an abundant life for every believer.
He makes us free to do that which prepares us for joy —
that which will bring the greatest happiness to us.

*I have often thought it would be a blessing if each
human being were stricken blind and deaf for a few days
at some time during his early adult life. Darkness
would make him more appreciative of sight. Silence
would teach him the joys of sound.*

*Now and then I have tested my seeing friends
to discover what they see. Recently I asked a friend,
who had just returned from a long walk in the woods,
what she had observed. "Nothing in particular,"
she replied.*

*How was it possible, I asked myself, to walk
for an hour through the woods and see nothing worthy
of note? I, who cannot see, find hundreds of things
to interest me through mere touch. I feel the delicate
symmetry of a leaf. I pass my hands lovingly about
the smooth skin of a silver birch, or the rough, shaggy
bark of a pine. In spring I touch the branches of trees
hopefully in search of a bud, the first sign of awakening
nature after her winter's sleep. Occasionally, if I am
very fortunate, I place my hand gently on a small tree
and feel the happy quiver of a bird in full song.*

Helen Keller

EVERYBODY'S LONESOME

by Inez Spence

Loneliness is universal. It is common to all. Loneliness can strike when one is surrounded by friends or can dog the footsteps of a stranger in a strange place. It brings nostalgia for the past and creates fear of the future.

Loneliness is many things. It hides behind sorrow; cringes when it feels ignored; yields to moods of despondency; fancies itself unloved and unappreciated; longs for the familiar; cries because it feels alone.

Years ago, when I was a freshman, a beloved teacher told me something I have never forgotten. Mary Scott was a tall, angular woman in her early fifties. In spite of her austere manner she was a popular figure on the campus. In repose her face was stern and her black eyes piercing. One quaked in her class if the lesson was unprepared — but very soon we learned to watch for her smile. It would begin in her eyes and then slowly the sharp lines would crumple into warmth and gentleness.

As my school years passed, my admiration for this rare teacher grew. She encouraged me to explore the world of good books. She helped me discover for myself new areas of study. It was she who noticed my intense interest in the manners and customs of the Bible lands and guided me into that field of specialization.

Mary Scott was quite alone in the world, entirely without family ties. But, somehow, you never thought of her as being alone or ever lonely. One day I talked with her about the loneliness I felt at times. She said, "Let me tell you something I learned a long time ago. I was alone in a large city, very alone and miserably lonesome. I spent hours in the public library reading and brooding. Opening a small book one afternoon I read these words.

Every heart knows loneliness. One may live in a house of luxury, or in a modest home with only limited comforts. One may live in shabbiness with only the bare necessities. It makes no difference. Every heart at times feels the ache of loneliness.

"I have forgotten the rest that I read but those words have remained with me. If loneliness is shared by everyone, I decided, then I can accept those times with understanding and plain common sense. Instead of dwelling on my lonely feelings I will deliberately set out to show cheerful friendliness to everyone I meet. Throughout the years I have practiced this. It has helped me to push loneliness into the background and to emphasize the pleasant things that each day brings."

My teacher could grade me only "E" for effort, I'm afraid. Too often I've been slow in rising above the lonely times. But her example has prodded me on to persistent effort. I have learned, too, that the most cheerful persons are not those least invaded by loneliness. They are the conquerors.

Never coddle loneliness. If you do, it will act as a spoiled child demanding more attention and pampering. Christ spoke often of joy and good cheer. Never did he put the emphasis upon happiness. That is a fleeting thing — something happens and the heart glows with happiness — but a telephone call, a letter, a spoken word, and happiness as quickly disappears, leaving the ache of unhappiness. Nothing, however, can destroy the joy that comes through fellowship with Christ and the cheerful spirit it nurtures.

A loneliness that is understood and faced is like a clean wound that will heal naturally. But many suffer from loneliness yet never understand its cause. This is the do-it-to-yourself kind of loneliness.

Today's market is filled with do-it-yourself kits of all kinds. By following instructions one can paint a lovely picture or turn a plain piece of furniture into a thing of beauty. Do it yourself, but always carefully follow the directions. How sad that a human heart can be lonely for pleasant contacts with others yet fail to follow the rules that make these contacts possible.

Myrtle Reiben lived alone in a modern apartment in a southern city. She had grown up in this city, married,

and raised two daughters there. She fluttered about
seeking news like a bee seeking honey. Her apartment
neighbors learned to expect the quiet opening of her door
whenever the outside door opened. Telephone calls
from her interrupted their early morning sleep. She
intruded upon afternoon guests or evening enjoyments.
Mrs. Reiben's pleasure in going places was matched
only by her ingenious ways of obtaining transportation.
Her desire to impress and her craving for prestige
were pathetic. And always she blamed others for
avoiding her.

Some very fine qualities were found in Myrtle Reiben.
She was friendly and eager for callers. She took pride
in keeping her nicely furnished apartment in perfect
order. Any responsibility given her by any organization
in which she was interested was faithfully fulfilled.

But Myrtle Reiben was a lonely person. Any indifference shown her was interpreted as a slight without
cause. Any refusal to grant a request was rudeness
on the part of the other. Firmly fixed in her mind was an
image of herself as a gracious lady admired for her kind,
sweet ways.

What a pity that Myrtle Reiben never really looked
within herself for the answer to her loneliness. The
answer lay there.

Sometimes we smile as we speak of husbands whose
work keeps them away from home much of the time.
We tease their wives about being "work widows."
I have watched with friendly interest two women face
this special kind of loneliness.

One couple moved to our city from a distant eastern
state. The husband's position meant almost continuous
travel. It was a most difficult time for his wife. She
never quite accepted it. She found no interests to fill
her days. Gradually her health began to fail and her
doctor told her that her nerves were causing much
of her trouble. She is waiting for the day that her husband
will retire so they can move "back home."

The second couple came from a northern city. Weekends
are the only time this husband can be home. They
have no children. His wife is a shy but charming woman
who finds those weekends the bright spot in her life.

But she didn't brood over her loneliness. She has studied music, and long hours of practice on the organ have brought her much pleasure. Now she has added the study of Spanish. Realizing that her shyness was keeping her from making friends, she began to accept invitations and to give them. She has made her days pleasantly full.

It is true that two different personalities react differently to the same conditions. One woman may have more endurance and self-reliance than the other. One may be more aggressive, the other may find that staying home is the easiest way to escape meeting strangers.

It is also true that healthy interest in others and participation in some interesting activities can make a lonely situation much more pleasant. Surely it's worth trying.

Everyone needs friends, the lonely, older woman most of all. Being a good friend is an art. Long-time friendships don't just happen — they are carefully tended.

What is friendship? Friendship is living on a two-way street. It is giving as well as receiving. Friendship is respecting the "no trespassing" sign that permits a friend his right to privacy and to his own opinions. It is confidence in the other's motives while not expecting perfection in his actions. It is being quick to praise and slow to criticize. Friendship is sharing experiences without depending overmuch on the other. It is enjoying a friend without monopolizing. It is diligently keeping the simple rules of lasting friendships.

Since friendships are so important to the lonely woman, wouldn't it be wise to stop now and then to take inventory? What characteristics do my friends see in me? Any irritating habits? Answer the questions below honestly and nudge yourself if any betrays you.

Do I have the monologue habit? Am I too talkative?
Am I inclined to be set in my opinions? Do I become argumentative?
Am I guilty of discussing family affairs with outsiders?
Am I quick to offer unsolicited advice?
Do I talk too much about my physical ailments?
Am I an inquisitive neighbor who pries into another's business?
Am I a gossip?

Do I feel possessive toward a friend and resent
the rights of her other friends?

A few years ago a prayer for the older person
was published in a city newspaper. It expresses some
very common needs. I liked its humor. The ability
to smile at one's frailties is a healthy indication that
the petitioner is a well-balanced, in-the-middle-of-the-road
kind of a person.

Prayer for Older Folks

Lord, thou knowest that I am growing older.

Keep me from becoming too talkative, and particularly
keep me from falling into the tiresome habit of expressing
an opinion on every subject.

Release me from the craving to straighten out
everybody's affairs.

Keep my mind free from the recital of endless details.
Give me the grace, dear Lord, to listen to others
describe their aches and pains. Help me to endure
the boredom with patience and to keep my lips sealed.
For my own aches and pains are increasing in number
and intensity and the pleasure of discussing them is
becoming sweeter as the years go by.

Teach me the glorious lesson that, occasionally,
I might be mistaken.

Keep me reasonably sweet; I do not wish to be a saint
(saints are so hard to live with) but a sour old woman
is the crowning work of the devil.

Make me thoughtful, but not moody; helpful, but not
pushy; independent, yet able to accept with graciousness
favors that others wish to bestow upon me.

Free me of the notion that simply because I have lived
a long time I am wiser than those who have not lived
so long.

If I do not approve of some of the changes that have
taken place in recent years, give me the wisdom to keep
my mouth shut.

Lord, you know that when the end comes I would
like to have a friend or two left. Amen!

Author Unknown

*There is nothing unusual about being lonely. Neither is it
limited to those who have lost their companions.
A wedding ring is no insurance against loneliness,
for some of the loneliest hearts are tied by a marriage
vow.*

*Young hearts can know its torture. Wanting
desperately to be accepted by their peers but feeling
left out, unwanted — this is a dismal, lonely experience.
Shy natures, sometimes thought to be unfriendly,
know their own special brand of loneliness. The blight
of loneliness has left its ugly mark on the lives of
little children, hungry for love and security. Mature
hearts are as vulnerable as the young or very old.
No, there is nothing unusual about being lonely.
But it must never be allowed to possess you — although
it will try.*

*I know many lonely women. Some go through
the motions of daily living but within them is a numbing
need that they do not know how to meet. I know others,
many others, who have used their loneliness as steps
reaching up to find new friends, helpful service, and
a satisfying life.*

*It is easier to recognize God's part in the bitter
experiences that come to us when we can look back
without tears or heartbreak. Then we find that they gave
us our sweetest times of prayer and the deepest lessons
in trusting. They taught us the reality of his presence
and the unfailing help that is found in his Word.*

*Only when sorrow covers the heart and we reach out
in utter loneliness to the Master are we aware of a new
song. It is a song of acceptance and submission. It
is a song of faith. It is a song to give to others. It sings
of a quiet confidence that the Master taught us in
love and compassion. It is a song that lonely hearts
about us need to hear.*

Inez Spence

THAT CERTAIN SOMETHING

by Arlene Francis

I was born in Boston, raised in New York, and died in daytime television. Well, that is not absolutely the truth. I had four remarkably enriching years on daytime television on a program that carried me to all parts of the world and gave me the chance to do a long series of interviews ranging from the premier of Japan to a push-cart peddler on West 67th Street.

Meeting strangers every day and helping them to expose, at the very least, capsules of their personalities has acquainted me with all sorts of charmers: real, false, and snake.

I have seen utter and complete charm in a Gloucester fisherman, and the total lack of it in a Back Bay matron or a debutante. I have seen grizzled bricklayers loaded with charm, and ladies-in-waiting who could be called ladies-in-wanting as far as charm goes.

Charm must come from within. As a reflection of a warm human spirit, it is a very individual thing. What is charming in one person might be false and repellent in another.

Alec Waugh, the British novelist, has these ideas about charm:

Being in the presence of a charming woman is like being drawn into a magic circle where everything is fresher, cleaner; where there is peace, warmth, comfort. Her smile is occasional rather than constant, making one want to bring it back. The charming woman puts a man on trial in the sense that she produces in him the desire to be his best.

From this description, we can draw a blueprint of our ultimate objective: to bring peace, warmth, and comfort to others. If, as Mr. Waugh says, charm creates the desire in a person to be his best, charm is also *created* by a person being his best.

Enid Haupt is an enormously capable woman who never lets an executive desk overpower her femininity.

She says:

A charming person is never petty or petulant —
rather she is one who is genuinely interested in people
and activities. Charm gives an automatic radiance that
magnetizes and, to my way of thinking, is the true essence
of beauty. Instead of fading with the passage of time,
the charm of a personality grows with the years. One
could even call charm a self-developed talent, for it
reflects individuality, intelligence, and warmth of spirit.
Almost anyone can achieve charm — its ingredients
are really only self-discipline and thoughtfulness.

The more interest you have in people and things,
the more robust your personality. And vitality and energy
of the mind are so much a part of charm that it actually
cannot exist without them. The more intense your interest
in things outside yourself, the greater your charm will be.

You, as a person, already have charm. You may
not be aware of it. It's your own very special charm,
and no one else can duplicate it exactly. It's personal,
as a dream is personal. It's not an imitation of somebody else's charm, and it's strictly nontransferable. You
can only get at it by releasing yourself — from the tentacles
of prejudice, fear, bias, unjustified guilt, self-pity, self-
centeredness, and a dozen other nuisances.

Charm is at the heart of our being and I'm naive
enough to think that it has to do with silly old-fashioned
qualities like honesty and integrity and — let's face it —
thinking of yourself, as well as of others.

Charm is bringing the best in every human being
to the surface. It's a self-generating thing. Charm
in one person often creates charm in others.

In total, charm is the best part of yourself
complementing every word and action with a kind of
humanity. In part, many individual things contribute
to it: your mind, your appearance, your feelings, and —
for lack of a clearer term — your spirit.

Your appearance and surroundings tell others what
you are, faster than you can say "Elizabeth Arden."
Good grooming attracts. Bad grooming repels. It's as
simple as that — and as axiomatic.

A personnel manager of a large firm told me that if
he has a choice of two secretaries, one well groomed

and the other sloppy, he'll take the first one every time —
even if the latter is a better typist and faster at
shorthand.

You don't need beauty to be charming, but you do
need to be well groomed and attractive. In some rare
cases, charm can shine through a shaggy exterior.
But it's a long gamble, and I wouldn't recommend it.
Besides, you owe yourself a little pampering so that
you can love yourself in the morning.

To be loved by people or to be loved by a person,
you must necessarily love yourself in the finest sense
of the word. If you appraise yourself by saying,
"Mirror, mirror on the wall, I'm the dreariest of them
all," you're liable to be pretty repugnant to others as well.

Again it's a vicious circle. If we don't like ourselves,
others don't like us. If others don't like us, we tend
to start a repetitive pattern so we make *sure* they don't
like us. Charm is impossible under these conditions.

We are all idiots at one time or another. We make
mistakes and we'll continue to make them. If we forgive
ourselves for these oversights, we'll be well on the way
toward thinking of ourselves realistically.

Charm is really the *best* part of yourself. It's the
throwing off of the bad part, and the highest and most
loquacious expression of the good part. It's not something
that is assumed or dragged into the picture. It's not
a new Easter outfit you put on for a parade up
Fifth Avenue. It's not even a self-conscious effort to be
charming, because charm loses itself the moment it
becomes blatantly self-conscious. The self-conscious
portion comes into the picture in your determining
to make an effort to find out the best possible insights
about your real self, and to become aware of the road-
blocks that are stifling your personality. To that extent
you *have* to be self-conscious. After that you must
proceed to get rid of self-consciousness.

If you think back over your experiences, chances are
you will find that the finest moments in your life were
those when you completely forgot yourself. The more
consistently you find total absorption outside yourself,
the greater your chances of being charming — charm

you will not be conscious of, the charm of being your absolute spontaneous self.

If any single aspect above all the rest is important to make the most of your charm, it is this development of interest in other people, other things.

I think that the Golden Rule is the most overlooked tranquilizer in the world, and that Saint Francis of Assisi was with it all the way when he prayed, "Grant that I may seek not so much to be understood as to understand; to be loved as to love." There is no substitute for it. Some people come by this naturally. Others have to work at it. The trick is to work at it until it becomes natural.

With this idea as an anchor, the other blocks to charm can be faced and thrown away as you go along.

Fear can be overcome, because you can't very well be afraid of anything when your mind is on something else.

Prejudice and intolerance evaporate because they are simply not compatible with genuine concern for others.

Shyness and embarrassment are lost because you don't have time to concentrate on yourself and your own problems.

Conceit and self-centeredness, of course, can't exist when you're thinking of somebody other than yourself.

Hatred, envy, jealousy, and greed are completely cancelled out.

Tension automatically disappears.

Boredom can't live in the same room with lively, radiant interest in something outside yourself.

No real shortcuts to charm exist, because charm is a reflection of the entire personality. However, some things are so fundamental they will give you a good boost while you work on the overall job. Let's take a look.

1/ *Get organized.* Lack of organization for the day can make people liverish more than anything I know. It's not a bad idea to plan your day the night before, and then you can sleep on the problems coming up and often subconsciously arrive at an answer.

2/ *Make sure you're well groomed.* The psychological value of this can't be overestimated. No one can be serene and confident feeling scratchy and ill-clad. Your

whole attack on the day is improved by the feeling
of well-being that good grooming brings to you.

3/ *Do one special thing for someone else as a surprise.*
Pick out a friend or a member of your family and
examine any ideas you can think of that would make him
happy. They don't need to be big things, but they can be
thoughtful things that will make someone else just a little
happier. In doing this, you'll be a *lot* happier.

4/ *Do one thing a day to make your home more pleasant.*
Plan to do one small thing a day, so that your improvement never stops. A new lamp for the bedroom. A
touch of paint on the bathroom cabinets. An experimental
recipe for dinner. A few new flowers for your garden
or your table. The reward of doing this will snowball
in direct proportion to the thought you put into it.

5/ *Force yourself to do one thing you've been
embarrassed to do in the past.* Perhaps you've been
meaning to call on a new neighbor, but you've felt
a little shy about it. Do it in spite of yourself. Things
that seem hard to do often dissolve when you *do* them.
Don't let imaginary barriers fence you in.

6/ *Read something worthwhile for at least fifteen
minutes each day.* Pick out one worthwhile book — and
try it on for size. Stay with it for at least fifteen minutes
a day, and gradually you'll neglect the clock, absorbed
in other worlds.

7/ *Think about someone you dislike — and wish him
well even if it kills you.* Our own pettiness and hatreds
detract from charm much more seriously than we're
inclined to think. Constantly to slander those whom you
dislike is to eat away at your own spirit.

8/ *Practice looking a person directly in the eye and
concentrate wholly on what he is saying.* This is one
of the most important attributes of charm — and often
the one most disregarded. Very few of us are good
listeners. Many times our attention, and with it our eyes,
wander all over the place when someone is talking to us.
We diminish our effectiveness if we dissipate our
attention.

9/ *Practice laughing at your own mistakes.* Do this
whether you are alone or with others. Try not to defend
your mistakes to others. Admit them graciously and

apologize for them if the situation demands it. Laugh at them if you can and you won't have to be afraid of others laughing at you. They'll be laughing with you.

10/ *Practice forgetting yourself completely.* As we said before, this is most important. But the problem is that you can't really forget yourself by *thinking* about forgetting yourself, because the minute you do that you're *remembering.* The trick is absorption — total absorption in something outside yourself. It's the only way. It's a *must.* Begin doing this *now!*

This business of being self-appointed judges as to what is or is not beautiful in others has always been with us and shows no signs of a quick demise. People do observe and judge one another's appearance, though this might well be done unconsciously.

Tell me, what is the first thing you notice about someone to whom you are being introduced?

"It varies with the individual," you answer.

Yes, it could be the sheen of her hair, the mod look, or her smiling eyes. True, but don't these answers boil down to one general term — appearance? *How one looks?*

Some people, like my friend Dorothy, have the faculty to recall with almost photographic accuracy a person's features and the complete outfit she was wearing. Many of us remember only the general impression (neat, faultlessly groomed, tacky, coordinated colors). But everyone remembers something about the way others look.

The old saying that man looks on the outward appearance but God looks on the heart could be passed off as an innocuous truism heard from early childhood; or this thought could cause one to do a double-take . . . reach for one's Bible . . . and thoughtfully read 1 Samuel 16:7: "The Lord seeth not as man seeth; for man looketh on the outward appearance, but the Lord looketh on the heart."

This says to me, "You, my child, are open to double

scrutiny — from people *and from* God. *People are looking at you."*

And so, in a few meditative moments, this commonplace verse can metamorphize: People are watching me. God is watching me. I am important!

You *are being observed: the way you* look, *the way you* act, *the way you* talk. *God is watching you, the* real you, *the unvarnished, down-deep you. You are important!*

Think of all the people during Christ's life here who looked at him. Yet all of his eighteen busy years between the time he was twelve and thirty were compressed into one simple sentence:

Jesus increased in wisdom and stature, and in favor with God and man (Luke 2:52).

Here we have another verse that bears meditation. Jesus increased in:

wisdom (intellectually)
stature (physically)
favor with God (spiritually)
favor with man (socially).

If God the Father thought it was important for his Son to increase in each *of these specific areas, important enough to have it recorded in his written Word, who are we to feel ourselves exempt from growth in any one of these areas?*

Marjorie Frost

2 THE WOMAN AND HER WORLD

HOW BIG IS YOUR WORLD?

by Char J. Crawford

Tell me, how long has it been since you eagerly toyed with a new idea? How many weeks, months, years has it been since your mind cried out for a new area of life to study? A woman needs to be alert, abreast of the times. Have you ever had the experience of being out socially with a group of well-informed people and finding that you have no real knowledge of the topics they are discussing? It leaves you with rather a "how-ignorant-and-uninformed-I-am" type of feeling, doesn't it? But when you get home again, what do you do about it? Do you forget it, or allow yourself to be challenged to greater heights?

We must let our minds feast on the courageous and noble things, and we shall find that our lives will be elevated to heights that we never dreamed were attainable. The areas of life that may interest me, you may not find quite so interesting. But, if our minds and eyes and hearts are open, we shall see many areas of life that arouse our interest, delight our souls, and tickle our curiosities. God has a perfect, intricate, beautiful design for each of the trillions of snowflakes that have fallen. Do we dare to doubt that he has a perfect and intricate and beautiful design for the life of each one of us? There is only one of each of us in this world; let us not be drawn too tightly into a mold. Be an individual thinker. What are your interests?

I'd like to suggest that you adopt a study plan. Let life be your university. Pick out some area of life that really interests you. Study every side of it, learn all that you can about it. When your thirst for knowledge on the subject is quenched, begin a new study on another subject. Such a rich, full, exciting world we live in: God's world! We, as God's children, should want to know as much as we possibly can about our world. "Learn as if you are going to live forever. Live as if you are going to die tomorrow."

Here are some "study" suggestions. Which of these areas interest you most?

Travel
It costs a lot of money to travel, but have you ever considered traveling via books? Take a lengthy European tour. Read about the traditions, customs, way of life, history, geography, and resources of each European country. Study them one by one. Such beautiful colored photographs and slides are available at your library that you can look at them and almost feel you're there. Travel to South America, to the Orient, on to Africa. A world tour — at no expense.

Poetry
A poet has a gift of God in his heart and at his fingertips. Through reading a poem we can look into someone's heart. There are poems of every variety: deep and profound poetry, light and lyrical gems, philosophical "treatises," and homespun humorous poems to add warmth and gaiety to life.

Child Psychology
I don't feel that most of us are "prepared" mothers. So few of our classes in school, so few of our experiences, have been geared to prepare us for the responsible role of motherhood. A great deal can be learned from those who have devoted their lives to the understanding of children and their growth mentally, physically, and spiritually. Read the available books on understanding children. Knowledge we acquire in this area can often be applied immediately. So many behavior and discipline problems could be eliminated if parents knew how to cope intelligently with them. Child psychology is an excellent study for those who don't have small children, too: Sunday school teachers, grandparents, good neighbors, and people who simply like children.

Flower Arranging
Are you the type of woman who enjoys working with her hands? Do you have a flair for the creative and artistic? Many excellent books and pamphlets are

written on the subject of floral arrangements. Working with flowers — colorful expressions of our Father's artistry — can be meaningful. Perhaps your service might be to arrange flowers to give to the sick and shut-ins.

Politics
Many women are keenly interested in politics. We must be well-informed voters. Do you stand for one party or another because your family has always done so, or have you done some independent thinking on the subject? Study party platforms, the history and legislative records of the parties, on a national and state level. Read all you can about candidates for office and what they stand for. We can never maintain a government "of the people, by the people, and for the people" unless we, the people, are interested and informed.

Art
Can you look deeply into a beautiful painting and "lose yourself"? Can you walk through an art gallery and appreciate the inspiration and feeling that originated the brush strokes? The Master, the greatest Artist, has painted and sculptured a masterpiece that can never be equaled: our world. He has created hills, canyons, mountains, rivers, but his greatest work is man. And to some men and women he has given the gift of artistry.

Education and Schools
Many schools are overcrowded, run down, and in poor condition. What can we do in our own communities to help? We can each be actively interested in our schools, in parent-teacher associations, in building programs, and in the actions of local school boards. We must narrow our national educational problems down to our communities and ourselves.

Music
To hear the works of a great composer should make one stand in awe of such God-given talent. Music has power to guide our emotions and feelings. Happy, gay music will put a smile on our lips; great and mighty choruses may send a chill through our bodies; a soft, lilting

song will soothe and comfort us, a love song will warm
our hearts, a rhythmic tune will set our foot tapping,
a great hymn will bring inspiration to our souls.
Christianity has come through the ages singing God's
praises.

You are not too old to play an instrument, if you
sincerely desire to learn. Or have you thought of joining
an evening class in music appreciation? Purchase season
tickets to a concert series. Let your musical tastes guide
your record selections, and include a variety of music
in your collection.

Sewing and Designing
To be perfectly honest, sewing on a button is a chore
for me. I must admit, however, that one of my fondest
ambitions is to learn to design and sew my own clothes.
Most of us have our own ideas about what colors and
styles we like best on ourselves. A talented seamstress
can see her ideas take form. She can sew to please her
family and friends, and save money, too. What a good
feeling it must be to receive a compliment on an outfit
you have made with your own hands, and perhaps
even designed with your own ideas. Creativity is
a treasure to be used, not stored away.

Writing
What a thrill it is to put your thoughts down in black
and white. Millions of words that could never be spoken
can be written. Courage can be found in the pen.
If someone would have told me when I was so eagerly
writing for the high school weekly that someday I'd write
books, I would have laughed. But here I am writing
to you the things that are overflowing from my heart.
A person must write from his own experience. Now
when new ideas are kindled in my mind, I feel restless
until I write them down in black and white and put them
in the file. Do you enjoy writing? Then, don't be afraid
to tackle pencil and paper. Put your heart and prayers
into what you write, and don't give up.

Youth Work
Our young people want to enjoy life and adventure.

Young people are vibrant! They want life in technicolor, and we adults must show them by our lives that in Christ we find happiness, power, joy, and adventure. Our Lord said he came that we might have abundant life. Christ offered the greatest challenge when he spoke two words, "Follow me."

Are you concerned about young people headed in the wrong direction? Then don't just sit there and read stories of teen-age violence and say, "Tch, tch!" Do something about it. Study delinquency problems and causes. If you are sincerely interested in troubled teen-agers and have the time, consider some phase of voluntary youth work. Consult your pastor or local youth commission for advice and information. Act now.

Bible Study

Of course, every Christian should be studying the Bible, but some of us would like to become real Bible students. Perhaps we haven't had the Bible training in our background that we'd like to have had. Perhaps our faith is new, and we are like newborn babes, sincerely desiring spiritual food. Where to start? Here are a few suggestions:

The new translations of the Bible help to make the Word more understandable. We can read the great truths written in our modern-day language.

Attend an adult Bible class on Sunday mornings.

Does your church have a mid-week Bible study? If so, attend regularly.

Since we are not all gifted theologians, consider this: Read from cover to cover an older child's recommended Bible story book.

Many Bible schools offer Bible correspondence courses. Inquire.

Read the Bible daily. Pray for understanding before you read, as you read, and when you have finished reading. God will answer your prayer.

Mission Work

How much do you know about home and foreign missionary efforts of your church? Where are the mission fields? What progress is being made? What are the conditions? What are the particular needs of the mission fields?

Your missionaries need your prayers, financial help, letters, gifts, and interest. God has called these men and these women to serve him in the mission fields. Remember that we are all co-laborers. "Go into all the world and preach the gospel to the whole creation." That means you and me, as well as those who have left their home in the name of our Lord. God bless them! And God help us to help them!

You don't have time to study? Funny, isn't it, how we can usually find time to do what we really want to do. Tuck the children tenderly in bed at night, and stop working. Use your evenings to relax and read the newspaper, magazines, your church publications, and books.

Develop your mind, elevate your thoughts, broaden your world.

THE THREE R'S OF BUSINESS

by Wilbert E. Scheer

Is this company a better place because of you? I hope so. Not only because of your company's reputation in the community, but also in terms of you, the worker. If this firm is no better because of you, then you have no business being here. If you took a job in the office only because you needed the money, or because it was convenient, then you have missed one of life's greatest opportunities.

The woman who works only for a paycheck is miserable indeed. "Man does not live by bread alone" — we all know that. We need to satisfy other basic necessities of life, one of which is to give something of ourselves, to do more than is required, to do it better than expected — in other words, to enjoy our work.

Life can never have a sense of fulfillment or completeness for us unless we are giving more than we are getting. Those who live only for themselves live little lives. Those who devote their lives to a cause greater than themselves always find a larger, fuller life than the one they surrendered.

We are not put into this world to see what we can get out of it, but rather to see what we can contribute to make it better than when we inherited it. Similarly, your company must be a better place because of you or you have failed in your opportunity to derive the job satisfaction to which you are entitled.

The Nature of Office Work

Office work is service work. It is performed primarily for the benefit of others. In a typical business, for example, the office is a service to top executives, to manufacturing, sales, and finance. The volume of office work is determined by factors outside the office. The kind of work is beyond the control of the office which must do it.

Office work produces no direct profit. On the other

hand, efficient office operations contribute to a company's profit picture. To make one dollar profit can be done either by increasing sales by $20 or more, or by simply reducing operating costs one dollar. You tell me which is easier.

Office work is a facilitating function. It is the essential medium through which the various activities of an enterprise are fused together. In business the many departments, such as order, accounting, payroll, purchasing, maintenance, and the like, are tied together in what we call administration or business management, which is the office.

You're Here to Serve Others

Underlying all office work is the service principle. The office is not in business for itself; it is there to serve others.

There may be times when some people, because of their position, try to "lord it over" the office workers. You might not like this, and I can't blame you. But if they didn't have work to be done, they wouldn't need you and you wouldn't have a job.

At the same time, you shouldn't look upon the people who come to you for answers, advice, or assistance, as an interruption or a bother. Every person whom you treat discourteously goes back to work disappointed or disillusioned. A frustrated person cannot be expected to do his best.

On the other hand, when you deal with the public, managers, and co-workers, and show them the courtesy and respect which you yourself like to receive, they are happier and so are you.

Narrow the Distance

In those cases where the working relationship between people is not as pleasant as we'd like it to be, we can narrow the distance between us by working either end. Since we have little control over the other fellow but full responsibility for our own actions, it would seem logical that we start at our end.

Many a preacher is in a better mood to deliver a stirring message because of the mood established by a good organist. Many a manager is more effective because of the cooperation received in the office. And many office beginners, the next generation upon whom you and I will have to rely, get off to a good start simply because people like you have tried to be sympathetic with their problems and helpful with their questions when they come to you.

People who depend upon you are not encouraged or stimulated by preaching or complaining. They are influenced not so much by what you do but by how you do it, not by what you say but by what you believe.

B-u-s-i-n-e-s-s

Those of us who really want to be successful in our daily work should realize that many kinds of people are in the act with us. Our personal effectiveness is directly related to our ability to get along with others. I'd like to show you how easy this can be.

The key word is business. When we look over any group in an office, factory, or store, we find all kinds of people. We may wonder what molds them together into an efficient unit. Represented are both sexes and different ages, background, education, national origin, religion, and family environment. But they have one thing in common: they are together in business.

When we look at this word B-U-S-I-N-E-S-S what do we see? We find the letters U and I. In fact, if U and I are not in business, then what is left is an assortment of desks and chairs, equipment facilities, methods — none of which gets anything done by itself. These inanimate components of business are there when we're gone, and nothing happens. It is only when U and I come back into business that business becomes alive again. Business is people.

Your Attitude Is Showing

We know about the three R's of our schooldays. There are also three R's of adult life. And by that I don't mean "romance at 25, rent at 45, and rheumatism at 65." The three R's of adult life are:

1/ Resources — training and other gifts we offer

2/ Resolution — what we decide to do with these
3/ Responsibility — the sincerity of purpose we put
   into life

Just as there are three R's of childhood and adult life, so there are three A's of business life: Ability, Ambition, and Attitude.

Ability establishes what a worker does. Ambition determines how much she does. Attitude guarantees how well she does.

Ability will get a worker a job. Ambition will bring her a paycheck. Attitude will lead her to success.

Attitude is defined as the "you" (the person) in the job. When ability and ambition in two persons are about equal, how does a manager select one over the other for promotion? This is where attitude becomes the deciding factor.

Appearance and Manners

What do others see when they look at you? Not how well you type, how thoroughly you fill out a record, how accurately you keypunch a card, or how pleasantly you answer the telephone. Yes, you're rated on the way you handle your work, but you're judged on the way you handle yourself. Good impressions serve as your silent saleswoman.

If you're going to work in an office, you must first of all look the part. Good appearance means personal neatness, cleanliness, appropriate dress, and overall good grooming.

Many times it may be difficult or even impossible to give a satisfactory explanation without embarrassment to an applicant who is turned down or to a worker who is denied a promotion. It's usually little things, which might seem insignificant; but like all little things, they soon add up to bigger things.

So take a look at yourself in the mirror — to see how you look. Then take a look at yourself in the mirror of life — to see how you look to others. Do you seem tired or alert? Does your appearance invite cooperation and inspire friendliness, or does it suggest to other persons that they should stay away? How pleasant is your tone of voice or your facial expression? A smile is the light

in the window of your face to let others know your
heart is at home.

A Sincere Desire
But it isn't enough to look the part, you should also act
the part. Good appearance should be supported by good
manners, rooted in genuine consideration of the viewpoints
and feelings of others. Good behavior is largely actuated
by a sincere desire not to offend.

Conducting yourself according to accepted standards
of office behavior comes easy when you have pride
in yourself, when you recognize that you represent
your company to the people you deal with. Your
manners then reflect dependability, a sense of responsibility, integrity, and good character.

Good conduct automatically embraces good personal
traits: courtesy, politeness, cooperation, and tact. I like
the definition of tact that says, "Tact is the ability to shut
your mouth before someone else does."

Good manners are not hard to cultivate when things
go well. But do they stand up when tested? When
co-workers and others are inconsiderate and uncooperative,
you should try not to share their faults. Remain steadfast
in your principles, and notice that the more you can do
to make them feel appreciated and respected, the more
they will appreciate and respect you.

Fits, Misfits, and Counterfeits
There are three kinds of people with whom we as workers
have to deal. They are the Fits, the Misfits, and the
Counterfeits.

The Fits are no problem, they just naturally fit in well
and cause us no difficulties. We have no right to brag
how well we can get along with these people for they
are Grade A to begin with and just naturally fit in with
everyone, including us.

The Misfits are more of a problem. Obviously,
they aren't so well suited for their niche in life and this
causes friction, some of which rubs off on us. But with
a little extra understanding, they will at least improve
their lot in life and thereby be less trouble to us.

In every group we have our share of the Counterfeits,

those people who are mentally cut on the bias. Nothing they do is right by our standards, and nothing we do seems to please them. These are the people who present a real challenge to us because they test our talents, patience, and ingenuity as we try to get along with them.

Judge Not, Mold Not

The interesting thing is that all these people, like us, are trying to find their place in life. Each one in his own way is trying to establish himself in some useful purpose, although often this is not clear to us. That's because we are inclined to measure everyone else by our standards, not his.

We run into difficulties when we attempt to make others over to fit our mold. At the same time, we would resent it if they tried to change us. We would be happier in our jobs if we could just learn to accept others as they are. We can do this if we will try to understand the other person, not judge him. Tolerance is an oil that takes friction out of life.

Short course in human relations

The six most important words: "I admit I made a mistake."

The five most important words: "You did a good job."

The four most important words: "What is your opinion?"

The three most important words: "If you please."

The two most important words: "Thank you."

The one most important word: "We."

The least important word: "I."

MOONLIGHTING MOTHER

by Martha Nelson

One-year-old Jimmie frets as he watches Mother dressing for her day at her teacher's desk.

Ten-year-old Mary complains about coming into an empty house after school. She resents having a sitter during the summer months.

Twelve-year-old Tom didn't report to school last Friday.

Friends of fifteen-year-old Bill go before juvenile court next week for possession of marijuana.

Husband Joe's job has become a rat race. And who is left to try to handle those lively youngsters? Mother!

One out of three working women have children under age eighteen; admittedly they have their problems. True, they have been reassured that the quality of time a mother gives her brood is more important than quantity. But they are finding that quality suffers when a woman is beaten down day after day by fatigue. And it takes a certain kind of quantity, unfortunately some of it impossible to schedule after hours, to provide the protection and security a child deserves.

Must the answer be either homemaking or employment?

More and more women, believing that their families deserve top priority, are finding their answer in part-time employment during the years of motherhood.

Today's young bride faces the prospect of some twenty-five years of gainful employment during her lifetime. She has been fortunate if she has had a vocational counselor or other interested adult who has guided her to prepare for a career that can "take" the interruption child rearing may bring.

If she has gained a vision of the full-time, part-time, full-time cycle of work outside the home that a woman may choose, she is indeed blessed. How wise the woman who is aware that there is time enough in a lifetime for both career and family.

Part-time work opportunities for women have been around for years. Enterprising women have found their part-time niche in direct selling (door-to-door, telephone, party-plan), retail selling, real estate, market interviewing, teaching, nursing, free-lancing in the creative arts, food services, and infant day care, to mention a few.

Many beauty operators and cosmetologists work on a part-time schedule, as do medical and dental assistants, library workers, and receptionists. Some women, such as seamstresses and drapery makers, have established their own small factories at home. Still others have thriving mail-order businesses.

One young woman, trained to be a home economics teacher, is putting her knowledge to work at home while her two sons are small. As a sideline, she raises, shows, and markets pedigreed dogs.

A young piano teacher instructs thirty youngsters and adults in a beautiful studio she has designed in her Oklahoma City home. She firmly limits her clientele to that number. She maintains that four hours a day, four days a week, is a big enough teaching load for a young mother and that she deserves Wednesdays as well as weekends for living without work interruption. This time is used for being a good neighbor, hobbies, entertaining, church work, or just brooding, if that is what her mood dictates.

In her relationships with her patrons, both children and adults, she has opportunities to express Christian love and concern for persons who otherwise would be beyond the sphere of her influence. Her college training is being conserved for the time when she may wish or need to utilize it on a full-time basis. She is wisely regulating her work, rather than letting it dictate to her.

A physical education instructor in Denver, the mother of two small daughters, counts among her blessings the part-time teaching position she holds in an elementary school. It started out on a half-time basis, increased last year to two-thirds, and now she's holding her breath for fear she'll be offered a full-time contract for next year. "But my setup is worth bargaining for. I just can't handle anything more," she says.

In several Massachusetts communities a partnership

teaching program was introduced in 1965. It uses a variation of team teaching, in which two certified teachers share one full-time elementary position, one taking morning and the other afternoon. The two communicate in the lunch-hour overlap and by note and phone. According to one study of the program's effectiveness, the children enjoy a "fresh face at noon," more personal attention, speedily returned written work, and the insights and specialties of two teachers instead of one.

A teacher working under the plan pointed out, "The children don't get under your skin as they do when you have them all day."

And a principal declared, "The teachers are half-time only on payday. We get about two-thirds of a teacher for half pay."

Part-timers are also proving themselves in the business world. A Christian business woman in Dallas saw an untapped resource in the American women who wanted to be homemakers first and foremost but who needed an outlet for their creativity and the sense of personal achievement that seems to come with gainful employment. Founding her business on faith and a financial shoestring, she recruited and trained women for hostess-plan selling of gifts and home accessories. Today, less than fifteen years later, nearly 3,000 women from Maine to Alaska call her "boss." Together they are grossing millions in annual sales.

This career woman motivates her employees to put people before profit and to express in their business dealings the principles taught in the Word of God. The changed lives of many of these homemakers as they move beyond the four walls of their own homes is evidence of the meaningfulness of such work for them.

One said, "This work has given me entrée with persons I would not have gotten to first base with, had I knocked on their doors as a church visitor. In planning with hostesses, I find they confide in me, and often I have the opportunity to be truly helpful. Isn't this what Christianity is all about — sharing beauty and love and encouragement and a word of testimony about God's goodness when it is appropriate?"

A clerical worker works hours that permit her to be at home when her eleven-year-old daughter is there. A co-worker said, "She is such an excellent worker that our boss is delighted to have her a few hours a day. She works right through the regular lunch hour and leaves in time to be home when her daughter gets in from school. No, she doesn't work during the summer either, but the boss is always glad to have her back when fall rolls around each year."

Admittedly the part-time position has some drawbacks. The expense of transportation, meals, and clothing may take the pay for a full day at work. The hourly pay may not measure up to that of the woman in the same work on a full-time basis. Vacations, holidays, sick leave, and fringe benefits vary for part-time workers, and the job-seeker should have clear understanding about these at the outset.

Some "underground disadvantages" suggested by Margaret Albrecht in her book *A Complete Guide for the Working Mother* may include: a wary attitude on the part of the boss that he's not getting his money's worth, a non-acceptant attitude on the part of fellow employees, the dissatisfaction in not always getting to see a task through from start to finish, and the frustration if one is working beneath her ability.

But a strong case can be made for the part-time employment for mothers when one envisions this scene: the wall-to-wall confusion in some homes where both parents are rushing about meeting job demands, the lack of communication between affluent parents and their children, the juvenile delinquency, drug use, or emotional problems surfacing in so many nuclear-age children. Some mothers have the stamina and resourcefulness to maintain a stable home life while holding down a full-time career; multitudes, however, are letting their home life slide in the process.

Many industries and professions are zeroing in on the resources of American women during their busy years as mothers. In the past few years, federal agencies have begun recruiting mothers as part-time historians, security personnel, budget specialists, and for other professional positions.

Hospitals are taking nurses any way they can get them: "You name the hours."

Secretaries, bookkeepers, and day-care workers have little trouble finding part-time positions.

While monetary success or status in the business world are seldom found in the career geared to allow for a family, the answer may lie here for the woman seeking a sense of personal achievement and self-fulfillment beyond her role as wife and mother. Such an arrangement can provide a continuity with her specialized field and keep her alert as she looks to the years when she will again be free to give herself more completely to a career.

I wished for home and husband,
  The wish was given me —
My heart and hearth are daily sparked
  With masculinity.

I wished for children. This request
  Was also granted me —
A nimble five-ringed circus
  Performing endlessly.

I'm ready for my third wish, now,
  Though squandered it may be —
A few dull moments, please, oh, please,
  Occasionally.

Geraldine Everett Gohn

THE TRUTH ABOUT CONSEQUENCES

by Evelyn Shafner

My friend Jessie tells me that she works at her 42-hour-per-week job because she needs the money. Her two sons are eight and ten. She is working to save for their college education and also to help maintain her beautiful home. Jessie's husband and mine earn the same salary, but her home is almost twice the value of mine. The furnishings are equally lavish.

Luckily, Jessie has a cooperative husband. He cleans up the breakfast dishes and kisses the boys good-bye, since Jessie must leave at 7:30 in order to reach work at 8:00, when her day begins. Jessie returns home around 4:30, changes clothes, and has a delicious, well-balanced dinner on the table at 5:30. Her husband and sons help her clean up afterwards. A schoolgirl arrives at her house at three o'clock to straighten it, greets her sons as they return from school, and stays with them until Jessie returns from work. Her husband arrives home about 5:30, just in time for dinner.

Jessie is well organized and efficient. She is also blessed with abundant energy and good health, but many Fridays after dinner with her family, Jessie has plopped into bed, unable to get up until the next morning.

I have seen her on such occasions in a state of complete exhaustion. She says, "I really should quit my job. I'm too tired to enjoy my house." Then she sighs painfully, "But I can't — I need the money!"

Material Needs Are Created

A single friend of mine made the observation that married mothers who work, claiming that they need the money, *create needs that impel them to work*. As an example, she cited the case of a mother of four (her youngest child in nursery school), who told her co-workers when starting to work that three major appliances in her home had broken down, her son began orthodontic treatment, the family needed a new car, and her husband was ready to break down if there wasn't some financial relief. Thus she had joined the working force. Three years later she was still working. The new car was two years old and her husband wanted to trade it in for a station wagon.

Perhaps work had become a habit with her, and she was finding it more enjoyable than being a full-time mother at home. To face that glaring revelation might produce ponderous feelings of guilt, so her valiant effort to maintain her purity of purpose was often punctuated by statements such as, "I'd love to stay home and take care of my kids, but we need the money."

It is true that situations arise in which the need for money is the prime reason for a mother to enter the labor force. Unexpected and overwhelming medical bills, home repairs, a large purchase such as a car to replace one nearly ready for the junkyard, or the down payment on a house — any one of these may cause a woman to leave her children temporarily and go to work.

Young adults need to be aware of the amount of money required to maintain a home as a married couple and to rear children. They should know that with each child added to a household, there may be a reduction in the standard of living for other members of the family. If it is the first child, it may mean that the mother will have to give up her job. Couples should plan for this reduction of income, so that when the baby is born and the mother quits working, they will not discover to their dismay that they cannot exist comfortably on one income.

As children grow older, their expenses increase. To help meet these expenses, I believe in having children earn money as early as twelve years of age. Both girls and boys can baby-sit or do yardwork. As they reach their mid-teens, they can obtain jobs as clerks, cashiers, waitresses, and ushers. Working is a vital component of education.

An individual arrives at greater self-identity as he receives feedback from the public, his co-workers, and supervisors. He establishes a stronger ego, because he is not completely dependent upon his parents for support. He derives greater understanding of what life is all about.

Working is more realistic than the textbook. If a child really wants to go to college, he can do so without his mother's financial help. Parents deny children an important part of their development when they don't require that they contribute toward meeting the expenses of their education.

There should be a balance between the working world and the academic world. Have you known people who had impressive degrees and high scholarship but did not attain the eminence they prepared for because they were unable to interact well with others? The ability to function well in interpersonal relationships is gained through experience. Thus it often happens that an academically-oriented individual who finds great joy in books has little time or inclination to mix with others.

The point is, it's valuable for children to work and contribute to the expense of their education. When they are deep in such a study as medicine, they may need financial assistance, but a mother does her children an injustice when she goes to work to pay the full expense of their education.

Money Can Imprison

There is a saying that money frees you. It gives you an opportunity to pursue objectives and diversions you couldn't do otherwise. Money also has the power to imprison. The thoughtless person seeks money at the expense of more potent, vital elements of his life. Money comes and goes. It can be earned again and again, but other things that are lost can never be regained. One of these is the time spent with a child.

Undoubtedly, grievous pangs of regret and sorrow have been experienced by older couples who, when younger, attached more importance to self-gain and monetary accomplishments than to nurturing their offspring and developing serenity within the home.

Particularly during the first five or six years, the child needs steady, reliable, concerned, loving care. Those most able to give this are his parents. This isn't to say that the care of a child should be relinquished once he has reached five or six years of age. No, the child must be secure in the knowledge that someone is there to care for him and be concerned about him, someone who is vitally interested in his welfare.

While he is in the intermediate grades of elementary school, the child still needs the responsive attitudes of concerned parents, even though he is attaining more independence.

By sixth grade, he may be asserting himself to such a degree that he barely needs mom and dad around. But don't let him fool you. If he has a stomach ache, if another boy wounds his pride with a punch in the jaw that sends him sprawling, or if his teacher scolds him unjustly, is he going to run to the stranger on the corner? No, he will seek his parents. He very much needs their care. That is, unless he has lost confidence in his parents because they have ignored him, not given him the attention he requires, and simply don't have time for him. He will bury his hurts within him, perhaps become a behavioral problem at school or merely appear as placid as before. But the hurt builds up within him because he has no one he can trust to reveal it to. There comes a time when he must finally spill it out, and the recipient is often a stranger, perhaps a psychiatrist or, unfortunately, the pusher on the corner who offers drugs, companionship, and belongingness.

All these years mother has worked, she has earned money and made life more comfortable. What a pity that much of it has to be spent on psychiatric help for the child!

I remember a first-grader I encountered in an upper-middle-income area school. The boy had a beautiful face and was exceptionally bright, but he had no self-control whatsoever. He couldn't stay in his seat, and his mouth was always moving. I consulted another teacher. "He's obviously disturbed," I said, "and I want to be cautious about how I discipline him."

"Ignore him!" she answered promptly. "The children are used to him, and you'll get used to his antics too. Actually, he's probably seeking attention, and when you give it to him you're only reenforcing his behavior." Her voice became quieter, as if she were confiding in me. "He's under psychiatric care. You see, both his parents have their doctorates. They have always gone to school or worked, and this boy has had one baby sitter after another. He has a very high IQ. Such a handsome boy too, but very mixed up. It's pitiful, isn't it?"

Fortunately, his parents were able to afford extensive psychiatric care for their son. Even with all of the medical attention he was getting, I wonder if he came out of it unscathed.

The Soundest Investment

Rearing a child has often been compared to building a house. The foundation has to be firm and strong in order for a house to stand over the years. If the support of the structure is removed too soon, it will collapse. Similarly, a child needs support from adults during his growing years, especially during the first six years. When that support is not forthcoming, or is removed too soon, the child is not able to build up a reservoir of strength to combat the stresses of life. In the case of the above-mentioned child, he didn't have the strength to tolerate normal classroom stresses.

If his parents had made an investment of five years in their son, the returns would have been bountiful. True, it would have meant five years from their lives — five years cut from the career progress of the mother, and more than a year of her income lost. Several thousand dollars can buy much security and many goodies. But consider how many thousands of dollars will be spent on therapeutic care for the helpless child who lost out. A psychology professor once told me that a person can never make up for lost learning and training during his formative years. The more I see and observe, the more I believe that statement. Surely the greatest gift the young boy's parents could have given him was their presence, attention, care, and concern during his formative years. No other gift will make up for it, not even the best and most expensive psychiatric and therapeutic care available.

So you need the money? Think of the consequences!

The idea of a "maternity sabbatical" — allowing
a woman time off to have a baby before she whips back
to her lofty pursuits — makes it sound as if parenthood
were limited to the labor room. There seems to be
some chance that the immediate future of the world
has something to do with the guidance and care
we give our children after they leave the hospital nursery.
Whenever we try to teach our children, by word
or example, what "responsibility" or "equality" means,
whenever we spend time trying to pass on some of
the hard-fought truths of living, we are, as someone said,
"involving ourselves in eternal consequences." And
when it comes to eternal consequences, I figure I want
to take care of my own.

I admit that there are years in any woman's life when,
no matter how she tries to arrange her time, she finds
most of it taken up in domestic duties. . . But even
during those years there is some leeway. We may be
on 24-hour duty, seven days a week, but we have more
free time than anyone working on the eight-to-four
shift. I don't mean sit-around-and-eat-bon-bon
free time, of course, but I do mean what-do-I-want-
to-do-next? free time, and that's almost as good.
And into this tight schedule we can shoehorn the time
and energy to develop our own individual interests.
Show me an investment banker who can take an hour
after lunch to practice his guitar, for example. Yet I have
two hardworking housewife friends who are able to do
just that.

Of course, many women may decide wisely that
their greatest contribution to the world lies outside
a family situation, or that their own completeness can best
be enjoyed by being on their own. For the rest of us,
however, the women of the middle ground, it is possible
to live free as birds within, and probably because of,
the family framework we have chosen. Even in our
busiest years, we can develop skills and interests
to use later when things calm down. Right now,

when the confusion of family life is at its greatest,
we can prepare ourselves for a quieter time to come.
   This is how we women of the middle ground live.
We are, if we have chosen this way, wives and mothers
first, and we work pretty hard at it. But, as our free time
and talents grow, we begin to use them. It's very simple,
really. Yet people keep telling housewives they can
truly find themselves only in the outside world. We
say that outside and inside worlds meet in the middle
ground upon which we stand, and that small acts, taken
in sum, can have major importance.

Joyce Kissock Lubold

TWENTIETH-CENTURY LYDIA

by Leslie Parrott

The most misunderstood women today are the working mothers. I'm not talking about the old sophism, "Men may work from sun to sun, but women's work is never done." I'm talking about the misunderstood mothers who punch a time-clock or otherwise meet a job deadline five days a week, eight hours a day, and then return home in late afternoon to get an evening meal for the family and assume the role of mother and wife. Theirs is a complex and difficult role.

In the value system of the agrarian society, which dominated this country from 1776 to 1946, the place of the mother was in the home. She might work a 16-hour day hoeing cotton, plowing corn, cooking for threshers, and canning vegetables — but she did it at home. She did this in addition to being a mother and wife, but she did this back-breaking work in her own home and on her husband's farm.

Since 1946 the family system has undergone a social and technological revolution. We still believe a woman's place is in the home, but in a different way. As one man said, "I believe a woman's place is in the home and I think she should go there straight from work." Working outside the home for money has been added to the list of options for women who are looking for ways to fulfill their lives.

It all started with World War II, when women were urged to leave their homes and assume jobs which previously had been the prerogatives of men. Under patriotic motivation more women learned what it was like to work in a man's world.

What the war started, the revolutionary years since then have continued. As some view the upheaval, women have been liberated and brought up to a more equal status with men. As others see it, women have been taken down from their lofty Olympian pinnacle, where they were given preferential courtesies and

71   *The Woman and Her World*

protection, to the valley of human struggle where they compete with men. Which of these views is correct doesn't really matter; the fact is that mothers are set free to work outside the home for pay without feeling they are different from a great proportion of other mothers in the community.

The other factor which has done the most to make possible the trend toward working mothers is the technological revolution. Since World War II the *development of electrical gadgets in the home and the development of food-processing services for the kitchen have taken much of the drudgery and demand out of homemaking.* In fact, the drudgery has been taken out of housework so far that one of the new mental health problems is the mother who is caught in the "split-level trap." This mother feels trapped in 1,400 square feet of suburbia which does not offer her fulfillment for her life or enough challenge for productive use of her time. Only one thing is worse than too much work, and that is not enough! With all the motivations and opportunities women have today, the phenomenon of the working wife is here to stay.

But the idea of working mother isn't new. It goes back at least to the first century. When the Apostle Paul visited Philippi on his first trip to Europe a working mother there became his first convert. Her name was Lydia, a dealer in the expensive purple dye used to color the fashions worn by the rich. The Scriptures don't mention her husband or children. But the Bible does indicate that she was converted and baptized *with her household*. Then, typical of a woman with great capacity to do many things well, she invited the four men — Paul, Silas, Timothy, and Dr. Luke — to stay in her home for the duration of their work in Philippi.

But whether you are from Philippi or Portland, working outside the home or inside the home or both, what are the factors that make a working mother easier to live with?

Bulwark of Love and Security
Whether Mother works at a job for money or not, the name of the game is the same. Home must be a bulwark

of love and security for everybody in it. Families caught in the bind between rising costs and family expectations must decide whether the additional responsibility of Mother working will be a threat to the family's love and security. It needn't be. Although Mother isn't the only factor involved in providing this love and security in the family, this is an issue which must be settled on the basis of personal and family priorities.

J. Edgar Hoover said about the delinquency problem: "The answer lies for the most part in the homes of the nation. Many of the cases coming to my attention reveal the shocking facts that parents are forgetting their God-given obligations and more children are being sacrificed on the altar of indifference as parents throw aside their responsibilities. Can we build homes without God, or have worthy parents who don't know his teachings?"

The wise old philosopher Pericles stood on the steps of the Parthenon on the Acropolis of Athens and looked out toward the Mediterranean, where he saw coming, figuratively, the might and power of the Roman Empire, which one day would engulf Greece. He said, "I do not fear the strength of our enemies from outside as much as I fear spiritual and moral declension of our families from within."

Three Big Decisions
Perhaps it is unfortunate that the three biggest decisions in life must be made while people are still young. (1) There is the decision about an *occupation*. In this day of proliferation of vocational specialties, students need to make earlier and earlier decisions on their life's work. For most people this decision — even if by default — is made in their teens. (2) The second great decision of life concerns *marriage*. Although many parents would be pleased if their children waited until they were older to be married, the tendency is toward younger marriages rather than older. The attitudes and patterns of behavior out of which decisions on marriage come are set most fully during the teen years. Presently more girls are marrying at eighteen than at any other age. (3) The final big decision made during the years of youth concerns

religious experience and a personal philosophy of life.
By the time young people are old enough to vote, the
major spiritual inclinations have been consciously or
unconsciously formulated.

The most important fact about these three decisions
of life is that the quality of the home has a greater impact
on them than any other one factor. Not even the church
can make up for the inadequate home. Only an occasional
child from an unsatisfactory home is rescued by the
church and lifted into a new level of decision-making
on life's big questions. Whether or not Mother works,
these three big decisions will still be faced. Her attitudes
toward her children and her husband, plus their attitudes
toward her, will have much to do with their effectiveness
in the three most important areas of life.

Kindness and Courtesy

Many mothers work as a means of fulfilling their lives.
The feminine mystique requires some kind of projection.
Other women must work to provide the minimal level
of living for their families. Other women work because
of a level of family expectation which cannot be met
with one paycheck. But, regardless of the motivation,
the psychological and spiritual needs of the family are
the same. Attitudes of kindness and courtesy must
provide the base for all other family purposes. If kindness
and courtesy are omitted, everything else at home is
discounted.

Euripides said, "A man's best possession is a sympathetic
wife." King Solomon said something even more
important: "Better is a dry morsel, and quietness there-
with, than an house full of sacrifices with strife"
(Proverbs 17:1). Someone else said, "Next to bread,
the greatest need for the human heart is for kindness."
The status and role of each family member changes
as time goes on, but the basic needs for kindness
and courtesy remain.

Almost everything a woman does in the home can be
hired done if money is available. Household help
can be brought in. The laundry can be sent out.
Lightning-fast meals can be heated in a radar oven.
But no one can be hired to give a home the fragrance

of a kind, radiant, happy woman. This is Mother's
major role.

Some studies show that in certain cases, mothers of
nursery-school children actually spend more time
with them than mothers of children at home. In other
words, some mothers who aren't working aren't really
doing much mothering. And some working mothers
are more relaxed, and plan more activities with their
children than nonworking mothers. It's not the quantity
of time spent with children, but the quality of that time
that's important. It's not how many hours a day,
but how much closeness, how much growing love
and understanding result from those hours. This takes
intelligent planning and personal inconvenience on the
part of any parent, under any circumstance.

J. Allan Petersen

YOU AND OTHER WOMEN

by Eileen Guder

Remember the old nursery rhyme about the little girl with the curl? "And when she was good, she was very, very good and when she was bad, she was horrid." Though I'm not a gambling woman, I would wager that those lines were written by a man. Beneath the childish jingle there lies a rather wry view of women.

But before we leap to the defense of our sex, let's take a long look at ourselves. The poem is right; we can be horrid.

All men are sinners: they can be arrogant, greedy, cowardly, cruel, or just plain ornery. But it pains me to admit that we women have some special, mean little sins that seem to be ours alone. They are often the things that men dislike us for. It may be that these sins are only the common sins of mankind, but shaped and twisted by the nature of women so that in us they have a special form. Whatever the reason for them, they do a lot of hurting, both to others and in the long run to ourselves.

I hardly know what to call the first unpleasant "little" sin. It's so vague and fuzzy in outline it's almost impossible to define. An attitude rather than a deed, it often leads to ugly words and actions. Perhaps the best way to label it is to describe it as a kind of secret competitiveness toward every other woman, antagonism masked beneath pretended friendship. Men are often competitive, but usually in an open way. They are out to be the best in sports or in selling or in school, but they compete openly. We women compete by regarding all other women as a threat to us *as women*.

I suppose it's natural that women feel threatened by other women. We are always in the position of waiting for men to make the first move, and that means we live in uncertainty. Our sins are the sins of the insecure, not the aggressor. But though this may explain our sin, it's no excuse. Just as we are told to forgive our enemies, to love the unlovely, to turn the other cheek, so we're expected to behave with Christian love toward other women. If that's against nature, we must remember that Christianity itself is against nature — as our nature is against God. Our nature is to be suspicious, selfish sinners. Only in Christ are we emancipated from that innate ugliness of being. We must be continually on the alert to step on this ugly sin in ourselves.

There are absolutely no rewards for this particular sin. Not only do we displease God, but we cheat ourselves of any possible good by closing off a relationship before it can get started. And we earn the dislike and contempt of men. They rightly suspect that a woman who doesn't like other women must have something pretty basic wrong with her.

Two other sins grow out of this spirit of competitiveness toward other women — as maggots grow out of garbage. The first is a particularly mean kind of gossip — telling someone what another person has said about them. I say this with shame, because I've done it; and I've been bitterly sorry each time. I doubt if there are many women who haven't done it at some time or other. Sometimes the hidden desire to wound is buried very deeply, so that we don't recognize it in ourselves. But it's usually there. What possible good can it do to repeat something (unless it's very kind) that another person has said? Does it help or build up in any way? I think not. And it always hurts. We are doing two things when we tell tales like this — we're putting the person whom we're quoting in a bad light, and we're hurting the person we tell it to. The hidden implication is that we, ourselves, agree with whatever it is that we're repeating and want our hapless listener to know it. But we haven't got the courage to come out and say it, so we hide behind someone else's words.

To pick up and repeat unkind little remarks from someone else is as bad as having said them in the first place, perhaps worse, because the story usually loses nothing in the telling. In some situations to do this can be outright slander, and in no situation is it ever good. This is a female trait I dislike and am ashamed of in myself, one that I fear and distrust in others. And its sister sin is just as bad — telling tales on someone.

One of the proofs or demonstrations to me of original sin is that all children are born talebearers. Self-righteous pride shines out of their little faces as they run to mama with the glad tidings of brother's naughtiness. As the little darlings grow up, they become more subtle about talebearing, but the same motives underlie it: jealousy and envy.

Talebearing has its own special style in the Christian world. I once knew a woman who always preceded the most damaging revelations about other women by saying piously, "We must all remember to pray for . . ." and then it would come. The variation on the theme was, "There is something that's really been a burden to me that I wish you'd pray about. Of course, we must keep this between ourselves, but. . . ." Either way, the story always got around.

Another kind of talebearing masquerades as concern for the person being confided in. "I just thought you ought to know," is quite frequently the prelude to this story. Sometimes it's the boss whose interests are being looked out for, sometimes a mutual friend. But always the story provokes tensions and unhappiness. There's an alternative to talebearing, however. Sometimes there is something wrong which needs to be aired, and the right person to go to is the one who did or said the wrong thing.

In an office, for instance, rather than complaining to the boss about the woman you have to work with, it's much better to tell the woman herself when she says or does something you don't like. This is more honest and saves burdening the poor employer with troubles in addition to his business worries. And it certainly makes for better relations in the office.

I know this is hard for women to do. We are ready to imagine all sorts of bad reactions, to invent a thousand excuses for avoiding a direct confrontation, but it's the only way. Even if it's difficult to face a woman with a grievance, suspecting rightly she may respond with anger, that anger is nothing to the wrath she'll feel when the tale is carried to her superior. Most of us are sensitive enough to recognize that the person who tattles on us really intends to put us in a very bad light, and we rightly resent it. And we also, I think, end up disliking the one who comes to us with a story about someone else.

It may take a while for us to realize that the kind, seemingly solicitous person is really nothing more than a tattletale, but eventually it sinks in.

Let me hasten to add that the things I'm most ashamed of, myself, the memories that still cause me to burn with embarrassment and remorse, are the times I've done this despicable thing. I know that God's forgiveness includes even this meanness, and for that I thank him daily. Adultery, embezzling, cowardice are not worse than this "small" mean sin.

Have you noticed that each one of these unlovely sins is effected by *talking?* I used to think of talking as distinct from action, but not any more. Talking is as decisive, as concrete as striking a blow or slamming a door. Talk can wound and cut and bite, or it can soothe and heal. As Christians we are commanded to be healers. It could be that in the eyes of heaven, words spoken are as definite in shape as acts, and this is why Jesus said that every word spoken shall be accounted for in the day of judgment. That is a terrible and sobering thought, for without God's forgiveness we should all be lost.

If, from all of the thousands of words in the language, you were asked to select the one that would influence your life more than any other, could you pick the right word?

I call it the "magic word," and it is "Attitude!" Once we are grown and on our own, this word actually controls our environment, our entire world.

If you are curious about what kind of an attitude you have, a simple test will tell you what it has been up to this point in your life. Just answer this question with a "yes" or "no": "Do you feel the world is treating you well?" If your attitude toward the world is good, you will obtain good results. If your attitude is excellent, your results will be excellent. If your attitude is negative, little that is positive awaits you. And if your attitude is just so-so, you will live in a world that isn't particularly bad, nor particularly good, just so-so.

Adopting a good, healthy attitude toward life doesn't affect life and the people with whom we come in contact nearly so much as it affects us. As it says in the Bible: "As ye sow, so shall ye reap."

It would be impossible even to estimate the number of jobs that have been lost, the number of marriages ruined by poor attitudes, all because people are waiting for others, or the world, to change toward them — instead of being big enough and wise enough to realize that we only get back what we put out.

In thirty days you can change your world and your environment by making this simple test. For thirty days treat every person you meet, without a single exception, as the most important person on earth. You will find that they will begin treating you the same way. You see, every person, as far as he is concerned, is the most important person on earth. How does the world look at you? Exactly as you look at the world.

Earl Nightingale

LIVE ALONE AND LOVE IT

from CORONET

Every live-aloner needs some sort of stiffening to her day: a spine, a *structure*. Otherwise, she risks deteriorating into a blob — bored, depressed, restless, lonely. Psychologists talk about "structure hunger" which, if it isn't satisfied, often leaves you feeling that every day is Blue Monday.

A job makes a big difference in morale, not to mention the money it provides, though it's perfectly possible to structure your day successfully without a job.

Some jobs are lonely and unsociable, and exactly what a live-aloner doesn't need. After all, you're already spending lots of time alone, aren't you? But other jobs have plenty of friendly, human contact that's as warming as a fur coat on a winter day. A switch from a lonely, unsociable job can be worth the trouble. One girl I know, bright, young, friendly, came to New York five years ago from Des Moines and got a secretarial job in a one-person office, even though she'd been voted the most gregarious girl in the class. Two weeks on the job, and she began to bite her nails. By the third week she was back at the employment agency, and within a month was working as an editorial secretary on a women's magazine. Her life is now full of daily stimulation and plenty of people, male and female, several of whom have become good friends. In fact, around deadline time there's so much going on at the magazine that it's a relief to escape to the tranquility of her apartment, wash her hair, and fall into bed.

If you've spent years depending on a husband, you're inclined to rate your abilities so low that you're discouraged to begin with. You might feel there's nothing you qualify for (even if you did teach high school mathematics in 1952) except perhaps, hopefully, a Christmas saleswoman job in a department store. Or you may wonder if you can learn typing, or does your age stand in your way? *Brushing up* are words that loom large in

the mind of a woman who is thinking of trying to get
back in the job market. *"Maybe I can brush up
on my shorthand. Maybe I can brush up on stenography.
Maybe I can brush up. . . ."* A dozen bottom-of-the-
barrel jobs occur to her.

But this is actually the perfect time for a live-aloner
to think, "What have I always wanted to do?"
"What would I *like* to do?" And not, "I might be able
to qualify as a stenographer."

"What would I like to do?" is an exhilarating thought,
thick with possibilities. Why not aim for work that you'd
enjoy, work that's pleasurable? There are a dozen jobs
that would suit your taste, your personality, a lot better
than a dozen others. Some jobs will fire up your ambition,
give you a goal, make it impossible to be bored, evenings
alone or not. You may get irritated and frustrated
and angry and exasperated, and maybe you'll feel over-
worked, but you won't be bored. The job will give you
too much personal satisfaction for that.

Maybe you'll have to go back to school to get a
particular job that intrigues you. Well, why not? You
have days or evenings to take courses. No one's going to
complain if instead of cleaning the closets or doing the
laundry you're out taking a course in accounting or
French or bookkeeping.

If you'd like to develop a specialty or have some talent
but you think, "It's too late" or "I'm too old," that's
nonsense. Plenty of people bloom late (you may be one)
because they didn't get a chance to bloom earlier.
After all, Paderewski didn't start to become a concert
pianist until he was in his fifties. Some successful women
writers of children's books, like Laura Ingalls Wilder
who wrote *Little House in the Big Woods,* and so on,
began writing in their sixties. The Roman statesman Cato
started to learn Greek when he was in his eighties,
George Eliot started writing in her forties, and Grandma
Moses picked up her first paintbrush when she was
seventy-eight.

Enjoyment is the thing. If you're going to have
to work, have a good time at it, whatever it is. Use your
time alone, to grow. I know one live-aloner who in her
forties entered Cornell with only an indifferent high

school record, a sum of borrowed money, and stubborn determination. After an admittedly costly, hard-working time she emerged a full-fledged psychologist. It took her years, and she's still paying back the money she borrowed. But she is rapidly earning enough money to pay simultaneously for a good apartment and good-looking clothes. She is also adding to a small collection of paintings on her living-room walls, and she has dozens of stimulating friends. Four years ago, she would rather have been almost anybody else she knew. Now she says she can't think of anyone she'd rather be than herself. If you're in your thirties, forties, or older and can get up enough nerve and enough money to become a professional anything-at-all, you'll get a lot more than only a paycheck.

Of course you may not feel like blooming late or blooming at all. But you'll generally have to know at least some skill if you're going to have a halfway decent chance at a worthwhile salary and an enjoyable place to work, with people you'd like to know. Being a good typist is a great asset. Typing is the best door-opener to interesting jobs, as any reputable employment agency will tell you. Typing is an important skill, when you want to get back into the job market, or even if you want to switch from a lonesome office to a lively one. One good thing for the live-aloner is that typing is the entrée into the active, hectic world of advertising, broadcasting, publishing, and a dozen other exciting fields. Typing can be a foot in the door to dozens of careers, even some you may not have thought you wanted. But once you're in an exciting office, it can act like the smell of grease paint to actors in the theater.

Any number of women alone who have solid incomes are tempted to do volunteer work as a way of "doing something." Besides, it's for humanity isn't it? And unselfish. It is fine to be noble and think of volunteer work and what you can do for humanity. But the way to accomplish most for humanity (and yourself) is to select a volunteer area that is related to your own personality, whether it's working with children, fund-raising, helping the elderly, or whatever, and then boning up on the subject first. Learning anything from an efficient system of filing, to office management to start with, if you're going to help out in a charitable organization's office, can make your volunteer work worthwhile. Otherwise, you'll just be a nuisance.

There are some live-aloners for whom, for one reason or another, a job isn't feasible. If you're among those women, you're going to have to create a backbone for your day if you hope to skirt a Blue Monday kind of existence.

Without a job, you can develop other interests, you can become involved in helping a political party, you can take a course in anything from botany to medieval literature. You can take advantage of all the free or inexpensive daytime weekday activities.

But the point is to *do* these things. And for that you need a schedule. It doesn't matter what kind of schedule, as long as it gets you up, out, and into action. One of the most successful live-aloners I know is a teacher who retired after thirty years of teaching the history of art. Every morning her alarm clock goes off at 7:30, and she gets up and follows a planned day, already jotted down in advance on her calendar. It might be anything, but it is *specific*. Since she hasn't much money, it is generally free or inexpensive. She has overcome that bugaboo of live-aloners — the uneasy feeling of *I don't want to go alone*. She goes wherever it pleases her to go.

"*Any* schedule" is the idea. It doesn't necessarily have to involve getting up early in the morning — there's no particular virtue in greeting the dawn. But the important thing is to have a schedule that includes some kind of self-growth, some passionate interest to follow. Pick one and follow it. There are plenty around, from ecology to music to working to push your present mayor out and a better one in.

Faith is . . .
. . . cooperating with God
in changing me,
rather than

taking refuge in
piously
berating myself.

Pamela Reeve

A FEW KIND WORDS FOR FEMININITY

by Ruth Stafford Peale

The other day Norman and I were taking a plane from Newark. Sitting near us in the big air terminal was another couple. The man was a gentle-looking person with an air of patient resignation. The woman, who wore slacks and had her hair cut severely short, was as positive and assertive as her husband was meek and retiring. She was the one who tipped the porter, who carried the tickets, who strode up to the desk to ask for flight information. She spoke in a loud, authoritative voice. Her gestures were commanding and decisive. We watched this oddly matched pair with fascination until their plane was called and they disappeared from view.

"Do you suppose," Norman said, "she's one of those militant feminists who go around putting stickers on advertisements they don't like, saying 'Unfair to women?' "

"Well," I said cautiously, "I don't know about that. But it's easy to see who runs the show in that marriage."

"I don't understand it," my husband said. "Of course, I don't understand quite a few things, but what I really don't understand is what's so good about a masculine woman or a feminine man!"

I'll have to agree with my husband. If the good Lord chose to divide the human race into two distinctive sexes, I don't see why anyone should try to blur the distinction. It seems to me that a man should possess — and occasionally display — the basic characteristics of the male animal: aggressiveness, combativeness, a drive to be dominant in most areas, including marriage. I also think that unless a woman is willing to look and act and be feminine, she's never going to be a success as a wife or a mother or even as a person.

Sometimes I think European women understand this better than American wives do. Recently I read an interview with Madame Louis Jourdan. She was talking to Eugenia Sheppard of the New York *Post* about marriage and the contrast in attitudes here and abroad.

Said Madame Jourdan: "The way a French woman treats her husband is different. You cater to him all the time. He's the head of the family. We French women enjoy being wives and not competing. American women are very independent. I admire them, but we don't want to be that way."

Why don't they want to be that way? Because they value their femininity too much; their femininity and the rewards it brings them.

Here's Madame Jourdan's formula for a long marriage . . . and she's talking to other wives: *"You have to keep making it attractive."* What a lot of wisdom packed into seven words! Madame Jourdan is saying that marriage is something you can never take for granted. It's not a machine that will run along predictably and accurately, like a clock. The variables are always changing. You have to keep working, adjusting, changing with them. If you don't, you're lost.

Of course, feminists would object to the implication that making a marriage work is primarily the woman's responsibility. But on the deepest level it really is. Since the human race began, woman's elemental role has been to attract and hold a mate. There are many other roles she can and does play, but this one is basic.

I agree with the feminists in some things, such as their claim that women should receive equal pay for doing the same job as men, and have equal opportunity for advancement in any field. But I can't go along with some of their more strident demands because it seems to me that instead of viewing the male-female relationship as complementary and mutually supportive, they regard it as a competitive struggle.

When women vociferously clamor for the right to compete with men, they become essentially combative — which is a masculine trait. They may insist on doing everything that men do, but inevitably in the process they become more like men. And obviously the more masculine they are, the less feminine they can be.

The trend away from femininity in this country is nothing new; it has been going on for years. Most of the change has come about during my lifetime. I think it really got under way after the first World War, when along with the right to vote women also insisted they had the "right" to drink, smoke, swear, and put aside standards of sexual conduct that they had maintained for generations. This drastic change in values was very apparent by the time I got to college, and it has been accelerating ever since.

Whether or not this "emancipation" of women had anything to do with the subsequent appearance of ugly manifestations in our society — the decline of everyday honesty, increase in crime, sexual permissiveness, erosion of discipline, disrespect for law, contempt for authority, increasing reliance on violence as a solution to problems — is something that can't be proved. But to me it seems highly probable that a direct connection exists.

Take a sensitive and intuitive genius like Irving Berlin: What is he saying when he writes a song with words as nostalgic and wistful as these?

The girl that I marry will have to be
Soft and pink as a nursery.

Is he just sketching a lacy and impossibly romantic Valentine, or is he trying to remind us of the days when America was stronger and better because its women had an identity and an integrity and an appeal that has been lost?

Along with this flight from femininity (and perhaps because of it) has come a corresponding feminization of men. Certainly in terms of dress and appearance the difference between the sexes has steadily diminished. The other day I saw a cartoon in which, having just married a shaggy couple, the minister was saying plaintively, "Now will one of you please kiss the bride?" Funny? Well, yes. But also a little depressing. The more alike the sexes become, the less exciting relationships between them are bound to be.

This whole trend works against the powerful polarity that is built into sex differentiation, the force that makes male-female attraction the deep and thrilling thing it can be. Not long ago I was with a group of young women where this subject of feminine liberation came up. "Men," said one of them scornfully, "don't want us to be their equals. Look at the way women are portrayed

in a magazine like *Playboy* — mindless, brainless objects
for sexual gratification, nothing more. It's time we put
an end to this sort of exploitation. Who wants to be
just a plaything for some man?"

Well, no one wants to be just a plaything, I agree.
But what sort of sexual partner is a woman going to make
if this kind of negative thought, this sense of grievance
and resentment, is uppermost in her mind? Noncooperative,
at best. Downright frigid, at worst. If, indeed, with
such a hostile attitude she's able to attract a man at all!

I don't pretend for a moment that the lavender-and-lace
type of woman portrayed by Mr. Berlin could come back
and function successfully in today's streamlined world.
That dream girl is gone for good. But if modern women
are wise, they will make a conscious and deliberate effort
to retain some of her qualities: the gentleness, compassion,
idealism, yes, the purity that men once expected from
their wives — and still hope for and still need, whether
they admit it or not.

*Instead of withdrawing, we are to go out and
communicate with the world. We need to discover how,
practically, we can initiate and develop friendships
with non-Christians and then realistically, relevantly,
and lovingly explain to them the gospel of Jesus Christ.*

*The art of friendship has been lost by many Christians
because they feel their time is being wasted when it's not
invested in a specifically religious activity. To be
a friend may involve listening to a neighbor's troubles
or participating socially with him in non-religious activities
that are of mutual interest. Coffee klatches and
other social activities aren't necessarily a waste of time,
even though no opportunity for a direct reference
to the gospel develops at the moment. If we are
committing our time to the Lord, the Holy Spirit will,
in His time, give natural opportunities to speak
about the Savior.*

Paul E. Little

3 THE WOMAN AND HER HEALTH

NINE STEPS TO A LONGER LIFE

by Blake Clark

"How can I feel better and live longer?"

For the answer to this question, some 200,000 people a year come to the famed Mayo Clinic. Since the turn of the century, when brothers William and Charles Mayo started the clinic in the small town of Rochester, Minnesota, this medical mecca has been sought out by more than two million persons — kings, plumbers, presidents, artists, farmers, executives.

Though they come with every malady known to medical science, what they really want to know is, "How can I feel better and live longer?"

"What do you tell them?" I asked ten of the leading members of the Mayo staff (average experience at the clinic: 20 years). Their answers are based on observations of thousands of individuals, many of whom they see year after year, and are colored by their distress that a large number of these people could have prevented their own illness or early death. Indeed, many need not have come at all.

Here are the steps that these doctors recommend for longer, healthier days on earth.

1/ *Realize that a longer life is chiefly up to you.*
"To a greater extent than ever before," says Dr. Bruce E. Douglass, chairman of the division of environmental medicine, "barring accidents, longevity is up to the individual." The enormous gain in life expectancy in America is a gift of modern medicine, research, and public-health measures. The top killers at the beginning of the century were infectious diseases — pneumonia and influenza, tuberculosis, diarrhea and enteritis, diphtheria. They accounted for one-third of all fatalities. Now, thanks to hygienic and medical advances, all are far down on the danger list.

Today's major killers, says Dr. Douglass, are the diseases of the middle and later years. Arteriosclerosis and cancer account for 75 percent of all nonaccidental deaths among adults. Yet the alert individual can do *more* than the doctor to protect himself from getting these disorders. Knowing this gives us the incentive to be less fatalistic — and to take better care of ourselves.

2/ *Have a periodic medical checkup.* This is your first investment in future health, says Dr. Albert Hagedorn, section head in hematology and internal medicine. Chest X-rays may reveal an early lesion, the cardiogram an indication of arteriosclerosis, blood pressure tests a susceptibility to hypertension. If so, you can take preventive action at once.

It is especially in the crucial age group from forty to fifty that today's killers creep in. "We find that if you weather this dangerous decade," says Dr. Douglass, "and continue to take care of yourself, there can be many years of smooth sailing to the seventies and beyond."

3/ *Don't ignore symptoms.* "I think of a young lady from Wisconsin who ignored a vaginal discharge," says gynecologist Dr. Mary Elizabeth Mussey. Her cervical cancer was discovered too late. A woman may greatly diminish her chances of dying of this type of cancer, adds Dr. Mussey, if she goes once a year for the painless, inexpensive "Pap" test, which detects malignant cells in time for successful treatment.

"Just this morning," cancer specialist Dr. Harry Bisel said in dismay, "a girl in her early thirties admitted she'd watched the lump in her breast grow until it was the size of a baseball. Breast cancer is the Number 1 tumor we see, and we can cure three out of four if we treat them early." If they have time to spread to the lymph nodes in the armpit, the chances for cure go down to one in four.

"People have a great ability to ignore symptoms," observed Dr. Kenneth G. Berge, section head in internal medicine and professor of clinical medicine. "All of us here have seen patients who have endured repeated chest pains without telling anyone. They say, 'I was afraid it was my heart and hoped it would go away.'" But an early visit to the doctor frequently means the difference between living in fear of a disease that doesn't exist and taking proper care of one that does.

4/ *Reduce your weight steadily each year.* "Most

patients," Dr. Douglass told me, "come here believing
that it's normal to gain as they grow older — a dangerous
misconception. As we age, we gain fat at the expense
of muscle. If you keep the same weight at sixty that
you had at thirty, you may be carrying a hazardous
excess." Remember: fat people usually don't grow old.

5/ *Stop smoking.* The doctors who know tobacco best
hate it most. Heart specialist Dr. Daniel C. Connolly used
to smoke forty cigarettes a day. But, seeing the tragic
effects on patients, he and most of his twenty-two
colleagues in cardiology stopped. "Patients are highly
motivated to quit *after* a heart attack," he said. "We'd
like them to get the motivation first."

"My specialty is hardening of the arteries," said
Dr. John L. Juergens. "I tell my friends who are artery
surgeons that I can do as much for a patient's legs
by getting him to quit smoking as they can by operating."
Dr. Juergens has followed closely the progress of 159
cigarette smokers suffering from advanced arteriosclerosis
of the extremities. Of seventy-one who stopped smoking,
none required amputation. But of the eighty-eight
who continued to smoke, ten had to lose a limb.
"Nicotine," says Dr. Juergens, "is a potent constrictor
of arteries. I tell patients, 'It's your cigarettes or your
leg.'"

Dr. David T. Carr, who has treated hundreds of persons
with lung cancer, hates cigarettes with a passion. He
considers them the Number 1 health hazard in diseases
of the chest. Stopping smoking, he says, is one thing
millions of individuals can do to protect their health
and prolong their lives. Tobacco is not going to be
outlawed, he tells patients. You alone can save yourself
from its lethal effects.

6/ *Watch out for alcohol.* Dr. Gastineau says that
the average person doesn't realize how quickly alcohol
creeps in for the kill. Liquor carries a lot of calories,
he points out. "A two-ounce martini before lunch
and a couple before dinner and you're taking in nearly
600 calories a day. Eventually, in a certain number of
cases, fat accumulates in the liver and leads to cirrhosis —
a *preventable* cause of early death." The drinker may

not realize that the liver can be damaged over a period
of time without causing pain.

7/ *Exercise regularly.* "Once considered an indulgence
for a few, exercise is now a must for all," declared
Dr. Douglass. Fit, responsive muscles squeeze the veins
and force the blood back toward the heart, lightening
its load of pumping the blood through the circulatory
system.

How much exercise? Dr. Donald Erickson, Mayo
staffer in physical medicine and rehabilitation, has
a rule-of-thumb. "Exercise until you're somewhat short
of breath. Like any other muscle, the heart needs deep
swings of demand — maximum work, maximum rest."
For the normal person, he recommends brisk walking,
jogging, swimming. "The pulse rate must increase, the
breath get short." By exercising regularly, he says,
the individual can do more and more all the time, greatly
benefiting his cardiovascular system, physical vigor,
and mental alertness.

8/ *Be optimistic.* Physiologically, happiness is healthy.
A depressed person suffers a slowing down of all his
metabolic processes. A merry heart does good like
medicine, runs the proverb, but a broken spirit dries
the bones. "You can will yourself to be ill," warns Dr.
Hagedorn. "A case of nerves is not just 'in your head,'
but is as real as a heart attack." The nervous system has
a job, like the heart, and its functioning is affected
by stress, such as extra responsibility and futile worry.

"Our patients have similar problems," say Dr. Hagedorn.
"Yet we see certain of them die young because they
lack a positive attitude." A physician friend of his
had a myocardial infarction and literally died of fright.
"Yet Presidents Eisenhower and Johnson had similar
attacks," observes Hagedorn, "and took the attitude that
they could handle them, and did."

9/ *Take a vacation.* Relief from everyday strains restores
the joy of living. Your vacation must be sensibly planned,
cautions Dr. Berge. "To some, a week camping with
the family in Yellowstone is not a rest but a nightmare."
Just get away from your work routine and do something
you enjoy. Happiness may be as close as your own
garden.

These are the recommendations of some of the world's most highly regarded medical men. Following them might easily extend your own life-span by ten to thirty years.

For the first time in history — it's up to *you*.

To those of you who are so strangely created that you can eat all you want to eat of anything without adding pounds, I will only repeat: Count your blessings. But those of us who are overweight have an extra hurdle to overcome. We must overcome our rebellion at being put together metabolically as we are. Nothing whatever is accomplished by complaining bitterly that your husband can "eat like a horse and stay thin as a rail." If you can't, then just proceed from there.

1/ We must accept *ourselves as we are. We must stop asking, "Why it is that every bite I put into my mouth goes to fat!" If we remain in this attitude, we are secretly blaming God for creating us as he did. We may not admit it, but it's true. And as long as we resent him, even subconsciously, we won't be able to do the next thing. We must know him and we must love him with a love strong enough to make sacrifices for his sake when no one is looking.*

2/ We must be willing *to begin making these sacrifices. He has given us all "choosers." Our part is to use them. I have never lost weight on a diet I started tomorrow. The only time I've ever been able to lose weight is to choose to start now.*

3/ The love-offering. *Make a list of all the rich foods you love with an unholy passion! The list is necessary only in nailing down your determination. So much has been written about caloric content of food, no one really needs to do any research here. The spiritual point is this: When you bake a cake or a pie, or when dessert is passed at a dinner or a banquet,* smile *and say, "No, thank you." It's really just as easy to say as, "Yes, thank you."* And in your heart, right at that moment, make a picture of yourself handing that rich dessert or that bowl of mashed potatoes or that homemade roll directly to the Lord as a love-offering!

When we deprive ourselves of something we love, we feel put upon. But when we give something we love to Someone we love, it's a different thing. I can promise you this will work. It has worked sixty pounds worth for me and I expect it to work for the remaining twenty.

A woman's grooming, her adornment, her size are definite indications of who is at the controls of her life.

Is Jesus Christ at the controls of your life?

Or are you?

Eugenia Price

TAKE TIME FOR YOURSELF

by T. Leo Brannon

"I always feel so guilty about leaving the children when I take a day for relaxation," said a young mother after a day away from home. Her experience of guilt and remorse is common in a day of harried suburban living, working mothers, and a highly organized society.

Like most young mothers, she felt a desperate need to get away for a while, but then was overcome with feelings of guilt for having left her children. Such feelings partially annul the benefits derived from the experience of getting away from home responsibilities. We feel this sense of guilt because we think that it implies neglect of duty, lack of love, and a too-selfish interest.

In recent years the tendency has been to think of the solution to problems of family life exclusively in terms of togetherness. Parents have been admonished to spend time with their children in order to develop the child's feeling of belonging, and thus strengthen his sense of security and happiness.

Undoubtedly there are blessings and benefits for families who make it a practice to play together, work together, and live together. Yet a time comes when it's equally important for both parent and child to get away in an experience of solitude. Such experiences have good effects for both parents and children that have been grossly ignored. These experiences may be just as productive of healthy family life as being together. In fact, one of the sure evidences of healthy family life is that the members are free of one another, yet bound to one another.

It's well to remember that primarily we are individuals, which implies something of a solitude. The psalmist reminds us that "God setteth the solitary in families" (Psalm 68:6, KJV). In some ways, we can never get away from being solitary persons nor should we try. The human situation in a special sense is inescapably lonely. It is alone that we are born into the world.

Alone we hear and answer God's call to us into the
community of the Christian congregation. Alone we
pray, and alone we die.

Parents Must Watch Their Needs
So something of both the hermit and the companion
is in all of us. Frustration of either of these aspects
of personal life results in feelings of loneliness. It isn't
unusual to hear persons express the feeling of being lonely
in a busy crowd or in the midst of family living. Just
as every person needs the experience of belonging
to a fellowship of persons, he also needs to be alone —
apart from groups of responsibility. Association with
others is actually helpful only to the extent that one can
endure being alone.

That we belong to the fellowship of the family will
give us meaning and support in times of solitude.
Dietrich Bonhoeffer, in his well-known book *Life Together,*
has warned, "One who wants fellowship without solitude
plunges into the void of words and feelings, and one
who seeks solitude without fellowship perishes in the abyss
of vanity, self-infatuation, and despair." The wisest
course for us, then, is to give attention to both the hermit
and companion aspects of our nature.

Someone has said that the first principle for successful
parenthood is: "The parents must survive." More than
just survival is required, however. Continuing development
and growth are required of parents. Wise parents must
not neglect themselves if they are to provide a wholesome
and healthy atmosphere in the home, and if they are to be
the kind of persons who enable children and youth to
mature into personhood.

So much attention has been given in the family life
literature of recent years to the needs and rights of the
young that there has been serious neglect of the basic
needs and rights of parents. Let it be said with force
and clarity that husbands and wives must not be careless
in their own personal growth or the development of their
marriage relationship. To do so invites trouble and distorts
parental love into a form of attention and affection
that smothers their children. They must provide for
each other to get away at times and also to be apart

from the family with each other. (Children are most
dependent on the emotional state of the parents and
the health of the marriage.)

Renew Energies
Perhaps a careful accounting of the profits derived
from getting away from the family will help to relieve
the feeling of guilt for those parents who suffer from it.
Being a parent is a demanding role, one that tests
the wisdom of a Solomon and the strength of a Samson.
It's an awesome experience, at times nothing less than
plain frightening. Therefore, it's tragic when feelings
of guilt enter in to paralyze strength and distort thinking.

One of the first benefits to the parent in getting alone
is the opportunity to renew vital energies. Constant
responsibility drains away energy and tires body and mind.
Mother's normal day is filled with the routines of
motherhood and household duties — diapers, dishes,
menus — with little opportunity for quietness and solitude,
much less any time for sharing emotions and experiences
with her husband. Some time of quietness and solitude
is essential if these vital energies are to be renewed.

Solitude also offers opportunity to drain off the growing
resentments and hostilities that have built up in the
dailiness of family living. Conflicts and agitations are
the normal results of living within the space restrictions
of the home. Seldom is there space enough for the
individual member of the household to find the quietness
needed for regaining inner control and sloughing off
the ordinary agitations that develop from close living.
For this reason, if for no other, regular times of solitude
are essential.

After such times of being alone we are able to return
to the family circle and meet others with different attitudes
and with freshness. LaRochefoucauld has wisely said,
"Absence diminishes little passions and increases great
ones, just as the wind blows out a candle and fans a
flame." As we go apart, we are actually refining our
true family emotional life and reinforcing its structure.

Simple reflection, in quietness and solitude, upon the
significance of family members and their meaning to us
is of inestimable value to family life. Strange and

paradoxical as it may seem, being alone can bring us closer together. Appreciation and understanding are deepened; essentials are clarified; purposes and goals are purified.

Children Gain Independence

Likewise, there are definite gains for the child who is left by a parent. Here is the necessary opportunity for the child to test his ability to face reality without the strong, dominating presence of the parent. As long as the parent is around, the child is relieved from facing these realities alone. Part of the maturing process for him is developing the ability to face life alone.

This should be done, of course, in short testing periods. As parents, we are responsible to develop a mature person with a sense of personal significance, balanced with a sense of the importance of other family members. Providing a house, clothes, and food for our children doesn't complete the requirements of parenthood; developing mature persons is the larger goal.

With the parent away, the child is also freed from the continual unrelenting restraint of the overriding authority that looks over all his actions with an eye of criticism and judgment. Even the most lenient parent represents this sense of outside authority to the child. Being free from this authority allows him to check out personal control over actions and individual autonomy. This may be a more difficult aspect of parenthood than constant care and supervision. Remember that children, too, chafe under constant restrictions and supervision. Relief comes with a period of separation.

Most important of all, the child is permitted freedom to assert and develop individuality. Parents are directly responsible to help their children learn independence and self-reliance. The child's dependence may make Mom and Dad feel important and loved, but dependence won't help the child develop a mature, healthy personality.

Parents need to move out of the immediate sphere of action in order for a child to assert rights and prerogatives and learn to be an individual. Such freedom implies trust and confidence, of course, if bitter explosions of rebellion are to be avoided.

Certainly this isn't an exhaustive discussion of the benefits to be derived from apartness from the family group. But here is sufficient reason for no parent to experience any feeling of remorse or guilt about wanting to get away from the family. Such experiences are just as loving and just as beneficial for a strong, healthy family life as being together.

The wisdom of the ancient philosopher is relevant for modern parents:

The bow that's always bent will quickly break;
   But if unstrung will serve you at your need.
So let the mind some relaxation take
   To come back to its task with fresher heed.

Don't mistake one week of vacation a year with the family as sufficient relaxation. Take regular times apart for meditation and thought, relaxation and refreshment, play and pleasure, quietness and solitude. It isn't sinful to do so!

Then Jesus suggested, "Let's get away from the crowds for a while and rest." For so many people were coming and going that they scarcely had time to eat (Mark 6:31, TLB).

DON'T WORRY!

by John Edmund Haggai

"Died of worry" could be written factually on many tombstones.

Every other hospital bed in the United States is occupied by a mental case, and most of these mental cases are the result of worry.

The word *worry* comes from the Greek word "to divide the mind." Worry divides the mind between worthwhile interests and damaging thoughts. The Apostle James states the unhappy condition of the person with the divided mind: "A double minded man is unstable in all his ways" (James 1:8). Worry is the cause of heartbreak, failure, misunderstanding, suspicion, and most unhappiness.

Has any home gone "on the rocks" that cannot point to "the divided mind" as the cause? It may be that the mind was divided between the wife and another woman. It may be that the wife divided her mind between the husband and "mama." Her mind may have been divided between an inexcusably possessive pre-occupation with her children and her God-ordained responsibilities to her husband. It may be that the mind was divided between home responsibilities and selfish, personal desires.

Don't some children fail in school because of discord in the home — discord that divides their minds between their scholastic responsibilities and the possible outcome of the domestic "cold war"? Only the Lord knows how many businesses have been torpedoed by worry — the divided mind. It is slaying its tens of thousands. It is ravaging homes, leaving in its wake bitter and frustrated parents, as well as insecure and terrified children, all candidates for psychiatric care.

Worry is a sin, a blighting blasting sin, not an excusable constitutional malady nor an unfortunately inherited weakness. Don't think you can excuse yourself as a helpless victim of an uncontrollable condition.

Worry is a sin for two reasons: (1) Worry is distrust in

the truthfulness of God and (2) worry is detrimental
to the temple of God.

1/ *Worry is distrust in the truthfulness of God.* When
you worry you accuse God of falsehood. God's Word says,
"And we know that all things work together for good
to them that love God, to them who are the called
according to his purpose" (Romans 8:28).

Worry says, "Thou liest, O God!" If it is highly insulting
to call a man a liar — although the fact is that David
probably spoke the truth when he said, "All men are
liars" — how infinitely more inexcusable it is to accuse
the Sovereign God of falsehood. He is the God "who
cannot lie."

2/ *Worry is a sin because it is detrimental to the temple
of God.* "Know ye not that ye are the temple of God,
and that the Spirit of God dwelleth in you?" (1 Corinthians
3:16). Worry debilitates and even destroys the temple
of God which is *your own body,* Christian! Some of
the ailments caused by worry are heart trouble, high blood
pressure, some forms of asthma, rheumatism, ulcers, colds,
thyroid malfunction, arthritis, migraine headaches,
blindness, and a host of stomach disorders apart from
ulcers. It also causes palpitations, pains in the back
of the neck, indigestion, nausea, constipation, diarrhea,
dizziness, unexplainable fatigue, allergies, and temporary
paralysis.

Worry is a sin. The Bible is the only book that deals
adequately with the problem of sin. Quite logically,
then, we go to the Word of God to find the solution
to this problem.

"Delight yourselves in God, yes, find your joy in him
at all times. Have a reputation for gentleness, and never
forget the nearness of your Lord."

"Don't worry over anything whatever; tell God every
detail of your needs in earnest and thankful prayer,
and the peace of God, which transcends human understanding, will keep constant guard over your hearts
and minds as they rest in Christ Jesus."

Here is a last piece of advice. "If you believe in
goodness and if you value the approval of God, fix your
minds on the things which are holy and right and pure
and beautiful and good" (Philippians 4:4-8, Phillips).

Now here is the formula for victory over worry:

Praise plus *Poise* plus *Prayer* equals *Peace.*

Praise

"Rejoice in the Lord alway: and again I say, rejoice"
(Philippians 4:4). You say, "But I don't feel like
rejoicing, I don't feel like being happy." By that you
mean that the circumstances engulfing you are not such as
contribute to your happiness.

You are entitled to no particular commendation simply
because you rejoice when everything goes well. When,
however, you have made praise and rejoicing the habit-
pattern of your life, you have arrived at that place
where you not only bring glory to God but you set up
an immunity against worry.

Rejoice even on blue Mondays and black Fridays.
No condition or circumstance can justify worry. Worry
is a sin. Praise is an antidote to worry.

You say you have troubles? Of course you do.
We all have. When rejoicing has become the habit-pattern
of your life you aren't a *thermometer personality*
registering the temperature of your environment. You are
rather a *thermostat personality* setting the temperature.
Think and act joyfully and you'll feel joyful. It's true
you can't directly control your feelings, but you can
indirectly control them.

You can control your feelings by controlling your
thoughts and your actions. It's a basic law of psychology
that you will feel as you think and act.

I'll give you an illustration. Try it and convince
yourself. Go to a quiet room, stand with your feet about
a foot apart at the heels and at 45-degree angles. Gently
clasp your hands behind your back, smile sweetly, main-
taining complete relaxation of the body. Now start thinking
resentful thoughts.

Did you observe what happened? Immediately you
straightened up because of the contraction of your muscles.
You became taut. Your thoughts, actions, and feelings
are interrelated.

Carry this over into the items of your everyday life.
When you are depressed and forlorn and feel that you

have nothing but trouble, smile. Throw your shoulders
back. Take a good deep breath. Sing. God's Word says,
"For as he thinketh in his heart so is he" (Proverbs 23:7).
You cannot think *fear* and act *courageously*. Conversely,
you cannot think *courage* and act *fearfully*. You
cannot think *hatred* and act *kindly*. Conversely, you
cannot think *kindly* and act *hatefully*. Your feelings
inevitably correspond to your dominant thoughts and
actions. Therefore, in the strength of Christ, master your
thoughts and actions and thus dominate your feelings.

It is impossible for you to "rejoice in the Lord always"
and to worry at the same time. Further, you cannot
remove thoughts of worry and fear by simply saying,
"I don't want to be afraid. I don't want to worry."
Rather, you only crowd out negative thoughts by pushing
in positive thoughts.

In the strength of God, control your thoughts.
Let them be regulated according to the will of God.
Such thoughts will lead to inner poise that shields you
against the self-destructive and fear-producing thoughts
of worry.

Poise
Study the records of those whom the world calls great
and you'll observe that every one of them possesses
the quality of self-control. Many homes are wrecked
through lack of self-control. Well did the wise Solomon
say: "Greater is he that ruleth his spirit than he that
taketh a city."

Enthusiasm is another indispensable ingredient in poise.
Lack of enthusiasm is ruinous to happiness in the home,
success in business, the making and keeping of friends,
and achievement in any field. No great work has ever
been done without enthusiasm. To be sure, some people
seem to be born with greater capacity for enthusiasm
than others. However, this quality can be developed
by focusing your mind upon a worthwhile goal until its
attainment becomes your "magnificent obsession." Enthusiasm leads to achievement. A sense of achievement,
an awareness of accomplishment is indispensable to poise
and to peace.

The person who has totally surrendered himself to Christ

has a serenity, a poise, that bespeaks a peace that cannot be defined — "a peace that passeth all understanding" (Philippians 4:7).

A mother came to me greatly distraught mentally and emotionally. The anguish of her heart was torturing her body. She had been under psychiatric care for more than four years, during which time she had been subjected to shock treatments. She was a professing Christian and gave every evidence of sincerely wanting to do the will of God. After some brief but pertinent probing I asked her quite frankly if something had taken place in her life, whether years ago or more recently, that was constantly preying on her mind. She said there was. It was a sin committed during adolescence. I asked if she had confessed it to the Lord. She assured me that she had, over and over and over — probably a thousand times.

I said, "You see, actually, you're making God a liar. You confessed that sin once. God promised you absolute forgiveness as we read in the words of 1 John 1:9 — 'If we confess our sins, he is faithful and just to forgive us our sins, and to cleanse us from all unrighteousness.'

"The reason you're going through this torture is simply because you haven't surrendered yourself completely to the Lord. You don't trust him. You're not willing to take him at his Word. He has forgiven you, but you refuse to believe it. You refuse to forgive yourself. You are making the mistake of thinking that repentance is repining and that self-examination is brooding. Now, then, simply take God at his Word. Surrender your life completely to him. Surrender the limitations of your finite mind to the assurance of his immutable Word. He has forgiven you. Now in complete surrender — *believe it.*" The Lord has corrected the situation and she is now enjoying the poise that comes with surrender.

Paul's formula for victory over worry is praise, poise, and prayer. Having discussed praise and poise, we now come to that leg of the tripod without which the other two legs praise and poise cannot stand. That leg is prayer.

"Peace is possible only to those who have related themselves to God through Christ — who is the Prince of Peace."

Until you come to Jesus Christ as a self-confessed sinner and by faith accept the salvation he has provided, you are spiritually dead. Death means separation. You are separated from God. Therefore you have no peace. Nor can you have peace. Your only hope is in Christ, the Prince of Peace, through whom you have access to God.

Perfect Peace

"And the peace of God, which passeth all understanding, shall keep your hearts and minds through Christ Jesus" (Philippians 4:7).

Just as worry means "divide the mind," so we might say that peace is "uniting the mind," fastening it upon worthwhile goals and stimulating it with worthwhile motives. God is the Author of this peace. God is not the Author of confusion. This is a genuine peace begotten of God.

The assurance of this peace is conditional upon no outside circumstance, for this peace is possible only through Christ. A life without Christ is life without peace. Without him you have excitement, worldly success, fulfilled dreams, fun, gratified passions, but *never peace*. If you are to enjoy the peace of God over daily worries and cares and anxieties, small though they are — "the little foxes spoil the vines" — you must fix your mind upon him. "Looking unto Jesus" (Hebrews 12:2).

Keep your mind "stayed" on him. This will enable you to fulfill the Bible formula of Praise, Poise, Prayer = Peace.

Patients often tell me that they are just as tired upon arising as when they went to bed. Sleep refreshes our exhaustion from work, but not the weariness that stems from worry. Many people take their anxieties to bed with them. The best medicine for that is to count one's blessings and thank the Lord for his gifts and kindnesses.

S. I. McMillen, M.D.

WHAT TO DO ABOUT PREMENSTRUAL TENSION

by William A. Nolen, M.D.

Ninety percent of women in their reproductive years, roughly between 15 and 50, suffer from premenstrual tension. Some don't have much trouble — a little anxiety, perhaps, or a mild case of the blues. But others get so depressed that they can barely get out of bed in the morning.

What causes this monthly problem? Sad to say, no one really knows. The favorite theory, and one that seems most reasonable, is that it's a matter of hormone balance. Your ovaries produce two hormones, estrogen and progesterone. About a week before menstruation begins, the balance between the two hormones shifts; this imbalance causes your body to retain water. Your breasts may swell and become sore; so may your ankles and fingers. You may feel bloated and, in fact, may gain five or six pounds in the few days before your menstrual period begins.

What you may not be aware of is that your brain becomes water-logged too; and, theoretically, the brain swelling may cause nervousness, anxiety, and depression. When you get premenstrual blues, it's probably your hormones that are to blame.

However, the woman who is in the grip of premenstrual tension doesn't really care about her hormones. She's not interested in a scientific explanation of why she feels as rotten as she does. The women I see with this particular problem don't really care about much of anything; they just want to feel better.

There are a few things they definitely don't want: They don't want their kids making a lot of noise; they don't want to have unexpected guests for dinner; and they most certainly don't want to hear anyone say, "Oh, come on, cheer up. It's all in your head." In fact, they would like very much to hit with a baseball bat anyone, and particularly a husband, who utters that line. I have read that of all violent crimes committed by women, 62 percent are committed in the week before their period begins. Any woman who suffers from premenstrual tension will understand why.

Unfortunately, having outlined the accepted "scientific" explanation for premenstrual tension, I have to confess that doctors don't have a cure for it. Diuretics (drugs that cause water excretion) will reduce swelling of the breasts, ankles, and hands. They will even decrease the heavy feeling in the pelvis that some women note in the premenstrual phase, which is probably due to pelvic congestion. (Incidentally, this pelvic congestion sometimes causes increased sexual desire.) A low-salt diet will also help reduce fluid retention. But except in rare instances, diuretics and low-salt diets won't cure the nervous symptoms associated with the ailment. Take diuretics if swelling bothers you, but don't expect them to help your nerves.

Many women — at least 50 percent, according to certain investigations — will lose all premenstrual-tension symptoms when put on hormone pills. If your doctor recommends that you take these (and birth-control pills are one type of hormone pill), you may get rid of your monthly blues. However, one in ten women will find that her symptoms increase in severity when she takes hormones. If you're one of them, the pills are not for you.

But if you don't want to or can't take hormones, don't despair. Other help is available.

I'm not a big advocate of tranquilizers and mood pills, but if there's ever a place for them — besides in the treatment of mental illness — it's in the treatment of the tense premenstrual woman. The woman who suffers from anxiety and irritability, who snaps at her husband and children or snarls at her co-workers, really ought to take tranquilizers when she is suffering from premenstrual tension. The woman who becomes depressed, cries a lot and finds it almost impossible to carry on a conversation because she's so low, ought to go on mood elevators while she's "down." Women who suffer severely from premenstrual tension aren't their normal selves. They should take any medication that will bring them back to "normal" or close to "normal." This type of medication should, of course, be used only with the approval of your own physician.

Let me make clear right now that premenstrual tension is not the same as menstrual cramps. These pains are probably caused by contractions of the uterine muscle and usually don't occur for the first two or three years of menstruation. Sometimes they are mild, sometimes quite severe.

Treatment (except in rare cases of some unusual physical abnormality) is simple, and hasn't changed much since these cramps were first described more than two thousand years ago. Aspirin and heat to the abdomen are usually adequate. Sometimes a stronger pain killer is necessary; in very severe cases, hormone treatment may help. It's best not to get tired out, but women who keep active and continue to exercise usually get over their cramps more quickly than those who take to their beds. Emotional upsets seem to make the cramps worse.

Fortunately, after their middle twenties or after a pregnancy, whichever comes first, most women have very little trouble with menstrual cramps. They disappear spontaneously.

But this doesn't happen with premenstrual tension. And if you'll concede, as I will, that the most miserable person in the world is the woman in the grip of a severe attack of premenstrual tension, then you'll also have to concede that the second-most miserable person is whoever is closest to her. It is almost impossible to behave properly toward a woman with premenstrual tension. It's impossible to live or work in peace with her.

I probably sound like a male chauvinist pig. I'm sorry. Let me assure you that I am most sympathetic to women with this problem. I think they deserve all the medical help they can get: diuretics, hormones, mood pills, anything that will alleviate their distress. But I also feel that the woman who knows she is susceptible to premenstrual tension owes it to those who are close to her to help herself. If she doesn't, she isn't being fair to herself or to them.

Finally, one last suggestion: Most men don't know what premenstrual tension is all about. I confess that until recently, when I was preparing to write this article, I didn't know much about it — and I'm a doctor. I think I'd have been a better doctor and a more compas-

sionate husband if I'd learned more about it years ago.
So let me suggest that you ask those males who are
close to you to read up on premenstrual tension.
If they can be made to understand that it is just as real
a condition as, for example, pneumonia, it may help
both you and them to get through those bad days
without friction.

*Nearly everybody has been in a J. C. Penney Store.
But few people know about one of the most important
events in the life of J. C. Penney, the founder.*

*In the crash of 1929, J. C. Penney's business was solid
but he had made some unwise personal commitments.
He became so worried that he couldn't sleep. Then he
developed shingles, a disorder that can cause great
annoyance and severe pain. He was hospitalized and
given sedatives, but got no relief and tossed all night.
A combination of circumstances had broken him so
completely, physically and mentally, that he was
overwhelmed with fear of death. He wrote farewell
letters to his wife and son, for he didn't expect to live
until morning.*

*The next morning the great business tycoon heard
singing in the hospital chapel. He pulled himself
together and entered as the group was singing "God Will
Take Care of You." Then followed a Scripture reading
and a prayer. In Mr. Penney's own words, "Suddenly
something happened. I can't explain it. I can only call
it a miracle. I felt as if I had been instantly lifted out
of the darkness of a dungeon into warm, brilliant sunlight.
I felt as if I had been transported from hell to paradise.
I felt the power of God as I had never felt it before.
I realized then that I alone was responsible for all
my troubles. I know that God with His love was there
to help me. From that day to this, my life has been free
from worry. I am 71 years old, and the most dramatic
and glorious minutes of my life were those I spent
in that chapel that morning. 'God Will Take Care
of You.' "*

INSIDE INSOMNIA

by Jean E. Laird

Insomnia is, by all odds, the great underground ailment of modern society. In some, it inspires a quantity of drug-taking, and in others, who have a chronic inability to sleep more than three or four hours a night, it may lead to the psychiatrist's couch.

Insomnia is a merry-go-round. We are told that in most instances the victim uses his inadequate sleeping hours to release muscular and mental tensions he was unable to release during the day because he was too exhausted from lack of sleep.

Scientists say that our minds move from light sleep to deep sleep and back again to light sleep many times during the night, the average person having six or seven cycles of sleep, each lasting from seventy to ninety minutes. During the light phase, many persons approach wakefulness, and some may open their eyes and actually awaken. This wakefulness means nothing. *If you don't worry about it,* you'll have a better chance of falling back to sleep.

The experts in the sleep labs also point out that no normal person sleeps "like a log." Anyone gets uncomfortable from staying in one position while asleep, just as he would while staying awake. An average person turns twenty to sixty times during the night.

How much sleep should one get? The accepted standard for a good night's sleep, eight consecutive hours, is a social convention rather than a physiological requirement. The number of hours you require can be determined only by your own experience, and we are told that a certain amount of insomnia is natural and unavoidable.

There is, according to the scientists, no strict necessity for making up for the hours lost from sleep: if you have been robbed of a good night's sleep, you don't need to compensate for it by an afternoon nap. However, an afternoon nap, "even ten minutes," says Dr. Walter C.

Alvarez of the Mayo Clinic, "can make the difference between much fatigue at 5 P.M. and a good reserve of energy."

Is insomnia recognized as an actual disorder? There are, of course, the severe cases we have mentioned, for which psychiatric assistance is sought. By and large, though, while it is more common as a complaint than the common cold, doctors say that insomnia is self-curing. They add that the familiar "I tossed and turned all night and didn't sleep a wink" just isn't true in most cases.

As for your personal need for sleep, if you are in normal health, the chances are that if you habitually tend to go back to sleep after your alarm has gone off you should go to bed earlier. But if you wake up *before* the alarm goes off, you are probably allowing for more sleep than you actually need.

Does your brain require the restoration afforded by sleep? No, say the scientists in the sleep labs. This is because the brain contains no muscles: thus it *cannot* get tired. "Brain-weary" is just a manner of speaking. What passes for "brain fatigue" is a combination of tired bodily muscles and emotional factors — anxiety, perhaps, or boredom or a complex reaction to the monotony of a task done over and over again.

How long can one go on without a night's sleep and still function normally? Experiments conducted at the Walter Reed Institute of Research in Washington, D.C., show that after two days things begin to slip. First to go is the ability to perform tasks that require a certain amount of concentration. A person who operates delicate instruments or drives a car will find that alertness and vigilance diminish. Vision becomes blurred, and you experience lapses of memory. After seventy hours of sleeplessness, hallucinations begin to set in. However, volunteers in sleep experiments have found that exhaustion and mental fogginess produced by long wakefulness quickly disappeared after they had slept for the equivalent of a night or so.

Does the amount of sleep you get have anything to do with the area in which you live? Not really, say the experts. City dwellers have to contend with incessant noises, but their suburbanite relatives aren't much better off. Even if you have a home on the range, it may be right in the path of jet airliners or within earshot of the whistling midnight train.

Maybe our relatives in past centuries didn't have to contend with screeching brakes, but they listened for the telltale noises that meant a band of Indians was about to descend upon them. Or they awakened to the sounds of a wolf ready to have a banquet in the chicken coop.

Scientists agree that modern man sleeps a lot less than his ancestors did, for many reasons. In bygone days, people did more physical work than they do today. Even if they had a leisurely day and weren't tired, they couldn't read or write after dark without getting up repeatedly to fill the lantern or trim a lamp wick. Electricity makes it possible to read half the night without straining the eyes. Electricity brings us 24-hour radio programs, and the late-late show on TV keeps getting later. We have, in other words, a lot more to stay awake for than our ancestors did.

Will it help us to sleep if we turn down the heat in our bedroom? The sleep labs say no. Man's own internal thermostat will fight back. The discomfort of being chilled will tend to keep us awake and make us shiver. Shivering speeds up body metabolism, and this heightens wakefulness.

Why not take a sleeping pill and be done with it? Medical authorities state that more than a hundred over-the-counter sleeping pills are available to the public without prescription. While these pills are mild, they do act as central-nervous-system depressants, slowing down the brain centers that control such vital functions as respiration and blood circulation. No one knows the full extent of their effects upon the body.

What should you do if you have trouble sleeping? Doctors say that trying too hard or worrying too much about it can leave you wide awake staring at the ceiling. Before you know it, you can acquire a full-blown case of insomnia. Persons who have trouble getting to sleep, whether their problem is constant or only occasional, should remember these tips from the sleep lab experts:

1/ Try to relax. Will Grandma's prescription for a glass
of hot milk work? It may help you relax. Warm milk
and celery, strange as it sounds, most often appear
in the somnologists' literature as effective sleep-inducers.
Other ideas that may work for you include warm water,
hot broth, breakfast juice, or a slice of toast. You should
avoid monumental sandwiches, highly-seasoned snacks,
and rich desserts at bedtime.

Going to bed hungry produces stomach contractions
which keep most people awake. On the other hand,
a heavy dinner too late at night, though it may induce
a heavy sleep at first, is likely to produce discomfort
which soon interrupts this sleep.

2/ Naps may mean trouble for you if you overdo them.
Many "insomniacs" snooze most of the afternoon and then
can't understand why they have trouble getting to sleep
at night. Short naps can be beneficial if you take them
on an occasional basis, relying on them only when you
are extremely fatigued.

3/ Try to wind yourself down about an hour before
bedtime. This means no arguments, no TV mysteries.
Try to avoid anything that will make you alert, nervous,
or upset.

4/ Get to bed at a regular time, and your body will
become accustomed to winding down at a certain hour.

Don't expect to drop off into peaceful sleep every night
the minute you hit the pillow. Even the best sleeper
has trouble at least one night in ten. And we don't lose
as much sleep as we think. Hospital nurses are well
accustomed to receiving complaints in the morning
from patients who say that they lie awake all night —
whereas, when these same patients had been checked
on routine rounds, a reverberation in the form of snoring
could be heard halfway down the hall.

One thing to remember: nobody ever died from
insomnia. It does no permanent physical damage, and
some loss of sleep won't impair your working efficiency.
Even if you don't sleep, just lying comfortably stretched
out in bed, with relaxed muscles, will provide sufficient
rest to carry you through the next day, say the experts.
Sleep must come eventually. No human can remain
awake too long.

*Avoid the mistake of concentrating overmuch upon
your feelings. Above all, avoid the terrible error
of making them central. Don't spend too much time
feeling your own pulse, taking your own spiritual
temperature. Don't spend too much time analyzing
your feelings.*

*You must talk to yourself and say: "I am not going
to be dominated by you; these moods shall not control me.
I am going out, I am breaking through." So get up
and walk, and do something.*

*I cannot make myself happy, but I can remind myself
of my belief. I can exhort myself to believe, I can
address my soul as the psalmist did in Psalm 42:
"Why art thou cast down, O my soul, and why art thou
disquieted within me? Hope thou . . . believe thou . . .
trust thou."*

*Turn to the Lord Jesus Christ himself. Don't sit down
and commiserate with yourself. Don't try to work
something up but — this is the simple essence of it —
go directly to him and seek his face, as the little child
runs to its father or its mother. Seek him, seek his face,
and all other things shall be added unto you.*

D. Martyn Lloyd-Jones

MENOPAUSE — SOMETHING TO LOOK FORWARD TO?

by Sally Olds

"Menopause is one of the great eras in a woman's life," a prominent gynecologist said recently. A surprising statement? Yes, to those women who have suffered some of the real, troubling symptoms of this myth-shrouded time of every woman's life. It might also surprise most younger women who haven't yet experienced menopause and are extremely apprehensive about becoming "menopausal": that time of life often associated in their minds with mental illness, sudden aging, and loss of femininity.

Most post-menopausal women, however, would unhesitatingly agree with the above statement by Dr. Luigi Mastroianni, Jr., chief of obstetrics and gynecology at the University of Pennsylvania Hospital. Women who have been through it know that menopause doesn't have to be bad. In fact, a recent study conducted under the auspices of the Committee on Human Development of the University of Chicago found that women who have been through menopause have a much more positive view of it than women who have not.

One woman said, "I've been healthier and in much better spirits since the change of life. I've been relieved of a lot of aches and pains."

And another: "I feel like a teen-ager again. I can remember my mother saying that after her menopause she really got her vigor, and I can say the same thing about myself. I'm just never tired now."

A summary of current knowledge about menopause, including its symptoms and their treatment, shows that women have little to fear if they only know what to expect at this time of life.

The word "menopause" refers to the end of menstruation. When a woman has had her last menstrual period, she has attained her menopause. Technically, the time span of two to five years during which the woman's body undergoes the various physiological changes that bring on the menopause is known as the "climacteric." Since the entire stage is popularly referred to as the menopause, that is the term we shall use here.

Interestingly, figures seem to indicate that the more children a woman has, the more likely she is to experience an earlier menopause. The median age of menopause for the childless single woman is 50.4 years; for the mother of one or two children, 49.0 years; and for the mother of three or more, 48.5.

A woman usually recognizes the onset of her menopause by a marked change in her menstrual pattern. She may have a heavier flow than normal, a scantier flow, or she may completely miss periods. These menstrual changes signal the fact that other changes are taking place within her body's endocrine system.

New York gynecologist Sherwin A. Kaufman, who has written an excellent book on the menopause, *The Ageless Woman,* has counted a total of fifty different symptoms women associate with their menopause. Some of these symptoms are directly related to hormonal changes within the woman's body. Others are due to the natural process of aging, which begins even before birth and continues throughout life.

The most common symptom of menopause is undoubtedly the hot flash, or flush. One woman described hers this way: "I would wake up in the middle of the night, burning up. My face would be dripping with sweat, my nightgown drenched. When I went into the bathroom to dry off, I looked in the mirror and saw a face as red as a beet."

The flashes usually last thirty to forty seconds and may, in extreme cases, appear every fifteen to twenty minutes, although they tend to average four or five a day.

The exact cause of these flashes is unknown. There seems to be some basis for believing that decreased estrogen production is involved, since the administration of estrogen usually brings dramatic relief.

To complicate the picture, however, we have to realize that for some women flashes go away with no treatment at all. Other women, despite low estrogen levels, never have flashes. Emotional stress seems to trigger flashes in other women.

Many menopausal women suffer a generalized anxiety

and depression, which may be attributed to a variety of factors. It seems to be one of nature's less playful tricks that menopause often hits a woman at a time when she is facing other problems. A woman who devoted her life to raising a family suddenly finds herself with grown children who don't need or want her assistance. A career woman may suddenly find herself pressured by younger women and may feel she can go no further in her profession. The middle-aged woman looks in the mirror and sees wrinkles and gray hairs.

In addition, the woman in her forties or fifties faces what anthropologist Margaret Mead has termed "the closing of the gates," the realization that she can no longer bear a child. Even if becoming pregnant is the last thing in the world she might want, many a woman is depressed by the certain knowledge that having more babies is no longer possible.

Is it any wonder then, with the onset of all the physiological changes of the menopause as well as the social and psychological, that a woman experiences some anxiety?

A hormonal deficiency may sometimes contribute to a woman's depression, and in such a case, the administration of estrogen will relieve it. No amount of hormones, however, can cure an anxiety caused by non-hormone-based family or financial problems.

There is one specific marital problem that hormones *can* relieve. With advancing age, the vaginal tissues of some women become thin and shrunken. They lose their elasticity and become dry and easily irritated. For a woman suffering from this condition, known as atrophic vaginitis, sexual intercourse can be very painful. She tends to avoid intercourse, thereby creating a marital problem where none may have existed before. Fortunately, this condition can be easily remedied with estrogen pills, creams, or suppositories, which restore the vaginal tissues to their normal state.

Most women secretly fear that menopause itself signals the end of their sex lives. This isn't so. Women can go on to enjoy just as satisfactory a sexual relationship after the menopause as they have before. In fact, some women, freed from the possibility of an unwanted pregnancy, report that their appreciation of sex is better than ever.

The one hormone that is most effective in treating the symptoms of the menopause is estrogen. Virtually all gynecologists prescribe estrogen in some degree for some menopausal patients, but there is great divergence of opinion as to who should receive estrogen, how much she should get, and when she should begin and end therapy.

Estrogen therapy is not all roses. It has side effects which some women find extremely annoying. One of these is the tendency for the woman taking estrogen to experience "breakthrough" bleeding, vaginal bleeding that comes at irregular times. Some doctors control this by purposely producing bleeding by prescribing progesterone in addition to the estrogen. Thus, the woman will have artificial menstrual periods on a regular basis, as often as every month or as seldom as twice a year.

Other unpleasant side effects are weight gain and swelling, breast tenderness, nausea, and increased cervical secretion. These can sometimes be eliminated by lowering the dosage or by switching to another brand of medication.

Many women are afraid of estrogen because they fear it may cause cancer, but Dr. Herbert S. Kupperman, associate professor at New York University Medical School, says, "There is no evidence in the human to indicate that estrogens are carcinogenic (cancer-producing). Estrogen therapy has been in use increasingly since 1940. However, there is no evidence in the literature of any increase in either endometrial or breast cancer in the intervening years."

However, estrogen does seem to stimulate existing cancers, and to aggravate noncancerous conditions such as cysts in the breasts. For these reasons, doctors ordinarily will refrain from prescribing estrogen for those women who have had cancer or other abnormal conditions of the breasts or reproductive organs.

People have always sought a fountain of youth, and some today believe estrogen is just this. Despite claims made for estrogen face creams, and despite the beneficial aspects of estrogen in treating certain very specific symptoms, estrogen doesn't work miracles. It helps a woman slide through her climacteric more easily, but it doesn't keep her from growing old. The fountain of youth is yet to be discovered.

Sometimes, a young woman who hasn't yet arrived at the menopause will require surgery involving her reproductive organs. The most common such operation is a hysterectomy, or removal of the uterus. Another not unusual operation involves removal of the ovaries and is called an oophorectomy. Whenever possible, a surgeon will attempt to leave the patient at least one of her ovaries, so that estrogen will continue to be produced in normal amounts.

In some cases, the physician may feel he has no choice but to remove both ovaries, thus producing a surgical menopause. The woman stops menstruating and is likely to suffer hot flashes and other menopausal symptoms. Since the decrease in hormonal production is much more abrupt than in a natural menopause, her symptoms are likely to be more severe. Such a woman usually receives immediate estrogen replacement therapy, either for a brief period or possibly for the rest of her life.

Every woman wants her menopause and the years that follow to be a "great period in her life." She wants to enjoy a time of life when she is no longer burdened by the physical needs of small children, no longer worried about the possibility of pregnancy, no longer tied to the humdrum day-to-day obligations of housekeeping.

She wants to enjoy the "second honeymoon" of the later years, when husband and wife have more time to be with each other. She wants to enjoy the gratifications of career or civic responsibilities, to which she can now devote more time.

The wise woman will have prepared herself for this time in her life by developing interests through the years that can now engage her mind and her capabilities. Even if she hasn't, there is no time like the present to begin. Many employers seek out the maturity and ability of the older woman. A society in the throes of change needs the involvement of capable, mature women in important social action programs.

The menopause may be the closing of one gate — but it

can also be the opening to a rich and satisfying time of life.

The stresses of living are not nearly so responsible for a host of debilitating diseases as are our faulty reactions to those stresses. The office of a physician is filled with people suffering from nearly every disease in the book because their minds are beset by a thousand worries about their finances, their health, or their children.

S. I. McMillen, M.D.

4 THE WOMAN AND HER MARRIAGE

WHAT DOES A MAN REALLY WANT IN A WIFE?

by Robert H. Schuller

Of all the persons in the world, none are more important than that crowd we call *wives*. "Behind every successful man is a great woman" is a famous and truthful statement. Someone else put it this way: "Whether a man winds up with a nest egg or a goose egg may depend on the chick he married."

Now for the million-dollar question: What does a man really want in a woman?

Consecrated Concubine

A man wants someone who can fulfill his biological needs. So he seeks a sexual partner. Every healthy husband needs a concubine, not in the usual immoral sense of a sexual mate outside of marriage or in addition to a legal wife. The truth is every wife should provide her husband with the sexual pleasures solicited from a concubine. "My wife is my one and only concubine," one satisfied man said to me recently.

We must never forget that God is responsible for this thing called *sex*. God designed and created male and female. "And God saw everything that he had made, and, behold, it was very good" (Genesis 1:31). Commenting on this verse, Charlie Shedd once added, "And among the best of God's good things is sex at its best."

Many counselors agree that sex is a primary cause of problems in marriage. The challenge to wives is to become successful playmates with their husbands. Dr. Marion Hilliard wrote about a patient, a minister's wife, who had come to her sheepishly with her problem. She and her husband had sexual intercourse once a week, on Sunday nights. It left her exhausted the next morning when she had to face an enormous weekly washing.

"I've tried to persuade him that this is very difficult for me," the minister's wife complained, "but it's no use. Is there something I could do about it?"

"Certainly," replied Dr. Hilliard promptly, "wash on Tuesday."

Confidante

Deep though the biological needs may be, man's social
needs are even deeper. He needs one person to whom
he can truly open up his heart, his hurt, his hopes.
Man wants in a woman someone who can listen to him
as he thinks his way through his dreams, and aches his
way through his problems.

Marriage, with a commitment to confidential continuity,
provides man with a mate to whom he can totally expose
himself, body and soul. If he feels assured that this wife
is his and his alone for life, then he can trust her with
his private, intimate feelings. You don't totally trust
a person with whom the relationship has a strong possibility
of impermanence.

Companion

What does a man want in a woman? He wants a warm
friend, an understanding companion.

A study was made of 1500 marriages and the Number 1
complaint of men about wives was that they talk too much
and don't listen enough.

This is the pattern in most adulterous triangles.
Wandering husband: "I first became attracted to the other
woman because she was so understanding. It wasn't
a physical, sexual thing. It was simply that she wanted
to listen to me and it seemed my wife never really wanted
to listen. It started out as a warm companionship, that's
all. Somewhere it got out of hand."

Virginia Graham offered five suggestions on how to stay
happily married. I particularly like her final point:
"Try to look ahead to a day in the distant future when
someone will ask you how you've managed to stay happily
married for so long. I hope you'll be able to answer the
way I do. 'It's easy,' I say. 'I married my best friend.'"

In "Woman's Guide to Better Living 52 Weeks a Year,"
Dr. John A. Schindler wisely writes, "Love is the combination of sex and deep friendship. The trouble with a
lot of love is that it's mostly sex and very little friendship."

Conscience

Most men might not admit it, but they do expect women
to be the conscience of their lives and their communities.

My wife is my conscience, and I respect her for it.
How she helps me! But being the conscience doesn't mean
that a wife is to *change* her husband. Ruth Graham,
wife of Billy Graham, said: "A wife's job is to love
her husband, not convert him." But retain the spirit
that can advise or gently correct. When the wife ceases
to be the symbol of the Ideal, all of society will begin to
deteriorate. So be a kind conscience.

Creative Climate-Controller

What a man wants in a wife is someone who can set
the mental climate-control to positive thinking. Be a
possibility-thinking woman. The wife can be her husband's
biggest booster. Wives, nothing is more disastrous
than neglecting to boost and bolster his morale.

For this reason the most important quality of a
successful wife is possibility-thinking. If a man is dreaming,
only to have his wife squelch his dreams and throw cold
water on his exciting plans, the marriage is headed for
the rocks. No man will ever leave, or stop loving, a
positive-thinking wife who feeds his enthusiasm and self-
confidence.

Virginia Graham wrote in *Good Housekeeping*:

Everyone needs what I call a Chinese Room
to which you can retreat and more or less get reacquainted
with yourself. Go in there alone and make a mental
market list of what you're doing right, and what you're
doing wrong.
In your Chinese Room, you may come to realize
that while you keep your house in perfect running order,
and you never forget to put eggs, butter, and bacon
on your market list, and you never let the flowers wilt
in a vase, you may be a lot less careful about how
you're running your marriage.
A big mirror in your Chinese Room is a must. Take
a good look in it. You may see that not only
your hair needs a touch-up, but your mind does, too.
You may feel that you're over-hubbied, but maybe
you're really over-hobbied, and hubby hasn't been
over-happy for quite a while. Come out of your Chinese
Room with the words "I love you" at the top of your
mental list. Then say the words out loud.
If your mate seems hard of hearing, it's probably
only that he hasn't heard the phrase in so long, he can't
immediately recognize it for what it is.

You create a positive mental climate by being a cheerful, happy woman. Pity the man who, tired from a day's work, has to come home to a depressed, fatigued, self-pitying woman. Be proud of your role as a wife and a homemaker. What could be more important?

You create a positive mental climate by being patient. (That's putting off till tomorrow what you'd mess up by doing today.) Practice the act of tactfulness. (That's changing the subject without changing your mind.) Above all, cultivate the habit of acceptance. (That's loving persons as the imperfect human beings they really are. It's the exercise of *mature love*.)

Now generate a positive mental climate by encouraging your husband to succeed. Know your husband, support your husband. Be his biggest booster. Be proud of him and let that pride show. Be a possibility-thinker. Be careful in your response to his positive ideas.

Don't say:
It can't be done.
We can't afford it.
I'm too tired.
But the children . . .
We don't have time.
It's impossible.

Do say:
Sounds great.
How can we swing it?
Let's see how we can possibly do it.
Let's find a way to do it.
Let's think of a solution.

A woman has the power to break man's spell of gloom and restore his soul. Man knows this, and therefore he turns to woman in his hour of need.

But few women know how to give true sympathy. Their greatest mistake is that they try to help him solve his problems — to rescue him: to offer suggestions, or to help lift his burdens, or to remove his obstacles.

These are mistaken approaches. All of these things hurt his pride.

It isn't practical help he needs from you. He comes to have his soul restored, his self-esteem reestablished, and his self-doubt removed.

Build him up by offering him approval, hope, and admiration, and whatever you do, don't let his gloom rub off on you.

Be happy and optimistic regardless, but don't necessarily expect an immediate response in him for your efforts.

One of the functions of woman is to be a comfort to her husband: To shed joy around, and cast light upon dark days. *Don't fail him in his hour of need.*

Helen B. Andelin

"LOVE YOU?— I AM YOU!"

by

Arthur A. Rouner, Jr.

If one thing is true in all the world it's that everyone wants to be loved. You can make it a rule: there isn't anybody, anywhere, who doesn't want to be loved. The most bitter people-haters have chosen to be that way because they feel ugly and unloved.

That means that the world can be won by love. Minds can be changed, angry attitudes overcome, perverse personalities transformed. Love can do all that.

There's a little bit of God in all love. Maybe it's that element in love that reaches out in such openness and gentleness, takes the other person by surprise, breaks down his defenses, and reconciles him. So when you're dealing with love, you're dealing with the most potent force the world knows.

Love is the most vital force affecting our lives. You need to be loved as a tiny baby if you're to have half a chance in the world. Mental disorder very often dooms the unloved young. And the worst battle of the soul for the growing number of aged men and women is the feeling of being rejected and unloved. And in middle life, at the height of his powers, the man who says he needs no one, nothing but his work, is fooling himself. He is striving for someone's love, the love of wife, children, secretary, or maybe the world "out there."

And the way love is fulfilled, the way it is most exciting and rewarding, is when it is shared — when each one gives something to the other. And all you really have to give, in love, is yourself, your heart, dreams, deep feelings, song, spirit, into someone else's keeping.

He gives to you, and you give to him. If only one person is giving, it's idolatry and not love. It's hero worship or goddess worship, but it's not love. Nothing is coming back, nothing is being shared.

Of course, if you do share, you're taking a risk. Because true love doesn't give away something cheap or dispensable. True love gives away itself, its inner

For Women Only

things, its secret things. It's your innermost being that you give to your lover, and the unwritten plea that goes with it is "Please don't trample on me. Don't ridicule me. I've no defense, no hidden retreat left if you don't take me, and accept me, and love me back!"

Love given is precious. It must be held with gentle hands, and cherished, and defended. It's a little like the beautiful rendering in *The Living Bible* of Paul's words to the Corinthians: "If you love someone you will be loyal to him no matter what the cost. You will always believe in him, always expect the best of him, and always stand your ground in defending him" (1 Corinthians 13:7).

Love is sharing, taking the other's part, identifying yourself with him. And if you don't give yourself away into the other's keeping and receive that one into your own keeping — well, it isn't really love!

Jesus gave this as the acid test of love: "Greater love has no man than this, that a man lay down his life for his friend." That is what he did, finally, for all of us. He gave himself, completely. And if he hadn't gone all the way, if he had stopped somewhere short of death, we would know that he loved himself more than us. There would then be no redemption, no salvation.

Giving your life away, not only to the other person but for the other person (which is very much the same thing) is the final test, then, of our love too. Most of us in this life are not pressed to that extremity. We dream of living a lifetime together with our loved one, and reaching old age rich in shared years and shared memories. But true love believes that it's always ready to go that far for the other, and lives in the assumption that if ever put to that ultimate test for the loved one, it wouldn't fail.

And yet, it's this giving, this sharing, this entering into the life of the other one that scares us most about getting married. And young love makes much of holding something back, of "being myself," of "refusing to lose my own identity in my husband's or my wife's identity."

The significance of married love is that two lives become one life. They become one common enterprise, one shared experience, one single adventure. Anything that touches one can't help touching the other. No victory or defeat can come into the life of one without also coming into the life of the other.

That's what it's about. "No man is an island entire to itself. Each man's death diminishes me." That's how John Donne expressed human relationships. Ruth said, in her beautiful words of commitment to one she loved: "Whither thou goest I will go, and where thou lodgest, I will lodge; where thou diest, I will die; thy people shall be my people, and thy God my God." Or, as a great modern medical missionary, Jim Turpin, says: "Love you? I *am* you!"

In marriage it's this that is symbolized by the act of sexual intercourse. Here the yearning of the heart and body for complete physical sharing draws two people together and is fulfilled. The two lives become the one new life, even to the point of literally conceiving new life. For Jesus said: "And they twain shall be one flesh." God's will and purpose is for a man and woman in love to become one life, not just in spirit or mind, but even in body — "one flesh," as the Bible says. In marriage, sexual intercourse becomes the complete giving of oneself to another in love. Not only do you say it, you do it. Intercourse is the most powerful nonverbal expression possible. It's a gift you give.

And if conceiving children in sexual intercourse puts us, from time to time, directly in the plan of God's purpose for life, then it is logical to think that he intends a man and woman to be living with each other in a relation of such commitment and permanence, that they can be the instruments for bringing these little human beings into the world, preparing them to make their contribution of promise and destiny in the world. And what can that commitment be, other than marriage? What can it be but two people committing their resources, their personalities, their common caring to each other for the long future?

And is that so bad? Is that the permanent loss of individuality? In giving himself to another person in marriage does the partner lose himself in that other one? Has he given something away that can never be taken back, or that is somehow lost forever?

Not as God would have it. In his plan it's an adding

to the other person, not a taking away. Because he is
loved, each one receives a new dimension, new security,
and therefore new joy and freedom. The lifelong struggle
of every human soul to be loved has found fulfillment,
has achieved its *raison d'être*. And that haunting fear of
never being loved is overcome, so that the personality
now is more fulfilled, and more free to be himself.
Youthful worries can be put aside. In the strength
and sunshine of another's love, the lover can go out
and share himself gladly with the world, and give to the
world the love that God has so uniquely given him.

Personality and identity aren't denied in marriage.
They are fulfilled and given a chance to flourish. If
marriage is entered into in love. If it has faith at its
heart. Admittedly, that's a big "if." People can destroy
each other in marriage. They can use the marriage bed
and the whole marriage relationship as a scene for taking
out their own frustrations on another human being —
dominating, defeating, even destroying him.

But that isn't marriage's fault. That is not something
commitment and the holy relationship of a lifetime do.
That is something selfishness and lovelessness and
demonic pride do.

What's beautiful is the shared life together God gives us
with another person. That's why marriage is worth
preparing for and preserving something sacred of oneself
for, in order to bring your best self to it.

Robert Louis Stevenson was a man fulfilled and
deepened by his love and marriage. He wrote of his mate:

Trusty, dusky, vivid, true,
With eyes of gold, and bramble-dew.
Steel true, and blade straight
The Great Artificer made my mate.

Honor, anger, valor, fire,
A love that life could never tire,
Death quench or evil stir,
The Mighty Master gave to her.

Teacher, tender comrade, wife,
A fellow-farer true through life,
Heart-whole and soul-free,
The August Father gave to me.

*Your marriage stands little chance of improvement
until you change. All the prayer you can cram into
your schedule won't change a thing in your home, until you
change. And should you say, "I will change when he
does," you're really saying that you consider something
else more important than a successful marriage.
The only real progress in saving a disintegrating marriage
comes when the offended party honestly prays, "Lord,
change this marriage, beginning with me!"*

John D. Jess

SENSITIVITY AND YOUR SEXUALITY

by Sandra S. Chandler

The union between a man and a woman is meant to be far more than mechanical manipulations. It should be meaningful and beautiful, a union of body, mind, and spirit. God didn't intend for man or woman to be the object of sexploitation by the other.

In order for sex to become more than an act, a couple needs to be aware of sensations. The sensation of anticipation, expectation. The sensation of one body reaching out to the other. A brief — but lingering — moment for each to bring the ultimate in sexual fulfillment. This is our goal.

Since intercourse involves two people, barriers to sensitivity are almost inevitable. Some interfere with the mind, but they affect the physical response. Barriers include environment, hygiene, attire, and the lack of understanding and openness a couple may face within their marriage.

Let's begin with the environment. Look at your home. What is the first thing that hits your husband when he walks in the door? An atmosphere of calmness? A feeling of comfort? Clutter inhibits relaxation for some people, so pick up that living room.

Two other rooms must be kept clean: the bathroom and the bedroom. Clean towels, a throw rug on the floor, a small vase of flowers, and crisp curtains on bathroom windows will go over with the man in your life. You spend a third of your life together in the bedroom (at least you should). You aren't awake all that time, but the mood you set when you are may determine the quality of rest you get.

Do your best to keep the house the way you think your husband likes it. He will usually hurry home if you do.

Change your bedding at least once a week. Dust whenever it is needed. Make sure the bedspread and covers are clean. Vacuum up specks of dirt and lint from the floor.

Last but not least, use candles or oil lamps for a cozy atmosphere. I give candles as bridal-shower gifts, and with them I tell about the beauty of love by candlelight.

While your husband is showering — get your shower first — turn down the bed, place a little perfume behind your ear, and light the candles. (All this preparation will be wasted if you use candles that drip. Nothing thwarts lovemaking like the smell of melted wax burning a dresser top. Use dripless candles or the kind in little glass containers.)

Not only should the atmosphere surrounding your husband be pleasing; the sight directly before him should delight his eyes. You!

I know what it's like to have children and to keep up with daily tasks. Or a job. But I try to have my face washed and my hair combed when my husband comes home. Better yet, I try to have on fresh clothes. When time permits, I shower before he arrives.

Men are vulnerable. They may see many young women during the day who are dressed as if they were modeling for the latest fashion magazine. Don't let it throw you if your man looks at these women, but make sure that when he arrives home he has something nice to look at that is his alone.

Better still, your squeezable, warm, receptive body may be the only thing that will erase some of the scars of the day. Remember, cleanliness spells "loveliness." Bathe regularly. Before retiring always wash the areas involved in love play. Dab a little perfume around the spots he loves most.

After a few years of marriage and several children, many women have neglected their figures or their wardrobe. Try to have at least one outfit that wows your husband. Dress in his favorite colors. I'm not saying conform to him completely, but do take him into consideration. After all, aren't you dressing to please him?

Give special thought to your bedtime attire. And give some thought to your figure. Equip your bathroom with a reliable scale so you can watch what happens to your weight. Getting in shape is up to you. Watch carbohydrates, sweets, and between-meal snacks and the problem will be half-licked. To lick the other half, exercise by walking, jogging, or regularly doing simple exercises.

You'll get discouraged about your diet. You'll find it difficult to exercise. Before you quit, think about those nights by candlelight when your body is given to your husband. Psychologically, a curvaceous figure can do wonders for your eagerness and ability for love play.

Before you seriously considered getting married you read and talked about sex. You may have picked up misinformation along the way. Possibly you expected ecstacy on your wedding night, and were disappointed. Enjoy the love within you on that night, and don't expect perfection. Frustration is frequent but normal. Lack of sensitivity is the biggest handicap; inexperience is another.

Tell your man how much love play you need, what you like and dislike. Be sensitive to his need for caressing — and learn when to go easy. You who have been or are married know how important this is. Don't hesitate to talk about your needs. It's senseless to suffer in silence. Foreplay and intercourse are more enjoyable and are a deeper expression of love when there is openness and sensitivity.

Some women are super-sexed; others couldn't care less. These are extremes. The important thing is how you can please your lover. Whatever you and your partner do is acceptable as long as neither of you finds it unpleasant or objectionable.

Some days all you want is lovemaking; other times you want to cool it. But be discreet. That's where communication comes in. How is your husband and lover going to know your highs, lows, and in-betweens unless you tell him how you feel? Until I opened lines of communication with my husband he had to guess my moods by my actions. Some weren't so pleasing, he told me later in gentle understatement. I know women who never outgrew that stage, and their husbands have gone looking for communication elsewhere.

Glandular problems also hinder sexual adjustment. We tend to forget that intercourse is a normal bodily function. If too much time elapses between sex acts, a man's semen accumulates and it may make it more difficult for him to delay his ejaculation. Thus there may

not be enough time for the woman to reach orgasm.
The problem of premature ejaculation may be overcome
if you are attentive to your man's needs. Don't become
too busy with trivialities at bedtime. He needs you.

Another factor that influences sexual relations is
the menstrual cycle. Because of a chemical imbalance
over the twenty-eight days (more or less) of your cycle,
your sexual desire will vary. Nature's plan is to make you
most interested in relations on the tenth to twelfth days
after your period. Keep your husband in mind. His desires
don't fluctuate as much as yours. He is likely to be
raring to go almost any night. You will receive enjoyment
through meeting his needs.

Sexual inhibitions cause some of the greatest hang-ups
encountered by those age twenty-five and over. Puri-
tanical attitudes in the home often produce these emotional
and psychological frustrations. (Parents should realize
how prudishness and ignorance harm their children.) Inhibitions are occasionally caused by unattractive physical
features such as obesity, scars, and birthmarks. These can
often be corrected or minimized through diets, cosmetics,
and surgery.

Two other fears often inhibit sex. They are fear of
pregnancy and fear of infertility.

Not long ago a woman with five nearly grown children
told me she thought part of the problem of her sex life
was that her husband didn't want any more children.
I asked her what method of birth control she used. Her
reply: "None." No wonder relations were strained!
I told her to see her gynecologist pronto.

Other women fear infertility. Sometimes a young woman
will think unceasingly about what she will do if she can't
become pregnant. Unfortunately she is so wrapped up
in her thoughts that she ties her body in knots and
brings upon herself the very thing she dreads.

If you have an infertility problem, talk to a doctor.
Realize that fears may be groundless; if you are intellectually informed and physically healthy, it will help
you solve your problem.

Men have related problems. A man who is afraid
of impotency can cause heartache for his lover as well
as himself. You can help by your sympathy, love,

and positive remarks. Never ridicule or show irritation.

Janice's husband had been on duty for a year in
Viet Nam. She expected a passionate session when he
got back. Surprise! He headed straight for bed, and sleep.
She let him. It had been a difficult year of separation.
Instead of quizzing him about a possible affair overseas
or what was wrong with him, she expressed her joy
at his being home. Then she curled up beside him
and dropped off to sleep too. In time Janice learned that
he feared impotency and therefore was afraid to make
any overtures to her. He didn't want to be a failure.
Her love, support, and patience not only helped her
husband overcome his problem, but it also brought
deeper understanding to their marriage.

The problem of infection can also impair sexual
adjustment. Various vaginal disorders seem to occur
for no reason. This is just part of being a woman.
At the first sign of vaginal infection see your doctor.
With proper treatment, your sex life shouldn't suffer.

Most barriers to a satisfactory sex life can be overcome
by common sense, sensitivity, intellectual understanding,
and experience. The barricades can be swept away,
if you're willing to work at it.

*"We are souls living in bodies. Therefore, when we
really fall in love, it isn't just physical attraction. If it's
just that, it won't last. Ideally, it's also spiritual attraction. God has opened our eyes and let us see into someone's soul. We have fallen in love with the inner person,
the person who is going to live forever. That's why
God is the greatest asset to romance. He thought it up
in the first place. Include him in every part of your
marriage, and he will lift it above the level of the mundane
to something rare and beautiful and lasting."*

Peter Marshall

Sex is celebration of love.
"Even though it should be obvious, it often goes

*unmentioned in Christian circles that the sex act itself
is perhaps the highest and most concentrated expression
of love humanly possible. In no other single act is man's
entire being so thoroughly embodied; no other act
comes so close to the losing of oneself in the unity
of two persons."*[1]

*Love is a constant, willed concern for the other person
and for the wholeness of that person. In the mutual
self-giving of sex we celebrate this intimate, self-forgetful
sharing in which each releases the other to fully "know,"
to truly love. In the "wonder of recognition" each
discovers the other in open-armed acceptance,
and in the other each discovers him/her self.*

David W. Augsburger

---

[1]Jerry H. Gill, "Love and Sexuality," *Eternity* Magazine (September, 1968) p. 11.

HOW NOT
TO BE
THE GIRL
HE LEFT
BEHIND
by Dorothy Carnegie

Every wife is responsible to train herself to live up to the social requirements of her husband's career. Whatever a man's occupation, his chances of getting ahead are increased by his wife's ability to get along well with others and her adaptability to social demands.

A state governor told me, off the record, that a large part of his success was due to having married a woman of tact, breeding, and charm. He himself had been born "on the other side of the tracks," brought up in a poor immigrant section of a big city.

"If I had married one of the girls in my own neighborhood," he said, "I doubt if I'd have had the incentive to educate myself and rise in the world. My wife, thank God, has everything I lacked. She has poise and background. Whether my job takes us among royalty, as it sometimes does, or into the areas of the underprivileged, she is equal to any situation."

Don't think that because your husband is now filling a somewhat lowly position, nothing is expected of you. The business, industrial, and professional leaders of tomorrow are all obscure young men today. Nobody starts at the top. Are you prepared to do your husband credit ten, twenty, or thirty years from today, when he is a leader?

Start today! If you have fears, prepare to shed them now. If you are awkward or tactless, learn to love, respect, and enjoy other people. If you feel a lack of educational background, don't hide behind that threadbare excuse, "I never had a chance to go to college." Take courses in night school. If you can't afford that, run, don't walk, to your nearest public library.

The wife he left behind him — because she couldn't keep up with his career — is no longer a sympathetic figure. She's regarded as either too lazy or indifferent to take advantage of the endless opportunities for self-improvement that surround each of us.

No one ever knows how the future is going to open up. But it is wise to be prepared for opportunity when it arrives.

Learning to make and keep friends, and to get along with others, is one basic way to prepare for the time when your husband achieves a position of importance. This is one skill that will always help your husband, whatever his occupation or station in life. If he himself is clumsy in handling people, a tactful wife will help make up for his blunders. If he is diplomatic in his human relations, a wife must be also — to keep him from looking ridiculous, if nothing else.

While gathering material, I had an enjoyable interview with the personnel director of one of America's largest corporations. He told me that he sometimes gets so absorbed in his work that he forgets to be careful of other people's feelings. "But my wife is never too busy to be nice," he told me proudly.

"Why, just the other day, I roared into our dry-cleaner and told him I wanted my suits cleaned in such-and-such a way and no fooling! He looked at me sadly for a minute and then said: 'I like it better when your wife comes in.'

"Everybody likes it better," this executive continued. "She's hearts and flowers with the world. She honestly loves people and takes an interest in them.

"When we pass the Greek shopkeeper in our neighborhood, my wife greets him in his own language. Another block down the street, she says hello in Italian to the man who sells fruit. They don't even notice me, and why should they? It's my wife who takes the trouble to learn a greeting in their native tongues. That is typical of her desire to please. She gets results, too."

I don't know this lady, but I would like to — wouldn't you?

The woman who inspires friendliness and good will is a priceless asset. A busy man often concentrates so hard on the technical aspects of his job that he fails to build the warm, human relationships that enrich life. How fortunate for him if he has a wife who creates an atmosphere of warm-heartedness wherever she goes. Such a woman will never be left behind while her husband goes ahead. She is his good-will ambassador to the world.

A wife can render another important service to a successful man (or to one she hopes will be successful). It requires a great deal of love, sensitivity, and timing. If it is not skillfully done, it can backfire disastrously. It is this: She can keep success from going to his head.

There are times when a man needs whittling down to size if he is to keep his perspective and not become a swell-headed egotist. The woman who can do this successfully is worthy of undying gratitude, and she usually gets it. Disraeli spoke of his wife as his severest critic and praised her for it. She kept his feet on the ground.

Another successful man, of our own time, told me that his wife's kindly deflation when he most needed it had been a major contribution to his happiness.

All of these women knew how to live up to their husbands and be a credit to them. They did it by their ability to win friends everywhere, to hold their own in any social environment, and to keep their husband's feet on the solid ground of reality.

Any woman who can do this will not have to worry about being "the girl he left behind him."

A wife is the silent partner in her husband's business success. It will never be known how much a man's success is due to his wife's confidence in him. Her shrewd foresight has been sound and helpful. Few men will attribute their success to their wives. Some do give them credit for wise judgment in business affairs.

One man has been so much more successful than other men. Is this success due in some measure at least to the "reverence" his wife has shown him? That is the scriptural program. "Her husband is known in the gates when he sitteth among the elders of the land." He has won a place of honor in the community, and his wife had a large share in the winning of it.

Elsie D. Helsinger

WIN HIM TO CHRIST
by Jill Renich

As Merle started supper, Jim went out to mow the lawn. Seconds later the back door flew open and Jim stood there enraged.

"Why didn't you get gas for the mower the last time you had the car? You knew the tin was empty. Why don't you look after things around here? The least you could do is see to the gas. You expect me to do everything. All you do is sit around gabbing with your friends! If you'd *do* something once in awhile. . . ."

Furious anger and hatred flared up in Merle. Another one of Jim's unfair accusations! Bitter words poured into her mind. Her mouth opened. "Now, God!" she prayed and closed her lips. *This is it,* she thought. *What she had faced and decided to do in Jim's absence must be put into practice now, in his presence.* Instantly she prayed for love as she confessed her anger and resentment to God.

Jim slammed through the kitchen into the living room. He threw himself into a big chair, storming abusively all the while.

God, you love Jim, Merle prayed. *Fill me with your love for him now.*

As Jim ranted on, Merle walked into the living room. Jim glared. Merle looked into his anger-filled eyes and said softly, with deep sincerity, "I love you, Jim." Jim was staggered. Where was the defensive ugliness from Merle which made his violence more justifiable? It was as though the walls of the room were crumbling.

Thus began Merle's creative, positive demonstration of God's way to live in the home. This was the end of fighting back, the end of nagging.

She memorized 1 Peter 3 and Ephesians 5:22-24. Prayer became her first as well as her last resort.

Merle prayed in times of crisis. She prayed while doing housework. The task of homemaking became filled with love. Ironing became a time she could pray for Jim and ask the Lord to fill her heart with love for him.

For Women Only

Cooking became a means of pleasing her husband.

Now, God-given concern for Jim enables Merle to stand in her husband's shoes and "tune in" to his outlook on life. What made him feel as he did? What kind of love and understanding did he need? What made him suffer? What made him happy? What encouraged him?

A God-worked submission began to follow in every area of her life. Jim saw Merle's change. He saw her active dependence upon him. He saw his responsibility for "their" actions, which drove him to find God. This made a man of him.

In time he submitted to God as Merle had submitted to him. As Jim began to love Merle with Christ's love, "submission" melted in that love. Merle was free. She no longer had to account for everything. She was free to use the car and the checkbook. Through submission Merle had proved herself a worthy wife, willing to please her husband. She ceased to be a competitor, and became a trusted companion.

Jim's attitudes also began to change. He became considerate of his wife. Merle thanks God that Jim didn't yield to her former self-centered and childish behavior. She saw how unlovely she had been. God worked a change in her to his glory. Even their sex life became meaningful as each became concerned for the happiness of the other.

What about your situation? Has your love for your husband grown through the years? Are you closer? Are you more understanding? Has your Christianity separated you from your husband so you no longer share his interests? What about friends? How do you treat his in comparison with your own Christian friends?

God has a plan to win your husband to himself. In 1 Peter 2:9 God says, "Ye are a chosen generation . . . that ye should show forth the praises of him who hath called you out of darkness into his marvelous light."

Then this passage goes on to show how this is done. You are to abstain from lust, be honest, submit to those in authority, and fear God. Servants are to submit to their masters. Children are to submit to their parents. Christ, our example, submitted to the will of God. Now in 1 Peter 3:1 God says, "Likewise" — in the same

way, with the same attitude — wives are to submit
to their husbands. Submission is an attitude of heart.
It's not so much what you do, but the attitude in which
you do what is right. Submission includes adapting to
your husband with love, insight, and empathy. Remember,
he is the one responsible to God for your home. God's
instructions to him are to love his wife with the same
tender love Christ has for his bride, the Church
(Ephesians 5:25).

God's way is positive and creative, *never nagging*.
It challenges and demands all that a woman has
spiritually and mentally.

"You wives must adapt yourselves to your husbands,
so that if some of them do not believe God's Word,
they will be won over to believe by your conduct.
It will not be necessary for you to say a word, for they
will see how pure and reverent your conduct is. You
should not use outward aids to make yourselves beautiful,
as in the way you fix your hair, or in the jewelry you
put on, or the dresses you wear. Instead, your beauty
should consist of your true inner self, the ageless beauty
of *a gentle and quiet spirit,* which is of great value
in God's sight. For this is the way the devout women
of the past, who hoped in God, used to make themselves
beautiful."

How is your conduct in the home? Are you a joy to
live with? It's easy to be nice to people outside the home,
but what is your attitude toward your husband? Your
children? Do you give them the love and consideration
you would give a guest?

What is your attitude to homemaking? Do you delight
in keeping a lovely home that will be a credit to your
husband? Have you trained your children to respect their
father? What is your reputation in the church and
community?

Outward Beauty
Many women depend on their outward beauty and
cultivated charms to win their way. God doesn't despise
attention given to personal attractiveness, for the Bible
refers to a woman's care of herself in the Song of Solomon
as well as in Proverbs 31. God loves beauty and

cleanliness. But God also makes it clear that we are not to rely upon this. It's delightful to see a woman who has done all she can to make herself attractive by using colors and clothes best suited to her, but real charm comes from the inner beauty of a meek and quiet spirit.

Study yourself. What could make you more appealing to your husband? Being too busy is no excuse for not keeping yourself attractive. You owe it to your husband and to your own self-respect. How do you look at the beginning and end of the day? What image does your husband carry in his heart as he leaves for work in the morning and as he returns home in the evening? It takes effort to lose ten pounds or to set your hair, but it is worthwhile.

Once I stayed in an apartment building where the other women were very friendly. We often had coffee and chatted together. But at four o'clock one of the women would excuse herself and dash home to shower, change, straighten the house, and put her baby into a clean dress. At five-thirty this wife, looking sweet and fresh, would be preparing supper when her husband came home. I guessed they'd been married about a year and a half, which seemed a long time to continue such care and attention for her husband. Out of curiosity I asked her how long she'd been married. "Seven years," she said happily.

Inward Beauty

When Fred and I were first married we lived with Ellie and Ben. It was a joy to live in the atmosphere of love and graciousness that pervaded their home. Their marriage hadn't always been that way, they assured us. They married with Christian ideals. Ben, a naturally gentle man, saw his need to be lovingly firm. In answer to prayer, Ellie changed from a naturally domineering woman to a gentle and submissive one. Only God could have worked her meek and quiet inner beauty.

God can create meekness and humility in a proud woman. What are your areas of pride? Will you entrust your husband to God? Will you leave the consequences of his actions with God? Will you let God create a quiet spirit of trust in you?

Why is a meek and quiet spirit of such great price
in the sight of God? Because humility isn't natural
to any of us. It can come only through deep trust in a
loving God during difficult and trying circumstances.

What is your attitude toward God? Does your conduct
show you revere him and his standards for your life?
Does your husband see your love for God and his Word,
or does he see that church bores you and that you
seldom read the Bible with pleasure? Does he see,
when you pray, that God answers?

As you obey God in practical loving ways, God will
work for you as he did for Merle. It wasn't easy
for Merle to be a loving wife, but day after day,
as she spent time with God, she prayed about how to be
to Jim what he needed. *She talked less and less to Jim
about God, but talked more and more to God about Jim.*

Do you harbor resentments from past injuries? Is
your spirit unforgiving for real or imagined hurts?
All such attitudes can hinder the work of God. Forgiving
your husband doesn't make his wrong right, but it does
clear the way for God to work. Have you been critical,
unappreciative, cold, accusing? Sin causes fermentation
that later bubbles up into anger and frustration.

For God to alter your attitudes, you first need his
cleansing from wrong attitudes and actions. Then you
need the infilling of God's Spirit of love, and finally
you need to ask your husband's forgiveness for your wrong
attitudes and actions. As you respect and obey the
laws of God's love, he will begin his transforming work
in your home.

Some husbands become more demanding and
unreasonable as they resist turning their lives over to
God. This is a time of suffering for many a wife.
Only an abiding, steady trust in God can sustain her
through these trying days, weeks, months, and sometimes
years. Maintain a spirit of prayer for your husband as you
try to think understandingly of him. His life isn't easy,
especially not now, since added to his daily grind is
his inner struggle. Are you able to stay positive toward him?

Expect God to work in your situation. Wait patiently.
Wait expectantly. He will not fail.

There are four reasons why women shouldn't try to change men:

1/ *It causes marriage problems.*
2/ *It can destroy love.*
3/ *It can cause a man to rebel.*
4/ *It doesn't work.*

The very heart of Christian doctrine is: It is ourselves we must change. *We have been told to cast out the beam from our own eye first, and then we will more clearly see the mote which is in our brother's. Women who try to change their men trample on their freedom, and violate righteous principles.*

The only hope that a man will change is for you not to try to change him. *Others may try to change him, teach him, and offer suggestions, but the woman he loves must accept him for the man he is.*

Helen B. Andelin

FILL THE VACUUM

by Patricia Young

One of the least discussed aspects of marriage is that inevitable time when a partner dies. As must be expected, such loss leaves a vacuum, whether there are young children to be raised or whether they have grown up and moved away. Indeed, the woman left with young children shouldn't expect to find solace merely in having the children around. While a joy in themselves, they have their own life of school and sports. Once they are bathed and bedded down for the night, the hours can be as long as eternity.

Because many married persons refuse even to think about the possibility of a mate departing before they do, most are left unprepared for the challenges of readjusting to their new role. Many feel that their life is ended, their usefulness gone. Some will refuse to accept the fact and spend their remaining days poring through the memories of the past.

To be sure, memory is a precious gift. But it can't and shouldn't take the place of reality. Indeed, over-indulgence in memory-invoking can only lead to the shadowy world of the past, ultimately cut off from the world of the living.

It can help every married couple then, to think and talk about the time when one or the other will be alone. Think about whether you will remarry. Whether you would consider selling the house and moving into an apartment. Whether you should move closer to a relative, take a job, or perhaps become involved with a pet project for which you previously never had time.

Beyond natural grief, the first rule of recovery is acceptance of the fact that a loved one is no longer of this world, that you are *not* going to wake up and discover that it was all a bad dream.

Step two is to avoid self-pity. While sympathy and condolences will come your way naturally, don't let this natural understanding and consideration of friends

and neighbors produce the feeling that the world's
greatest tragedy has come to you alone. Everyone in the
whole world dies eventually. Most people experience
the parting of one or more loved ones. Acceptance
of your new role, new routine, and sometimes even new
financial security — without self-pity — will help shorten
the period of adjustment.

Many widows fail to recognize that a lifetime of routine,
married habits, family customs, and familiarities must
change. Not next month or next year, but immediately.
To mark time and make ineffectual promises to get going
sometime in the future is to find oneself listening for his
voice, to wake up anticipating his touch or his steps.
To avoid this agony, a new routine must be instituted
immediately. Rather than staring at his empty chair
every time you walk into a room, remove it or have it
re-done. Change the position of the kitchen table overnight
and then settle down to breakfast in a new robe with
the morning newspaper and a radio in the background.

If anything, it's wise to have company, particularly
on weekends. In addition to those helpful friends who
come around, begin seeking new contacts. Many other
women are in your position. Hundreds of spinsters
have learned to live a life of single happiness.

Since bedtime will evoke especially tender memories,
try going to bed later. Move the furniture around.
Keep a stack of books, the daily newspaper, knitting
or some other hobby on hand. Cry if you want to,
and get it out of your system. Then sit up and paste the
rest of those snapshots in an album. Even in public,
when something comes up that provokes a tear, cry it out
without apology, then smile and talk about a new recipe
you're going to try.

Together with a readjusted home routine, a new hairdo,
and rearranging the furniture, the greatest readjustment
must come through social contacts and outside involvement.
After a lifetime of doing things together — visiting
other married couples, eating together at favorite spots —
a whole new concept of social relationships should be
embarked upon immediately.

Don't sit at home expecting new contacts to come
to you. At first, you'll have to take the initiative.

Get the names of other widows and spinsters. Telephone them and explain your position and even your loneliness and you'll have made a new friend. Volunteer to take office in a church club, the ladies' hospital auxiliary or community center. Become involved in a political club, horticultural society, public library, children's aid, orphanage, or Great Books program.

Don't wait to figure out whether you will care for these involvements. Jump in with two feet. You can always weed out interests later.

Recognize the fact that perhaps for the first time in your life you have time available for all the things you would have liked to do. This can only be a personal choice. One woman I know finally got around to taking up ventriloquism and wound up entertaining children at a local hospital. Another bought a greenhouse and developed her interest in growing orchids. In any event, immediately launch into filling your time — even if it merely means slinging hash at a downtown restaurant.

Most important of all, don't look upon widowhood as the phasing out of your existence or usefulness. It can and often does mean the beginning of a completely new and different fulfillment. Many women have been known to take over a departed husband's interest in business or politics with great success.

Rather, widowhood should be looked upon as entering a new kind of existence. In childhood, we live in a world of school and parental authority. We enter a new area of experience and responsibility when we enter the business world. Courtship and marriage are another step, as is raising a family. Widowhood is still another world to be explored and adapted to so that we are able to fulfill ourselves as creatures of God. For while he granted us the privilege of union with man in matrimony, he didn't create us as "married couples" but as individuals. We can only give the best of our stewardship to whatever role he wishes us to take on.

5 THE WOMAN AND HER CHILDREN

WIFE OR MOTHER?

by Henry E. White, Jr.

A mother-child syndrome has developed in the American family. The principal role played by females in the United States as generally seen by society and women themselves is that of mother. One indication of this is that we have a Mother's Day. Quite noticeably we do not have a Wife's Day.

In a research study conducted in Chicago, 622 housewives put their role of mother above the role of wife. A majority of them said that their children were the most important persons in their lives. Further, they were asked how they viewed their mates. At the top of their responses was "provider" and halfway down the list was "husband."

The role of mother is important. But she fulfills another role which in some ways is more vital and essential — that of wife. Most women are mothers (in the operational sense) for only eighteen to twenty-five years. They are wives from forty to sixty years.

This is a role which has not received the acclaim it needs and should have.

Christianity emphasizes the husband-wife relationship. This is distinctive when compared with other religions. Other religions stress the parent-child relationship and the roles of father and mother. In the Old Testament men were enjoined to leave their parents and cleave to their wives, thus becoming one flesh (Genesis 2:20-24). Although addressed to husbands, this admonition is also applicable for wives. It is an extremely valuable principle on which to found family living.

We have not followed this biblical entreaty, and as a result we have created many contemporary family problems. When the wife (or husband) doesn't view the spouse as the most important person in her life, and when the marital relationship isn't seen as central, the hub of the family may well disintegrate. As a result, the couple will be less happy and therefore will have less interest in supporting and spending time with the family.

One unsatisfied husband put in words what many other American partners have felt. He said that he didn't particularly care about going home. What was there to go home to?

When young wives spend all of their time with and for the children, to the neglect of the husband, jealousy and resentment can be engendered in the mate. Children can see, hear, and sense the unhappiness of their parents. This detrimentally affects their lives as far as happiness and security are concerned. Their personality development is retarded.

When a husband and wife are pleased with their marriage, the children have a better chance of being reared in a happy home. When the emotional needs of the couple are met, the needs of the children are more likely to be met. Happiness comes downward from the husband and wife to their children. Rarely does it proceed upward from the children to the married couple.

Growing up in such happy homes, children see love demonstrated. They learn how to solve problems. They are then someday better able to implement in their own marriages what they have previously experienced.

In the home where the mother role is predominant, overpossessiveness of the children by the mother may occur. Since this kind of wife doesn't have (in essence) a companion and a lover, she may attempt to make a "husband substitute" out of her children. She may focus all of her emotions on her children. As a result she may attempt to control their lives by keeping them with her. In some severe cases she may attempt to prevent them from marrying even though they may be ready for marriage.

This can eventually cause the youth to have deep resentment toward their mother.

Homosexuality may result from this type of relationship. For example, a mother is very strongly possessive of her son. He has practically no positive identity with his father. The relationship between the father and mother is distant, also. Therefore, the boy might be reared as a female, or he may grow up with no strong male model to emulate. It would be only natural for him to see himself more like his mother.

In some cases a woman might not have a husband who loves her and spends time with her. She could develop strong antagonism toward her husband. In turn, she may easily communicate her frustration and low regard for her husband to the children. In so expressing her resentment, she may cause the children to develop a low esteem or even hatred for their father. This situation can cause role confusion in the mind of the child.

By emphasizing the role of mother and de-emphasizing the role of wife, women often create for themselves an extremely depressing valley of sorrows sometime in median adulthood. When the children are grown and gone, both husband and wife must readjust to a household where only two adults live. And that period of living with the marriage partner only will probably last twenty to thirty years. If the foundation for that two-or-three-decade relationship has not been laid and nurtured during the child-rearing years, that marriage can easily develop severe problems.

For example, Jan marries. Her husband becomes increasingly involved with his work and outside activities. Two children are born, and Jan spends most of the next several years caring for them, being a good mother.

She and her husband spend little time together, share few common interests and activities. They grow farther and farther apart emotionally. Suddenly the children are grown, off to college, and married.

Jan finds rather abruptly that her children-companions are gone. She is no longer a mother in the child-rearing sense of the term. The role she has played so faithfully for twenty-five years has been terminated. ·Her entire womanhood which has revolved around being a mother has collapsed.

As a result she feels useless, unneeded, and at her wit's end. What to do with herself becomes a nagging question. Her primary reason for living is gone. She is anxious and depressed.

How different the picture would have been if Jan and her husband had continued to be lovers and companions. She would have seen herself as a wife and then as a mother, with her husband as the principal person in her life. When the children grew up and left, she wouldn't have lost her complete role. She would still have been a wife. She would have been as needed as she was when she was first married.

Those years after the children are gone can be full of usefulness, excitement, and grandeur. Or they can be nightmares of loneliness. It all depends on how the earlier years are spent.

This mother-role concept is often forced. Women often *choose* to see themselves as mothers primarily and their children as the most important persons in their lives. This may be true because of an unwise marriage, a lack of psychological understanding, and the society. But many wives are *forced* into this unhealthy role-playing by the man of the house. Very often the hard-working, success-oriented, young, middle-class husband may get so involved with getting ahead in his business, going to civic clubs, or attending church meetings that he neglects his wife. He may even reject her need for love and companionship. Some, to have needs met, turn to extramarital love affairs. More often it is to the children, since this is a more acceptable alternative. Almost always they would have preferred to have their husbands as their companions.

Being a good mother is a high and holy calling. But being a good wife is a higher and more holy vocation. When women are wives first and mothers second, the lives of the husbands, the children, and the wives themselves are enriched. Marriage and the family are more characterized by unity and oneness from the top down. The center of the family is the married couple. Husbands and wives need to stress the primary role of the married woman, being a wife.

A child's most basic security is in knowing that his parents love each other. It's even more important than their love for him. He feels assured of being part of a strong, satisfying relationship and is certain he'll

*never be abandoned. Obviously, there are many ways
in which marriage partners can show their love. Their
mutual respect for each other, seeking the other's advice, fulfilling each other's unspoken desires, protecting
each other from criticism and misunderstanding: all these
demonstrate love. But along with these should go
the happy exchange of the physical expressions of love:
the pat, the squeeze, the hug, and the kiss.*

*The only people who really know how to express love
are those who have seen love expressed. A child knows
his parents more intimately, more honestly, than anyone
else in his life. Therefore, what he's going to learn
about love will come from watching them, day after day.
Before he enters kindergarten, he's acquired more
than 50 percent of his intelligence and personality
development — at home.*

J. Allan Petersen

DOES YOUR DAUGHTER HAVE A MINI-MOTHER?

by Abigail Van Buren

In this day of miracle makeup, weight-watching, and the mini-skirt, many a teen-age daughter is being cheated out of her birthright: A maxi-mother.

When Mother and her teen-age daughter appear together, how often they're told, "You certainly don't *look* like mother and daughter. Why, you look more like *sisters*." Mother's day is made, and Daughter, too, is proud of her look-alike mother who looks younger than her years.

Take a typical 13-year-old. Plagued with pimples and yearning to convex where she concaves, she smiles through her braces as she introduces an attractive, youngish, size 10 mom.

But comes a time when enough is enough. Daughter comes on as a *femme fatale* and starts to date.

The young man arrives Johnny-on-the-spot. Daughter, a little behind schedule, as usual, prevails upon Mom to entertain Johnny while she puts on some of the finishing touches.

Daughter makes her big entrance, and for openers Johnny says, "You didn't have to hurry. Your mom and I were having a great time. I wouldn't mind taking *her* out instead of *you*."

All in fun, of course, and Daughter manages a polite chuckle.

Yes indeed, every girl wants her mother to make a big hit with the Johnnys in her life. But let's not overdo it, Mrs. Robinson.

I don't know exactly when mothers started being "chums" and stopped being mothers to their teen-age daughters, but I have a theory.

Studies in human behavior reveal that one's actions are strongly influenced by one's appearance, so perhaps mothers stopped behaving like mothers and started acting like chums when they commenced to *look* that way.

Milady's fashions have played a significant part in making the modern mamma look younger than ever.

So what do we have? An alarming number of middle-age mammas who have all but abandoned their roles as mothers to become "girl friends" to their teen-age daughters.

Every girl needs a girl friend. Someone with whom she can gossip, scheme, and dream aloud. A trusted confidante with whom she can compare notes, agree, disagree, speak her mind, and be herself without fear of disapproval. Someone with whom she can let her guard down and talk freely about the sweet mysteries of life, and love, and — would you believe? — *sex*. A "best" friend who "sleeps over" now and then. And when she does, they let their hair down even as they put their hair up. And they lie awake until dawn, whispering delicious secrets they'd never dare to tell another living soul.

Girls even use words with each other they wouldn't dream of using with their mothers. We did. And so do they. It's part of growing up.

But every girl needs a mother, too.

A mother who will act her age, no matter how young she *looks,* and be content to let her daughter act her age, too — to grow up and mature normally in the natural course of events.

Shame on those ambitious mothers who rush their little girls into nylons, heels, padded bras, sophisticated hairdos, and theatrical makeup and let them go to all-night prom parties with a boy who got his driver's license last Monday.

And all this well-intended, too-much-too-soon rearing because Mother so desperately wants her daughter to be "popular" and have a "happier" girlhood than *she* had. (Woe to the girl who is being coached from the sidelines by a mother who never made the team!)

Every girl needs a mother who will instill in her daughter sound moral and spiritual values. A mother who will guide and discipline with a loving but firm hand.

A mother who will state the rules clearly, set the limits, and lay down the law, and not cave in when her daughter challenges her with remarks such as, "Times have changed, and everybody else can."

Every girl needs a mother who will tell her what she *needs* to hear — not what she thinks she *wants* to hear.

Girls need mothers with the courage to say no and stick to it, for today wise parents realize that their children don't always want what they ask for, and some are secretly relieved when they're denied privileges they aren't sure they're old enough to handle.

Lastly, every girl needs a mother who is willing and able to be an example for her daughter. Someone she can look up to, respect, and emulate. For no matter what Mother *says,* her daughter will be inclined to do as Mother *does.* (Witness the epidemic of divorces that runs in families; after Mother gets a divorce, it's easier for Daughter to gather the courage to do likewise.)

I have no statistics — only my voluminous mail — to support my belief that most mothers today are deeply concerned about their nearly grown daughters' boy-girl relationships. And with this in mind they try unceasingly to impress upon them the importance of "saving themselves" for their husbands, for a variety of reasons.

Some fear the worst. Pregnancy, with its attendant shame, disgrace, and heartbreak. Others are afraid that their daughters will become promiscuous and ruin their reputations. (Then what will the neighbors say?) And with others it's simply a matter of being a "good" girl or a "bad" one.

I am aware that many psychiatrists will argue that repressed or "frustrated" sexual expression makes frigid bed partners. I say that early and casual sex experiences, which are bound to be hurried, furtive, and in less-than-lovely surroundings, make for guilt, confusion, and a feeling of worthlessness, which is just as bad.

Most authorities in the field of human relations urge mothers to keep open the lines of communication between themselves and their daughters, at all costs, lest they break and further widen the generation gap between them.

"Communicating" (or, more recently, "relating") seems to be the order of the day. The In thing. Modern mothers are told to put aside their inhibitions, to get over their feelings of guilt, restraint, and modesty, and to talk freely and frankly about sex with their daughters in order that they may better "understand" each other.

Now, I'm all for "communicating" and a better "understanding," but, at the risk of appearing square and old-fashioned, I maintain that certain areas of discussion between mother and daughter are out of order after a girl has reached a certain age.

I refer specifically to those frank "woman-to-woman" talks, and I mean getting right down to the nitty-gritty.

First, I'd like to make something crystal-clear. I believe that girls (and boys, too) should be taught everything they need and want to know about sex. And that includes dating, mating, petting, begetting, the birds and the bees, and the whole ball of wax. But this should take place during the early years, when children are forming their attitudes about sex.

By the time a girl is in her teens, her mother will have told her all about the perils of promiscuity, pregnancy, and the Pill. She will be familiar with the possible consequences of illegal abortion and the risk of venereal disease. This simply for the sake of health and hygiene, without the "thou shalts" and "thou shalt nots." As a part of her religious and moral training, and long before she is actually aware of experiencing such sensations, a girl should have been told that all healthy normal adolescents can expect to feel strong physical desires that will draw them to the opposite sex.

This is the time for a mother to tell her daughter that this "feeling" is normal and nothing to be ashamed of but isn't necessarily "love," and that it's entirely possible that she will experience that "feeling" with perhaps a dozen or more boys before the "real" thing comes along. And may I add that when there is no special boy in the picture, a mother can more effectively impress upon her daughter that while this "feeling" may be difficult to control, it's not *impossible*. And no matter what the would-be young lover says, he prefers the girl he marries to be a virgin.

All this should be "communicated" long before a girl stands on the threshold of womanhood.

I think that the mother who discusses (or, heaven forbid, "debates") the pros and cons of premarital sex, or of taking the Pill with a teen-age daughter who is considering engaging in premarital sex or taking the Pill, is admitting to a terrible failure in her earlier mother-daughter relationship. If a mother has left the slightest room for doubt as to where she stands on these issues, it's too late for talking. Let a girl argue with her girl friends in defense of premarital sex, but not with her mother.

I've had letters from mothers who boast, "My daughter and I have a wonderful relationship. She tells me *everything.*" And then the mother goes on to say how "proud" she is to be regarded as so "broad-minded and understanding" that her teen-age daughter feels perfectly free to discuss the off-limits intimacies she's been having. A mother who listens to this kind of talk has allowed herself, whether she admits it or not, to be maneuvered into the position of becoming an accessory to the whole mucky business.

But some mothers do listen, and even though they may be secretly heartsick, they somehow give the impression that they are "grateful" for such confidences. I think a girl who would share such confidences with her mother, knowing full well her mother's deep convictions on the question of sex before marriage, does so primarily to implicate her and make her share the responsibility for the consequences, should there be any.

These poor misguided mothers who are so "proud" of being thought "hip, broad-minded, and understanding" have placed such a high premium on being able to "communicate" with their daughters that they have completely destroyed the mother-daughter relationship and have turned it into a relationship between two adolescents.

Today, when almost anything goes, when our society is saturated with sick, tasteless, downright dirty literature and entertainment — when vulgarity and nudity are passing as "art" and "realism," and when in the name of "freedom of speech and freedom of the press" our senses are assaulted by pictures we wouldn't have in the house and by words we used to see only on latrine walls — we desperately need mothers who still believe in modesty and manners and the old-fashioned virtues and aren't ashamed to say so.

Today more than ever we need mothers who love their little girls enough to spend the time it takes to teach them patiently the value of being feminine and gentle, yet morally strong and in control. We need mothers who will lay down the law and not compromise their principles.

And if getting down to her teen-age daughter's level and being her chum is the modern mother's way of closing the generation gap, then perhaps it's better that the gap remain open.

You must tell your children about the facts of life.
You must *tell them. You must not be deluded and wait.*
Too many of us do wait. In our country the average
child learns about the facts of married intercourse
from his parents five years after he has heard about them
outside the home. The average parent in our country
is five years too late! How many children actually find out
these truths for the first time from their parents?
One child in ten! Nine out of ten learn first on the
street — in the wrong place, in the wrong way,
at the wrong time, from the wrong person, and usually
incorrectly.

Don't mix up innocence with ignorance. "Oh,
she's such a sweet little innocent thing; don't disturb her
little world." Ridiculous! There is no relation between
innocence and ignorance. Innocence means being pure
of heart and free from sin. Ignorance is lack of informa-
tion or false information.

If we want to preserve our children's innocence,
we must tell them — tell them early and tell them enough.

Mr. and Mrs. J. C. Willke

LET YOUR SON GROW UP

by Carlyle Marney

The case histories of hundreds of thousands of emotionally immature husbands and fathers attest that somebody ought to talk to mothers.

Men are less important to their children than women. Consequently, more problem parents are mothers, even though many times mother is a problem because papa is no real father. And to whom is mother a problem? To her little son, of course, most of all.

Every normal mother wants her son to be a "real boy," a "big man." But if he develops so much self-assurance that he becomes self-assertive, she is scandalized and cries about it at night. If he develops so much courage that he gets competitive and goes in for football, boxing, or mountain-climbing, she is frightened and hauls him back behind the screen of her protectiveness, or else becomes feverish with visions of imagined injuries. She wants him to grow up, but she doesn't want him to grow up. Even though in principle she is all for his development, she nevertheless forbids it. By transferring the restricting fears of her own rearing, she begins to *smother*.

Then comes adolescence with its high narrow bridge to maturity. And one of three things happens: He breaks out in overt rebellion. He asserts his maleness in some petty vandalism, abuse, troublemaking, or delinquency. He breaks windshields, he deliberately disobeys, he's a "hard-to-handle" toughie. Or, he represses his hatreds and resentments. They reappear as hatred of the "female" and he makes a sorry husband for any woman foolish enough to marry him. Or, he surrenders to this loss of individuality and never breaks out. He is tied to you long after you are dead, with a cord that no future attachment can break. Pathetic, listless, sexless, futureless, he has "stayed small." He's a good son. He never did leave you and he never will.

I am a son and have had a mother all my life — a grand one, and smarter than either of us knew. She

knew how to turn us loose and thrust us to freedom
and opportunity. She, somehow, by God's grace, knew
instinctively what happens to little boys kept tied too long.
I salute her for loving me in a way to release both of us
from the natural selfishness of mother love.

I not only am a son, I know *your* sons. On fifty college
campuses, at a dozen air force bases, on several army
posts, at a navy school or two, I know your sons. I have
taught them briefly, at CCC camps and at high school,
college, and seminary levels. I have known them in
three or four jails, before the grand jury, in the work
of several churches, and in Scouting — all the way from
six on patrol to fifty thousand camped together at
Jamboree. I know your sons.

Out of sympathetic concern for all involved I keep
remembering those fine youngsters who have said to me,
"How can I get my mother's hands off me?"

The release a mother owes her son is emotional,
psychological, personal. The release she must give him is
the right to manhood, and she must prepare him for it.
Only in the womb is he completely hers; the rest of life
is a process of separation. Indeed this is just what
physical birth and its severed cord symbolize. This is the
meaning of birth — one soul cannot be kept within
another. And this is why birth is so difficult a process.
Growing up is so much a matter of separation — physically,
psychologically, emotionally — that some births are
never completed, and both mother and son are in labor
all their lives. How tragic, how difficult, is the life of
the half-born son. And how can he be born again
who has not yet been born the first time?

All of a mother's life with her son is within this process
of separation begun at birth. But to say "turn him loose"
is not to say "be unconcerned." You must give him
two things first of all:

Security-sense comes from the long, uninterrupted period
of psychological mothering. This is the time of suckling
and snuggling, the easy creation of habits not begun
too soon out of false pride, the sense of family, the
development of morals, the birth of beliefs, the sense
of the presence of God. These are the years when he
becomes not just son — he can't help that — but also

friend — and you can't bribe that. It's given and deserved, or it's lost.

Self-confidence is created by that gradual process of release to himself and to other helpers. You are concerned about where he's going, you fear he'll fall, yet you let him go. You push him out. You let him ride off alone.

All this raises the question, "What makes a mother smother?" First, when there exists a lack, an imbalance, a failure, a lack of mutuality at any level of marriage, the woman easily gives evidence of her instability, or insecurity, by her inordinate concern for and domination of her children. This is particularly true when the physical relationships of husband and wife aren't right. What really belongs to the husband-wife association is repressed, turned around, and changed — even perverted — until it forces its way into expression as so-called mother love (better called wife frustration). Again, and just as frequently, the mother's concern for her children becomes complete preoccupation when the father isn't really father, for there is a father-child responsibility too. Sensing the lack of support, shared authority, responsibility, and concern in her children's father, the mother, unconsciously or consciously, gradually tries to become both father and mother. The effect is usually smothering.

Second, as a factor in making smotherers out of mothers, is the social image, the ideal, that our way of life has idolized and made mandatory for its mothers. We go overboard in the maudlin expression of inane sentiment no real mother will tolerate, in place of the true spiritual reverence motherhood deserves. Our whole way of life joins in the chorus, creating an almost universal drift toward mother domination. The image clings, grows softer and more beautiful with time and distance, and becomes so potent a factor in our lives that honest, self-disciplined, confident mothers seem positively unconcerned alongside the rank and file who knock themselves out to keep their sons from growing up.

The third cause of smother-mothers, perhaps first in importance, is plain immaturity. Immaturity begets immaturity. We transfer our parents' weaknesses to the rearing of our own children. Immaturity also produces shallow levels of concern. The mother becomes so completely concerned over the child's eating, washing, and bathrooming, all of which must be done precisely in order, that she never sees what she does to personality, independence, pride, and future by her emphasis on purely mechanical functions. Wet diapers on a three-year-old or a sweet tooth in the baby's eating habits are such major faults to be overcome that no thought is given to the long-range effect of her spiritual neglect during the most vital months of young life. Horace Bushnell was a hundred years ahead of his times when he claimed that indulgence of suckling children may make dependent alcoholics of adults. Immature preoccupation with mechanics not only makes nervous wrecks of mothers, it also makes stripped characters out of little children who are thus taught mechanical and functional values that never grow into the spiritual values essential to real adulthood.

Karl Menninger makes a list of the crimes unwittingly committed against the child by some mothers: inconsistency, threatenings, objection to his activities because of her neurotic fears, refusal of reasonable requests, ignoring his efforts to be pleasing, breaking promises, quarreling over trivia, transferring her own anxieties, discussing him before others, embarrassing, neglecting, bribing, lying, shielding him from the consequences of his own acts, comparing unfavorably — inculcating a dishonest, hypocritical philosophy of life. These are hard words, but any minister, teacher, army officer, or judge who deals with sons knows they are true words.

Some Guides to Follow

Thou shalt not be inconsistent in order to keep him close.
Thou shalt not threaten in order to gain thy way.
Thou shalt not transfer thine own neurotic fears
    in order to control him.
Thou shalt not break promises in order to subdue him.
Thou shalt not quarrel over trivialities to keep
    the upper hand.
Thou shalt not bribe him to do what is right.
Thou shalt neither lie to him nor for him.
Nor shalt thou shield him in any other way from
    the consequences of his own acts.

Thou shalt neither embarrass, neglect, compare, nor tattle
  in order to dominate him.
Thou shalt *wean* thy son!

*O Lord, please bless these lovely aliens, my children.
They seem so strange to me at times, not even resembling
me in face or traits or body.*

*It is sometimes hard to believe that I had anything
to do with producing them, these vigorous strangers
going their own way with such vigor and independence.
The fact that I even clothe and care for them seems
an anomaly, as if I am just some loving outsider attending
their needs.*

*At times I protest this, Lord. I don't want to be
an outsider. I am lonely for the deeper attachments
we had when they were small. I feel a hungry desire
to know more truly what they think, to share their lives.*

*A kind of righteous indignation rises up, demanding,
"See here, if it weren't for me you wouldn't be here!
Pay attention to me, draw me in. Hey . . . I'm your
mother!"*

*Then I'm reminded of my own blithe, often incon-
siderate youth. You help me to see that this is nature's
way, however cruel, of cutting natal strings. I can't
carry them forever in my womb, or on my lap (only in
my heart). The burden of it would be intolerable.
For my sake as well as theirs, I've got to let them alone,
let them go.*

*So bless them as they make these fierce, sometimes
foolish, sometimes faltering strides toward independence.
Give them strength — they're going to need it! Don't let
my self-pity sap their progress. God bless these
lovely aliens, my children.*

Marjorie Holmes

DISCIPLINE FOR LIFE
by Dr. Fitzhugh Dodson

Our ultimate goal in disciplining a child is to help him become a self-regulating person. And the extent to which he will become self-regulating will depend upon the strength of his self-concept.

What can you as a parent do to help strengthen his self-concept and move him toward this ultimate goal? You can make use of the following teaching methods:

1 / An individualized approach to each child promotes a good self-concept in that child.

Intellectually, parents know their children are unique. Yet in practice, parents often try to use the same discipline methods on all their children, as if one were like the other.

We need to take time to study the individual characteristics and the "growing edge" of each of our children, whether they be introverts or extroverts, happy-go-lucky carefree children or serious, introspective youngsters.

2/ Giving a child freedom to explore his environment and assume self-regulation as soon as he is able at each stage of development builds a positive self-concept.

When he first grabs a spoon and indicates to you that he wants to feed himself, give him the chance. It's the same with all his other activities. As soon as he can dress himself, or brush his teeth, let him do these things by himself.

Many times we hesitate to let a child do various things on his own because, way down deep, we don't want to see him grow up. And yet what great things we can do for our children if we respect their urge for freedom and give it room to develop.

3 / Relying on the powerful force of unconscious imitation is a great builder of a positive self-concept in a child.

Children are terrific imitators. If we show good table manners by our own example, our children will imitate us when they grow old enough. Not at two years or at four years, but later. If we want our children

to respect the rights and feelings of others, we must begin
by respecting the rights and feelings of our children.

4/ *Letting your child learn by natural consequences helps
to build a strong self-concept.*

This is one of the most powerful tools we parents have
to enable our children to learn things.

A child doesn't eat at breakfast. Mother merely removes
the food from the table at the end of the meal and lets
the natural consequences take over. Before too long
the child will probably want a snack. Mother can then
say, "I'm sorry you're hungry. We'll have lunch at
twelve o'clock. It's too bad you have to wait so long."
The hunger the child experiences is a natural consequence
of not eating his breakfast. It promotes a far faster
change in his actions than any amount of scolding or
punishment by his mother would do.

It would be nice if we could rely entirely on the natural
consequences of inadequate behavior to discipline a child.
Unfortunately, natural consequences aren't always
sufficient. Sometimes we must find artificial or arbitrary
consequences to apply to the behavior of a child.

We can use three main methods:

1/ *We can deprive the child of something important
to him.*

Suppose your five-year-old scribbles on your living room
walls with crayons. Such behavior is "normal" for a
two-year-old. But it's an act of hostility for a five-
year-old.

When you discover it, you may immediately spank him.
That is one type of artificial but unpleasant consequence
for him. Or you might deprive him of some privilege,
perhaps saying, "Danny, you're old enough to know
not to draw on walls with crayons, so I guess you won't be
allowed to use your crayons for three days. That will
help to remind you that crayons are to be used on paper,
not on walls."

2/ *We can use social isolation by sending the child
out of his social group or to his room.*

Suppose your four-year-old is disrupting the play of
a group of children in your back yard. You might say
to him, "Charles, I see you aren't able to play well
with the other children right now. You keep hitting them

and causing trouble. You'll have to go to your room
and play by yourself until you tell me that you're able
to control your actions."

Always let him know that when his behavior is able
to change and he is able to play reasonably with the
other children, he can come back and play.

3/ *We can spank a child.*

I want to make it clear that there is a "right" kind
of spanking and a "wrong" kind. By the wrong kind
I mean a cruel, sadistic beating. This fills a child
with hatred and deep desire for revenge. This is the
kind that is administered with a strap or stick or some
other type of parental "weapon." Or it could also mean a
humiliating slap in the face.

The right kind of spanking needs no special para-
phernalia. Just the hand of the parent administered
a few times on the kid's bottom. The right kind of
spanking is a *positive* thing. It clears the air and is vastly
to be preferred to moralistic and guilt-inducing parental
lectures.

What you should do is to tell your child once or
perhaps twice what you want him to do or to stop doing.
Then, if he refuses to obey your reasonable request,
let him have it right then and there.

If you're quite honest with yourself, you'll find
that at times you lose your temper, fly off the handle
at your child, and yell at him or spank him, only to realize
afterward that what he did actually shouldn't have
elicited such a violent outburst from you. You were
really mad at your husband or your neighbor. Or just
cranky for some unknown reason. And you took it out
on your child.

What can you do in such a situation? Well, you could
pretend you are a holy paragon of virtue and that
your child fully deserved the scolding or spanking he got.
Or you can have the courage to say something like this
to your child: "Danny, mother got mad at you and
scolded you. But I can see now that you didn't do
anything that was really that bad. I think I was really mad
at something else and I was sort of taking it out on you.
So I'm sorry."

Your child will feel a wonderful warm feeling toward

you for admitting you are human and fallible. This will
do wonders for his self-concept, and yours.

I have said that the natural consequences of a child's
misbehavior may have to be supplemented by artificial
consequences. But even though these consequences
of a child's misbehavior are artificial rather than natural,
some basic principles govern their use.

1 / *The artificial consequences should be reasonably
consistent.*

If your child is deprived of his crayons one day for
scribbling on the wall, but is laughed at indulgently
the next day for doing the exact same thing, it will be
difficult for him to learn to stop scribbling on walls.

2 / *The artificial consequences should be immediate.*

For instance, if your child has misbehaved in the middle
of the morning, let the unpleasant consequences begin
right then. Don't put off the punishment until Dad
gets home that night. Say: "All right, Jimmy, I'm
afraid you're not going to be allowed to watch TV the
rest of the day, beginning right now."

3 / *If you deprive a child of something important to him,
the amount of time the deprivation lasts should be
reasonable.*

To deprive a five-year-old of watching TV for a month
is unreasonable. The punishment then becomes meaningless
to him. He has no incentive to improve his behavior
so that he may be allowed to watch TV again. To
deprive him of watching TV for a few days is meaningful punishment and does give him the incentive to
improve his behavior.

4/ *Never punish a child by depriving him of something
really crucial to him.*

I have known parents who deprived a child of
a birthday party as a punishment. Or of a special trip
to an amusement park which he had been looking forward
to for a long, long time. Such deprivations accomplish
little in the way of true behavior change. The child
reacts to them only with hostility and desire for revenge.
As a child sees it, to deprive him of something like
a birthday party constitutes "cruel and unusual punishment." And he's right.

5 / *The unpleasant artificial consequences should be as*

relevant as possible to the misbehavior.

If a child has scribbled on the wall with crayons, it's relevant for him to be deprived of the use of his crayons for several days. And he'll recognize the relevance and justice of such a punishment.

6 / Give your child a positive model for what he should do.

I know a puppet master who gives Punch and Judy shows for children. He understands the psychology of children very well. That's why children are so delighted with his shows. At one point in the show, Punch is riding on a horse, and the puppet master tells the children, "Now don't say 'giddyap,' because every time the horse hears the word *giddyap,* he'll buck and throw Punch off. Remember, don't say 'giddyap' to the horse!" Hardly has he finished admonishing the children what *not* to say, than the children are joyously shouting "giddyap!" Many mothers don't seem to understand the effects of telling a child *not* to say "giddyap." They are surprised and unhappy when their child starts shouting the psychological equivalent of "giddyap" to them.

We need to phrase our instructions to a child so that we tell him *what to do,* and refrain from telling him what not to do. Instead of saying, "Stop throwing sand," you can say, "Sand is for playing in, not throwing."

7/ Handle danger situations wisely.

By danger situations for a preschool child I mean such things as crossing a street, fires, boiling water, sharp knives, and poisons. The wise use of environmental control will keep some of these dangers inaccessible to your child.

But environmental control won't do the complete job. The key to helping your child learn to cope with danger situations is to teach him a healthy respect for the danger, without developing excessive fears in him. Allow him to experience the minor unpleasant consequences of his actions in situations which aren't dangerous. He will then be more likely to be cautious and to listen to you as a reliable guide to danger than if you've overprotected him and prevented him from experiencing the natural consequences of his actions.

The use of these seven positive methods will do wonders

to strengthen your child's self-concept and help him become a self-regulating person.

While we are disciplining our children and guiding them toward our ultimate goal of self-regulation, let's not forget they are still children. Our methods of discipline should enable the dynamic quality of childhood to be channeled into socially approved ways of expression. But our methods should never eliminate that vital and dynamic quality that makes kids act like kids!

The child who has everything done for him, everything given to him, and nothing required of him is a deprived child. . . . The parent who tries to please the child by giving in to him and expecting nothing from him ends up by pleasing no one, least of all the child. For in the end, when trouble results, the child will blame the parent for his gutlessness.

Larry Christenson

LIFT YOUR RECEIVER

by David and Virginia Edens

He asks you a serious question, but before you've had time to answer, he decides you don't know enough to answer it.

She calls you a tyrant for restricting her telephone calls, but turns around and brags to her friends about her parent's standards.

Who are these riddles? They are your teen-agers, half still yours and half belonging to their newfound world and friends. Their actions at any moment can be frustrating, pleasing, alarming, surprising. You wish time and again that you could understand what's going on inside their heads. Have you stopped to think that often they're wondering "what gives" with you? Maybe it's time to "lift the receiver" and listen to one another. Communication, whatever else it is, is always a two-way process.

Talking isn't always communication. In some families there's much talk but no real exchange of warm understanding. There's a big difference between the spontaneous conversation that teen-agers enjoy and a continuous prattle to secure attention. A teen-ager may talk continuously and say nothing that really matters to him, using speech as a defense against prying questions and holding back his real feelings lest his parents won't understand.

How can we prevent talk from becoming a barrier instead of a bridge? Good communication between parents is a foundation for communication between parents and children. Channels of love and understanding are kept open at all times. Paul said, "Let not the sun go down upon your wrath: neither give place to the devil" (Ephesians 4:26, 27). In paraphrase, "Never go to sleep with a quarrel in your heart. If you do, the devil is your roommate." Probably the six most difficult words in the family vocabulary are, "I was wrong; I am sorry." We can keep the lines of communication open between husband and wife and, if an honest look shows that they have become clogged with debris of everyday problems, we can do our best to open them again.

A teen-ager needs to feel free to talk to his parents, and parental attitude usually determines the extent to which this freedom is used. Have you ever thought, "I wonder why my child never asks questions"? The answer may be that he has been preconditioned to your attitude. If a child knows that a parent will go into shock or explode into criticism before he has even finished talking, he soon learns to keep his problems, experiences, and feelings to himself. If we laugh at the adolescent's confidences or repeat them to others, the confidences will stop. We do not have to be a teen-ager to respect his teen-age interests.

We need to remember that communication need not always involve speech. When we offer understanding through silence or grant privacy when we feel it's needed, deep communication takes place. A need that sometimes escapes the notice of parents is that the teen-ager must be able to find privacy when he wants it. A room of his own, a separate hobby area, a place where he can entertain without stumbling over other members of the family are ideal situations. Even if he shares a room with another member of the family, there should be separate areas set aside for study and for hobbies. The "I want to be alone" attitude of teen-agers is not necessarily a forecast of maladjustment (unless it happens too often). Rather it's a healthy sign that the adolescent can be creative by himself, can privately take stock of things, or needs to be quiet — alone.

Adolescents don't necessarily talk over all problems with their parents. They long to be independent. Mother and Father supplied the answers in childhood, but now the adolescent wants to find his own. Parents can respect his desire to keep things to himself and at the same time make it known that he can confide in them whenever he feels the need.

A change in family relationships develops during the adolescent years. A new type of communication between adolescent and parent emerges. Parents become standbys more than confidants. A full measure of trust and encouragement replaces the time previously spent in dressing, feeding, and tucking the child in bed.

Amid the changes and uncertainties, the adolescent
finds comfort in his dependence upon the stability of an
understanding parent. When values change all around
him and new ones are being formed, an adolescent finds
satisfaction in the unchanging values adhered to by
Christian parents. Parents' convictions about Christ, the
church, honesty, responsibility, duty, and discipline
are symbols of stability.

The emotional calm arising from reasonable limits set
by parents is often welcomed. The adolescent wants
the strength, privileges, and responsibility of adulthood,
but is uncertain of his readiness physically and emotionally.
He finds security in the mature judgment of parents
who have faith in the unchanging wisdom and love of
God.

Family discussion periods can keep the channels of
communication open between you and your child.
These discussions need not always focus on crises
or big problems. At the dinner table, at times when the
family relaxes together, or when friends or relatives are
being entertained, many things spark healthy discussions
— neighborhood happenings, community affairs, small
newspaper items. Parents can broaden the topics, stimulate
interest, and subtly introduce values about human nature.
Adolescents can learn to express themselves on subjects
that don't come out of textbooks. Families that are
accustomed to talking with each other about nonfamily
affairs (above the level of gossip) more than likely will
feel free to communicate with each other on personal
matters, an important necessity for adolescents.

Communication Checklist for Parents
Do you . . .

Allow time to be with your child?
Encourage your family to watch quality television
   shows together?
Read Christian periodicals and good books during
   leisure time, and talk about them together?
Show an interest in school problems and teen-age
   activities? Do you encourage your child to evaluate
   these activities with you, yet know how to retreat
   gracefully from running (or ruining) his interests?
   Make sure that both of you as parents share equally

the various problems of your teen-ager, with consistent approaches?
Maintain privacy and "separateness" in the home,
    for parents as well as teen-agers, realizing that each
    is entitled to his own interests and activities?

The adolescent often has mixed feelings about what is happening to him. He has that new-old feeling. One adolescent expressed his feelings this way: "I'm not what I ought to be, I'm not what I'm going to be, but I'm sure not what I used to be!"

The warm environment of a Christian home can further the development for which the adolescent strives.

Next to the after-school hour, there is no better time than after a red-hot basketball game or a washed-out date. All kinds of thoughts are racing through his head. "Boy, what a night!" Or "What a skag! How did I ever get hooked up with her?"

I take the cue from them. If they seem eager to talk about the evening, I ease myself into a chair and listen. On the other hand, if it appears to be a night when no talk is forthcoming and my sons or daughter want to "be alone," I go to bed after the first greeting.

Learning never to scold or lecture while the children unburdened themselves was my most difficult lesson. Eventually I realized that during these moments they couldn't look at themselves objectively. To advise or scold because they were "off the beam" would have been disastrous. Had I shown my shock at some of their musings, I'm certain that my role as a listener would have ended. I might not approve what they were thinking sometimes, but at least I can understand them better for knowing.

Early in the game I found that to be a good listener I must not give in to the impulse to share the confidences I gathered. Naturally, I shared them with my husband, but never with an outsider.

Helen H. Andersen

BUILD THEIR SELF-IMAGE

by Elizabeth Peterson

I suspect that all of us who work or live with children find them at times maddening, fascinating, frustrating, rewarding —

- but seldom dull. Out of interest or love we try to supply children with the food they need to nourish their bodies, with stories and music to enrich their lives, and with moral and spiritual values to nourish their souls. But we're also supplying them with pieces which they fit together to build self-images. Whether this self-image gives pain or pleasure has a great deal to do with the child's future happiness and fulfillment.

A healthy self-image is realistic, not conceited. I suspect that conceited people have very shaky self-images. This is why they have to run around "blowing their own horns," trying to reassure themselves and let other people know they have worth. But a person with a strong self-image has a comfortable feeling that he's a worthwhile human being.

Because we're human, all of us are terribly vulnerable to the damage that other people can do to us; when we're children we're doubly vulnerable. Similarly, children are most sensitive to positive measures to build or restore their self-concepts.

First, to help a child create a good self-image, it's important to be sure that the image he sees of himself as reflected in our behavior and attitude assures him that he is loved, capable, and respected. This starts in the cradle. When we cuddle our babies and coo at them and meet their needs, we're saying to them, "You and your feelings and your needs are important to me." We smile at them: "You're delightful!" This expression of love and interest serves as an inoculation against failure, but children need constant booster shots.

If adults are too busy with business or social life or whatever fills their time, crowding children out of their lives, children quickly get the message that they're not as important as these other things. Kids are pretty quick to catch on to the fact that we spend our money, our energy, and our time on the things that matter.

Second, we need to build a healthy self-image in a child by appreciating him for what he is, not for what he does. It helps if adult attitudes convey the message, "We like you because you're you. It's wonderful when you bring home a good report card or when you're elected patrol leader; this gives you a good warm feeling. But we love you just because you are you. *You don't have to win our love by your successes."*

So often as we go about the business of civilizing our children, we leave them with the feeling that they do nothing right. We let them know that we think they're pretty dismal failures. While we must civilize them, we need to let them know along the way that they do lots of things that please us.

Third, we must use each child's ability and interest as cues, instead of forcing our own ambitions upon him in attempts to realize our unfulfilled dreams. I remember seeing a cartoon of a scowling nine-year-old boy hacking away at a violin and saying, "I wish my mother hadn't had such a deprived childhood."

I feel sorry for middle-class children who grow up in families where it's taken for granted that of course they'll go to college, whether the young people have aptitude or interest in it or not.

The fourth ingredient in building a child's self-image is to see that he acquires skills. These image-building skills begin very young and progress with age: being toilet trained, learning to ride a tricycle, learning to take turns, learning the rules of social courtesy, learning to ride a bicycle, learning to take part in group discussions, and other appropriate things.

Such skills build a child's image among his peers. Children have to earn their own way. Those who have skills that other children respect are likely to be accepted by their peers. Throughout life all of us need the confidence that comes from doing small things well. And when children work diligently to achieve a skill, adults should celebrate their successes.

A fifth thing to remember in building a child's self-image is that both overprotection and domination weaken it.

When we make all the decisions for our children from the time they get up in the morning until the time they go to bed, we're saying, "I really don't think you're capable of even the simplest decision." That scarcely builds self-confidence.

Youngsters need experience in making decisions. If their first chance comes with crucial decisions at adolescence, both they and society are likely to suffer. Because decision-making takes a great deal of skill, appropriate chances to practice should begin early.

A sixth need is to be realistic about normal behavior. This is something I'd like to capitalize and underline, because all of us are victims of generations of adults who thought that children were little adults. They're not. They're totally different little creatures.

We expect three-year-olds, for example, to sit still through a 40-minute dinner hour. One study found that the average three-year-old, left to his own devices, is still for a total of seventeen minutes of his waking hours.

Parents need help in learning what is typical behavior at different age levels. Too often we make issues of things the children will outgrow. They're just acting their age, but we punish a four-year-old for "four-year-oldness" instead of expecting that this is the way a four-year-old will act.

Seventh, remember that acceptance of self includes the physical self. I think of one little boy who has a tragic case of cerebral palsy. At the end of a Sunday school session his father came to the classroom to get him, swept him up in his arms, wiped the saliva that drooled out of the little boy's mouth, and with much love in his eyes said, "Tell me what happened today." The affection between these two, the total acceptance of this little boy, permits a great hope that he will make it.

Little children can be very cruel to the overweight child. A friend, who in my opinion is one of the most competent clinical psychologists in Minnesota, says if you let kids get to the teen age with real weight problems — not plumpness, but obesity — the problems are difficult to unravel. This psychologist refuses to treat an obese teen-ager unless the parents will work with the doctor, too.

The eighth thing we must remember is to avoid

belittling, sarcastic, discouraging remarks and labels. When you tell a child, "You're a liar," "You're a thief," "You're lazy," "You're irresponsible," "You're stupid," "You're clumsy," you're attacking the child rather than the misdeed. Labels tend to become self-fulfilling prophecies. Children often live up to the labels we pin on them, which is why we should look for good ones.

No matter how hard you have to look, find something you can honestly praise in a child. Often the children who need this most are the children who make you really search to come up with something positive to praise.

And it should seldom be necessary to scold children before their friends. You can certainly take them aside. Otherwise the child has not only his guilty feelings and your anger to combat, but he has the diminished self on display before everybody else.

Wherever we possibly can, we should separate the child from the deed. To attack the bad deed, saying, "That's a terrible thing you did" is very different from attacking the child, saying, "You're a terrible child." We can correct his behavior without undermining his confidence in himself.

A ninth suggestion is to avoid comparisons and appreciate each child's uniqueness. I suspect that all of us as parents are trapped sometimes into saying things like, "Why can't you do your homework the way Susie does" or "Why can't you hang up your pajamas the way Johnny does?" This is unfortunate. We can compare a child with his own best self, but not with somebody else. We don't want to say, "You're less acceptable than the other person is."

A tenth thing we need to keep in mind is that constructive discipline is a key factor in developing a worthy self-concept.

Inconsistency in discipline brings problems. We make a lot of rules, many of them unnecessary, and we don't have the backbone to carry them out. I think we ought to make minimum rules, but then see that they are carried out day-in and day-out so that children know exactly what to expect.

Above all, love in home and church assures each child of his own worth. Then he will be free to make use

of his unique gifts, and in turn to affirm the worth
of others.

Happy is the family
  Whose members know what a home is for,
And keep the main aims in view;

Who give more thought to affection
  Than to the shelter that houses it;
And more attention to persons
  Than to the things amid which they live.

For a home is a shelter for love
  And a setting for joy and growth,
Rather than a place to be kept up.

It is a hallowed place,
  To which its members shall turn
With a lifting of the heart.

Leland Foster Wood

SHOW THEM COURTESY

by Mildred Martin

Adults sometimes use a double standard when it comes to courtesy. We feel that adults rate our best manners, but with children it really doesn't matter.

But it does matter. Children are smaller and younger than adults, but they are intelligent and know when they are treated courteously and when they are not.

I remember two people who were especially kind and considerate to me when I was a child.

There was an aunt who rolled out the red carpet when I came to visit. She treated me like an important individual and called me by name. She was a busy wife and mother, yet she took time to do things that would make the children happy. I still remember how she sliced the potatoes thin, and how excited we were to have real potato chips!

The other adult I remember was an elderly man who lived in our neighborhood. He never failed to tip his hat as we passed on the sidewalk. He made a ten-year-old young lady feel that at least one person realized she was almost grown up.

Perhaps if we were to treat children with more respect and courtesy they might grow up with the idea that that is the proper way to behave.

Ten Easy Ways to be Discourteous to a Child

1/ When you are watching *your* favorite television program do not allow the child to make the least noise. But when he is watching *his* favorite program, laugh and talk, and carry on a noisy conversation.

2/ When he offers his opinion on a family problem, dismiss his suggestion with an appropriate remark: "You don't know anything about it — you're just a child."

3/ Should he attempt to discuss his day at school with you, tell him you are tired of always hearing what that teacher is saying.

4/ If someone reports that he has been a naughty boy,

punish him before you ask him to tell his version
of the incident.

5/ Do not trust him. Suspect the worst of him.
Expect him to get into trouble.

6 / Do not bother to compliment him on an achievement.
After all, he is only a child. You do not want to spoil him.

7/ If he is downhearted, there is no need to
encourage him with a kind word, as you would an adult.

8/ Do not introduce a child by his name. Just say,
"Oh, this is Bill's little boy."

9/ When you meet a fat child, say, "You are a chubby
one, aren't you?" Or, if he is skinny, "My, how thin
you are!"

10/ If a child is playing within listening distance,
go ahead and talk about him — no need to wait
and discuss him behind his back, as you would an adult.

We should take time to be more courteous to children.
We are no busier than the one who said: "Suffer the little
children to come unto me, and forbid them not"
(Mark 10:14).

SAY "I'M SORRY"

by Ruth Hayward

Shopping with a neighbor, I waited as she was paying for a purchase. Suddenly she cried, "Oh!"

"What's the matter, Jean?" I asked. "Forget your wallet? I have enough to lend —"

"Oh, no, it isn't that." She drew out a bill and handed it to the salesclerk. "It's these. Cindy's gloves. She didn't have them to wear to school this morning. When I accused her of being careless and scolded her for losing them, she told me she'd given them to me after Sunday school yesterday. I didn't believe her."

"That's all right," I said, "just tell her when she comes home from school."

"Tell her? Indeed not. I don't want her to think her mother is so forgetful."

"But Jean, she has a right to know that it wasn't her fault."

Jean looked at me sternly. "Children have the right to look up to their parents as good examples — not as imperfect blunderers."

I protested again. "But we are *not* perfect."

"Why admit it, Ruth? After all, there is such a thing as pride."

I didn't say any more on the subject. I am so blundering in my own family relationships that I had no right to preach to my friend. But I still think that pride has no place in family relationships, whether between parent and child or man and wife.

No matter how perfect we want to appear to our children, we simply aren't. In spite of all our good intentions, we blunder. We are mistaken at times in our interpretation of children's behavior and sometimes we discipline unfairly. I remember a time when my daughter, Wendy, had to stay after school because she hadn't handed in her homework. When she came home I scolded her.

"But I did my work, Mommy," she declared. "I just

couldn't find it to hand it in."

"Wendy —"

"But I did. Please believe me."

I went on. "Didn't you look at TV quite a long time last night?"

"Yes, Mommy. But I did my work first," she insisted.

Knowing she wouldn't deliberately tell an untruth, I didn't press further. But I was sure she had forgotten. Later that night I was picking up papers on the coffee table. I had been working on household accounts the night before and had left my work there. Now, sorting things, I came across a piece of notebook paper. Heading it was the name "Wendy Hayward," then the title "Science." It was the missing homework.

I picked up the paper. My heart pricked as I realized how mistaken I'd been. I hadn't accused Wendy of not doing the work, but I knew she thought I didn't believe her. Hurrying to her room, I noticed she was turned to the wall. Hoping she wasn't yet asleep, I called softly, "Wendy?"

She turned over. In the dim light I could see she'd been crying.

"I found your homework, dear," I said.

She sat right up. "Now do you believe me?"

Taking her in my arms, I said, "Of course, I believe you. And it was very wrong to even make you think I didn't."

"But that's all right, because it turned out right. I should have put it right in my notebook, but I was in too much of a hurry to watch TV. Next time I'll do better."

"And so will I," I promised.

When I was first married, I made the mistake that so many young people make. I thought all quarrels and misunderstandings were the fault of my husband. Quite often, though, it was proved that I was the one at fault, but pride kept me from saying so. Being young, too, my husband had the same attitude.

But one night he came to me, his arms outstretched, saying, "Ruth, I'm sorry. It was all my fault."

Taken by surprise, I found all the anger and self-righteousness drained from me, and I said spontaneously,

"I'm sorry too. It was mostly my own fault."

That moment was a revelation to me. It made me realize that my husband was a reasonable, loving, understanding person. Most important, when I wasn't too proud to say, "I'm sorry," I made our life together much smoother and more rewarding.

And so it has been with our children. Conflicts between us have often arisen when I, as mother, have been mistaken and failed to admit it. False pride, based on a natural desire to be regarded as an ideal mother, has at times kept a barrier between a child and myself much longer than was necessary. When I have "swallowed my pride" and admitted I was wrong, I have found immediate, tender forgiveness and understanding.

Pity the poor mother who says to a friend in front of little Billy, "Oh, dear! I don't know what I'm going to do with Billy! He's so wild and naughty that I'm just worn to a frazzle. I don't know what to try next." And there sits little Billy, horns creeping higher, thinking to himself, "Heh, heh — have I got her in a frenzy! Wild I am — wild I'll be!" You see, it's true with children as of adults: we are what we are expected to be — in many ways. If that mother had been wise, she'd have said something like this, "I enjoy taking Billy visiting with me; he's such a gentleman!" Billy is thinking, "Who? Me? I am? Sure I am!" And chances are he will be. Don't ever underestimate the capacity of those little minds.

Char J. Crawford

MRS. BILLY GRAHAM ANSWERS YOUR QUESTIONS

Ruth Bell Graham
with Joan Gage

It's somehow reassuring to know that even in a religious household like Billy Graham's problems arise. After talking to Ruth Graham, it becomes clear that she has encountered most of the problems any mother of five would face — and a few more besides.

But in many ways Ruth Graham is well prepared to cope with the problems of being Mrs. Billy Graham. She draws strength from her childhood background and her serene faith in God, and has a fine sense of humor that lets her laugh at moments when another mother might miss the humor of the situation.

"I remember one time when Bill was away," she says. "We had four small children then, all terrible sleepers. I used to get up from three to seven times a night. One day I woke up in the morning looking a wreck — hair a mess, no makeup. I grabbed my bathrobe. Franklin was a baby and I didn't even bother to change him; I just picked him up and plopped him in the high chair. And that morning, every time Gigi the oldest child, started to say something, Bunny, the youngest girl interrupted her. Finally Gigi slammed down her fork and said, 'Mother, between looking at you and smelling Franklin and listening to Bunny, I'm just not hungry!'"

Mrs. Graham laughs at the memory and adds, "I thought to myself, 'This also has a spiritual application. We Christians sometimes take away someone else's appetite for the Lord by the way we live and by the way we appear and by the way we sound.'"

Ruth learned to deal stoically with running a household full of small children while her husband was away more often than he was home. "A mother ought to be with the children," she says. "Personally, I love it. I wish we could live a more normal life, but God never asks us to give up one thing without giving so much in return that you wind up almost ashamed of yourself."

She disciplined the children by herself. ("Did I spank

them? Heavens, yes," she laughs.) She also learned
to cope with home repairs by herself. "Although we
don't have a normal family life," she once said, "we
have a happy one."

Ruth spends part of her time answering letters from
people who turn to her for advice, often about problems
of child-rearing. She says she has no magic formula.
"The older I get, the less I know . . . the less of an
authority I become." But she agreed to answer some
questions about raising children to believe in God.

How do you introduce a small child to religion?
"You start off teaching children about God very simply as
being a loving heavenly Father who cares for them very
much and is watching over them constantly. Small
children can grasp deep spiritual truths with amazing
alacrity. In fact, we need their simplicity of faith.
Our daughters have very young children, and they pray
with them every night before they go to bed and tell
them very simple little Bible stories. I think that
spontaneous prayers are best for that age. Just,
'God bless Mama and Daddy' and right down the list,
winding up with, 'I love you.' I'm not sure how much
they understand, but they're getting the idea that
they're talking to someone who loves them and cares
about them.

"Someone has said that the best way to get a child
to eat his food is to see his parents enjoying theirs —
and I think this carries over into the spiritual realm.
If they see us enjoying our faith, they're much more likely
to do so themselves than if it seems some kind of drudgery.

"I believe the husband is the one, according to
the instructions in the Scripture, who should take the lead
spiritually and call the family to family prayers and
devotions. Sometimes the mother has to if the father's
not there, but I don't want our sons to get the idea
that devotions are just for women. I want them to
understand that it's their responsibility when they are
married."

*What do you tell a child when a prayer isn't
immediately answered?* "That God knows best and that
'no' is also an answer. I remember once when Ned
wanted a bicycle. He's so persistent! Morning, noon, and

night he was telling us exactly the type of bicycle, how many speeds, what color, what make, where to get it, how much it cost. We said, 'Absolutely not,' and we explained that Christmas was three months away. The next week he said, 'I've changed my mind about the kind of bicycle,' and went through it all again — different speeds, different colors, different handlebars. About a week later he'd changed his mind again. Well, by the time he finished I understood better than ever before why God doesn't answer our prayers immediately."

How do you train children to avoid such pitfalls as smoking, drinking, and drugs? "I told the children that if the Bible is explicit, that if God says, 'Thou shalt not,' then there's no argument, no question. But in areas where the Bible is not explicit, they have to weigh the pros and cons, face all the facts, and make up their minds what is right and wise for them.

"We have to teach them the difference between moral issues and nonmoral issues. Moral issues involve honesty and reverence for God — the Ten Commandments make it all pretty clear. Nonmoral issues would be fads, length of hair, mistakes.

"I think children are less likely to experiment when their lives are filled with wholesome activities and they're busy and have a purpose in life."

How do you keep children from being influenced by the actions of their friends? "First you must encourage them to make the right friends. Then be sure their friends are welcome in your home. You've got to be willing to listen to your children. And to their friends as well. But I wish I had a foolproof formula. I know one boy who is now in jail on charges of pushing drugs, and no boy ever had more godly parents."

What about when children reach the age of challenging their parents' religion? "I do think that it's important to try to answer their questions *when they ask them,* and not to be shocked by anything they ask. I had an experience in college where I lost my faith. This went on for months. I was miserable! It was as if the light had gone out. So I argued with everybody. People dreaded seeing me coming. Finally one very perceptive friend sat down and gave me all the cold, hard reasons

why we should believe in God. And then, at the very
end, he paused and smiled and said, 'But still, there's that
leap of faith.' And that was all I needed. But the
experience taught me that young people, when they
argue, aren't necessarily arguing from conviction, but from
concern and confusion. Someone once said, 'A boat toots
the loudest when it's in a fog.'"

*How do you protect your children from undesirable
books, movies, and so forth?* "When they were small I
could control what they saw, and I think this is all
any parent can do. It's important to teach them to *select*
all through life — books, music, films, the friends
they choose. A child who has never been permitted to
choose for himself will have a harder time making
wise choices when he is grown. I think a child whose
life is filled with wholesome things is less likely to have
an appetite for trash, even though he'll probably see
and hear and read some thing you'd rather he didn't."

*What if children start dating someone you feel
isn't suitable?* "I think this is less likely to happen
if a mother has a good relationship with her daughters,
if they admire and respect their father, and if, when
they start dating, they feel free to bring their friends home.
So often they might have a good time with someone,
but, when they bring him home, all of a sudden they
see — "Unh-unh, it's not what I want to live with.'

"Sometimes you can just lower the boom and break
the thing off. Sometimes you can get them to separate
for a year and look at things more objectively. And
sometimes there's not one thing you can do, except
hope and pray."

*Looking back, how has your faith helped you
with your children?* "It may sound strange, but looking
back over my life I'm most grateful for the hard places.
That's when the Bible really comes to life for me and
when the presence of the Lord is most real. It's not true
that Bill and I have had no major problems with our
children. But let's say this: Each crisis has taught us
so much more about God and also about compassion
and understanding for other parents.

"I remember one night at about one or two o'clock
in the morning, sitting and reading my Bible and

praying through a very difficult situation. It's funny, the problems involving the ones you love are so much more difficult than the ones involving just you. That night there came such an overwhelming sense of the presence, the immensity, of God. And such a flood of reassurance knowing that he was quite capable of handling such situations — in his own time and in his own way.

"In raising children, all you can do is your best. If your child ultimately grows up to honor God, consider it a miracle. We can do the possible, but we can't do miracles. So we should take care of the possible and leave the impossible up to God."

Americans think that children automatically know they are loved. That's not true; children have to be told over and over again. Often parents say, "It goes without saying that we love our children." It shouldn't go without saying. It should be said frequently. And you have to love children physically, too. There shouldn't have to be a reason to give a hug or a kiss or an affectionate embrace. Giving a child $10 and shoving him out of the house is no substitute for your presence.

I'm not saying that children are for everyone. I'm sure there are women who can have a full life without them. But those women who undertake motherhood ought to do it well. Science and technology have blessed us with many things, but thus far they haven't invented a substitute for love. Loving a child takes time. Loving her children — for her benefit, their benefit and, ultimately, society's — remains woman's most valuable role.

Princess Grace

MAKE GOD REAL
by Robert H. Lauer

One of the most awesome tasks a parent faces is to interpret God to his children. We want our children to know the Father, not an inferior and infantile and inadequate god.

This interpretive task is endless and begins at the moment of birth. At first, God is a smile, warmth, tenderness. The fact that you cannot communicate verbally with a baby doesn't preclude an interpretation of God to him. As Lewis Sherrill said: "When the infant encounters love he encounters God."

The way a mother holds her child, the readiness and concern with which she cares for his needs — these aren't mere mechanical skills by which the child's physical needs are met. They are his first instruction about God. Her attitudes tell him that God can be trusted, that God is love, that God is both able and willing to provide for his needs. Or, they tell him that God is untrustworthy, arbitrary, uncaring.

Both interpretive words and actions become increasingly important as the child develops. Interpretive words must be sincere and clear. Sincerity means that you don't pretend to have all the answers. You need not be a theologian. You need only interpret God as best you can. You are trying to give your child an understanding of God himself and his world in biblical perspective. For example, the birth of another child or an animal, the observation of plant life, are times to talk about God who is both Lord and source of all life. Six- and seven-year-olds are already interested in the heavenly bodies, and can begin to understand the orderliness of the universe and the care of God.

Ordinary activities and inevitable frustrations need clarification. A boy who had planted a garden and then neglected it was quite distressed: "Why didn't God water my garden?"

"Would that have been a good idea?" asked his mother. "Would you want God to treat you like a baby who has to have everything done for him?"

The boy thought about this and decided he didn't want to be treated like a baby. He learned something about responsibility and about God's order in the world. His understanding of God and of God's ways with man was far more realistic than it had been at the time he planted his garden.

Family worship is an excellent time to relate daily activities to biblical teachings. Happenings and sayings from school and home can illustrate truths about God. Your child begins to see that God has something to say about every facet of our lives. One small boy prayed during worship: "Thank you, God, for the walls and the wallpaper." No one laughed; he had learned to give thanks for all things.

Interpretive actions can be grouped under "examples" and "exposure." By examples, I mean those observable actions that unavoidably teach your child something about God. The whole pattern of home life must be included here. Through the expression of love, patience, kindness, and forgiveness in the home, the child can see God's love at work and God's power molding human relationships in a rich and desirable fashion. He learns that God is love, and that a loving God imparts something of his own nature to his children.

The father has an especially important role, for he is the key to the child's concept of the Heavenly Father. (See Psalm 103:13.) The father who takes time with his children interprets a Father who cares, and who will never leave us nor forsake us. The human father is responsible for making God's fatherhood understandable and acceptable.

By actions of exposure I mean those that expose your child to vital faith. This would include regular attendance at church, and also social and recreational activities that enable your children to meet and relate to others who have a living faith. Through them, your child learns more about the extent of God's influence, and the power of God to enable people to be happy and useful as they walk with him.

In the realm of interpretive attitudes, keep three words in mind: open, relaxed, respectful. An open attitude says to a child: "I'm available. I'm not too busy for you. I'm not afraid to talk to you about anything that concerns you." A relaxed attitude means an atmosphere that is free of threats. It says: "You needn't be afraid to talk to me about anything. I want you to be honest with yourself and with me." A respectful attitude says: "I may not agree with all of your thoughts, but I do respect them. I won't ridicule you."

Your child then learns that God is always available to him; that God wants us to be honest with him so that he may forgive and not condemn; that God respects our feelings and thoughts, and, in turn, demands that we respect him.

You may be thinking by now that virtually anything you say or do or think can tell your child something about God. You're right.

We wouldn't think of building a stone fireplace without stones, or of baking an apple pie without apples. Why then are so many people trying to build Christian homes without Christ? They try to maintain "Christian" principles, establish a "Christian" home and even use "Christian" terminology; but without the presence of Christ there cannot be a Christian home. The great and holy God must be living *in that home; he must be* living *in the hearts of those who call that house "home."*

How is it in your home? Do you know about Christianity, or do you know Christ personally?

Char J. Crawford

GIVE CHILDREN SPIRITUAL DIRECTION

by Patricia Hershey

Enjoy Daily Devotions

God gives each of us twenty-four hours a day. We take time for the things we think are important. Where in importance do daily devotions fit into your busy schedule?

Until you have children of school age, you have the whole day to choose from. Ideally it's a time when Daddy can join you, though for some families this is impossible. I believe it is our God-given responsibility to have devotions with our children even if Daddy cannot or will not be present.

Remember, it is during the preschool years that you are establishing habits. If devotions aren't part of every day, they will not become a habit. Thus it will be harder in later years for your children to establish their own daily devotions.

Songs. All children enjoy singing. Even before a child can sing, he enjoys being sung to. Music creates a mood. That is one reason why the songs for devotions should be carefully chosen. Notice the words of the songs. Many choruses convey an entirely different meaning to the child than is intended by the author.

Let's teach songs that will be meaningful. We start with action choruses. Each child takes turns choosing a favorite. The one choosing stands and leads the others. This is something that even the youngest can do and thus take part in devotions. By daily singing a hymn you'll be surprised how soon even four-year-olds will learn it. Then watch their faces shine when some Sunday at church the congregation sings their song with them.

Storytime. If you can tell the Bible story in your own words, do so. This is the easiest way to hold the very young child's attention. If you feel you cannot tell the story, then choose a picture storybook for children under four. The preschool age is a wonderful time to make your child acquainted with Bible characters. Have the Bible on your lap as you talk.

The story with a moral is also of great value. We

had been having a problem at our house with a child
who frequently cried. I had tried dealing with this
in various ways, but improvement started after I read
the story, "The Little Girl Who Almost Lost Her Name."

Use poetry freely. Children love to recite poems. The
beauty of a rhyme, even beyond the child's age level,
will hold his attention in a way no story can.

Bible verses. How sad it is that we teach our children
the ABC's and many other things we think they ought
to know before starting to school, but neglect the most
important knowledge of all: God's Word in their hearts.

Verses learned to fit the daily occasion will have the
most meaning to your children now. Some examples:
When there is quarreling, "Be ye kind one to another"
(Ephesians 4:32). When they are disobedient, "Children,
obey your parents in the Lord" (Ephesians 6:1). When
they are grumbling, "Do all things without murmurings"
(Philippians 2:14).

Scripture flashcards help to make memorizing fun.
We make our own by pasting or drawing a picture
on one side and the verse on the other side. The reference
is written beneath the picture. The older children
enjoy these so much they often use them for a game.

Missionaries. A world and a United States map
offer your children visual knowledge of missionary places.
Hang maps at their eye level. Place missionaries'
pictures as near to their country or state as possible,
adding a ribbon to pinpoint the exact location.
We put up only the pictures of missionaries that our
children have met. It's better for young children to have
personal interest in two or three families than a general
interest in a great many.

Prayer. Your whole devotional period should lead up
to this time of conversing with God. By praying as we
would talk, we change our children's attitude of boredom
to one of eager participation. I usually begin our prayer
time by thanking the Lord for something. Each child
gives a word of thanks, back and forth until all are
finished. Someone may then pray for one of our friends
who is in the hospital. The children again take turns
remembering this one and others.

What we are doing is moving from subject to subject

with everyone praying at least a sentence once, maybe
twice, while still talking about a certain thing. This
eliminates some of the impatience from the child
when he has to wait for others to finish a long prayer
before he can pray. Now he can pray just as soon as
he thinks of something he wants to tell the Lord.

Pray for specific things. This is a necessary personal
touch in teaching children to pray.

You can try all these ways of having devotions in the
home, but don't use all of them at once. Make each day's
devotions short and just a little different. Variety
keeps interest keen.

A profitable family devotional time doesn't just happen.
To achieve this goal requires preparation, perseverance,
and parental prayer.

*Many parents do nothing about their children's religious
education, telling them they can decide what they believe
when they're twenty-one. That's like telling them they
can decide, when they're twenty-one, whether or not
they should brush their teeth. By then, their teeth may
have fallen out. Likewise, their principles and morality
may also be nonexistent.*   Princess Grace

*When a child has been reared in a Christian home
and in a Christian church, when the temple of his mind
and heart has with deep reverence been prepared
for Holy Occupancy, the time will come when he will
inevitably have his own personal encounter with the Lord
of Life. This encounter will not be with a stranger,
for he has already learned to love him. It will not be
an encounter like a prodigal adult would have, which
would involve a complete change of direction and pattern
of life, but it will involve just as definite a decision
and just as definite a commitment to the Savior.
For when the time comes that a child or youth knows
there are two ways of life, he is old enough to make
his decision for Christ.*   Anna B. Mow

WIN THEM TO CHRIST

by Mildred Morningstar

An archer looks in his quiver, picks out an arrow, and fits it into his bow. Where he will aim the arrow is his choice, not the arrow's, for the arrow's task is simply to go in the direction it is sent.

The psalmist speaks of children as arrows: "As arrows are in the hand of a mighty man; so are children of the youth. Happy is the man that hath his quiver full of them" (127:4, 5).

A characteristic common to both children and arrows is the ability to be directed. Parents cannot totally determine the direction in which their children go, but parents can play a large part in formulating this destiny.

A thief using his seven-year-old son as an accomplice illustrates this truth. One night the father boosts the boy up to enter an unlocked window. The boy opens the door, and together the father and son rob the house. The father is determining the direction his son will go.

Another father sits down with his son after dinner with an encyclopedia between them. They explore the possibilities of a science project for school. During the subsequent project an abiding love for science is born in the heart of the son. The father is determining the direction his son will go.

Because children are easily directed when they are young, parents should give them proper spiritual training during this time. This training includes leading the children to Christ. Christ referred to the fact that children possess characteristics necessary for salvation when he said, "Except ye be converted, and become as little children ye shall not enter the kingdom of heaven" (Matthew 18:3).

One of the characteristics a child possesses is a tender conscience toward sin. A big sister, jealous of the baby, may grab the rattle and push the baby down. If she looks up and sees her mother, immediately a look of guilt spreads over her face. She senses the tendency toward sin within her; she cannot explain it, and it troubles her.

This attitude toward sin must grip a person before he can come to Christ. He must know that he has sinned. Many adults feel that children aren't sinners because they haven't committed great sins. However, Adam and Eve didn't commit murder to be driven from the garden: they simply disobeyed God. Every boy and girl is familiar with the sin of disobedience. As he lives without Christ, the child's conscience becomes more calloused. A sin that bothers him when he is six years old may not cause him a qualm when he's a teen-ager.

Besides a tender conscience toward sin, a child has a willing spirit. Since a parent can easily lead a child, this is the time to lead him in the right way: to introduce him to Jesus who is the Way (John 14:6). "The greatest field and the most hopeful field for evangelistic effort is the childhood of the world," stated Paul W. Rood in the foreword to *Teachers' Introductory Bible Studies* by J. Irvin Overholtzer. On the other hand, parents must remember that every child increasingly learns to want his own way (Isaiah 53:6; Matthew 18:11-14).

A group of young couples have recently come to the Lord, and their pastor has wisely instructed them to have devotions with their children each day. Two of the men compared notes. Tom said, "When I'm ready for devotions I go to the door and call down to the family room, 'Bible time!' Then the thundering herd tramps up the stairs. Eileen calls out, 'I get to sit on Daddy's lap,' and Betsy cries, 'I get to sit next to him.' They are keen and eager for the Bible story. It's making a big difference in our family."

Jack had a different story. "My kids are older than yours. They never went to Sunday school. They can't quite decide what has come over Dad and Mom since we've come to Christ. No thundering herd comes when I call. They are most reluctant. To them it's a drag." The time when Jack's children would be most willing to accept spiritual training has passed.

In addition to a willing spirit, the child also has a believing heart. He will believe almost anything he is told by someone he trusts. How important it is to tell him the truth. Jesus Christ is the Truth (John 14:6).

The characteristics necessary for trust in Christ are already present in a child. Parents and teachers can use this precious time to bring the child to the truth, to show him the right way, and to help him become a true child of God. The tragic mistake of many Christian parents is to wait until the child has outgrown these characteristics before they make an effort to bring him to the Savior. "Every Christian parent should be a children's evangelist," stated J. Irvin Overholtzer in *Teachers' Introductory Bible Studies*.

Some practical suggestions may prove useful to the person who wants to bring a child to the Lord. Every child has the right to know that his parents love him and want him. He also has the right to know that God loves him and wants him. Some parents mistakenly tell a child that if he is not good, God will not love him. But that isn't true, for God loves sinners. The adult needs to make sure that the child knows that God loves him (John 3:16).

Next, the child needs to know he has sinned. Parents have the privilege of spending many hours with their children, and they usually know when their children sin. An ideal time to explain sin and its effects to a child is immediately after he has sinned. C. H. Spurgeon, a great English preacher, said, "When a child is old enough to sin knowingly, he is old enough to believe savingly" (*How to Reach Children for Jesus* by Florence R. Kee).

In spite of this, when an adult deals with a child he should avoid the attitude, "I am very good, but you are a wicked little sinner." Rather his attitude should be, "I've sinned and you've sinned and we both need Jesus." He may convey this attitude by telling about a sin he committed in childhood, and then stating, "If that were the only bad thing I had ever done, I could never go to heaven unless Jesus had died for me. Now I have believed in what God has done for me."

It's important for the child to know that Jesus died on the cross to pay for his sins. The adult may explain, "Jesus is the perfect Son of God. He never did anything wrong. He never even had a bad thought, but he was punished for us." A brief description of what it meant to die on the cross will help the child realize what Jesus went through for him.

Show him that short portion in 1 Corinthians 15:3, "Christ died for our sins." Say to the child, "Let us change the word 'our' to 'my.' I want you to think of the bad things you've done, as we say together 'Christ died for my sins.'" The child may think quietly of the wonder of that act.

Next, tell the child that Jesus died for his sins. "God put them on Jesus. Jesus willingly died and was buried. He paid for every one of your sins. Would you like to tell Jesus that you have been bad and that you want him to forgive you?"

If the child says he wants to accept Christ, then the adult should ask him to pray a simple prayer. A prayer might be, "Dear Jesus, I am a sinner and have done many bad things. Thank you for coming to die for my sin. I am sorry for my sin. Please forgive me for my sin and come into my life. Amen." If the child doesn't want to accept Christ at that time, use other opportunities to explain the plan of salvation.

Which direction will the children go? Parents and other Christian adults can point children in the right direction.

6 THE WOMAN AND HER HOME

ARE YOU A "TRAPPED" HOUSEWIFE?

by Norman M. Lobsenz and Clark W. Blackburn

Many wives feel "trapped." The woman with young children, living in a community distant from close friends or relatives, without enough money to afford a regular baby-sitter, is so overwhelmed by the duties of being wife and mother that she spends her day virtually isolated from the outside adult world. She may be effectively imprisoned in her neighborhood if mass transportation isn't available and her husband uses the car for work.

Other wives feel trapped because their husbands are frequently away on business. The wife of a sales executive complained that her husband traveled more than half the year. Whereupon the suburbia-based wife of a young businessman retorted: "At least when yours is home, you have him! Mine leaves every day at 7 A.M., gets back at 7:30 P.M., brings home work to do after dinner, and falls into bed exhausted at midnight. He's there, all right, but he might just as well not be, for all I get of him!"

For others, life suddenly seems sterile. Today's young woman is educated to be competitive and independent, to use her mind, and to strive for achievements. Yet when she marries, she is expected to become a housewife and mother who derives her principal pleasures from these roles. Many women protest that their minds are atrophying, that they didn't need a college or business education to scrub floors, wash dishes, and change diapers. They yearn for something more, and feel guilty about not feeling fulfilled. *I ought to be happy,* they say. *What's wrong with me that I'm not?*

If more of them could admit this dissatisfaction without feeling guilty, they might be freer to explore other interests. But often the disillusionment and consequent guilt are projected into jealousy of the husband's freedom to come and go, of the allegedly "interesting" days he has, of his chance to move ahead while she is stuck in a rut. "One-third or more of our

cases," one marriage-counseling agency reports, "have at
their core the wife's boredom, her seldom-fulfilled hopes
of being entertained evenings by a husband who,
she believes, has had an exciting day."

The fact is that the overwhelming majority of men
haven't had an exciting day, but a day of hard work,
problems, tension, worries. They're too physically and
emotionally exhausted to play the role of courting gallants.
Rather, they'd like to be catered to by a wife who, they
in turn think, has had a peaceful day at home.

The greatest unhappiness arises when the trapped
housewife feels that intellectual interests and creative
outlets should be brought to her, that she shouldn't be
expected to seek out mental stimulation. These may be
harsh words, but the thousands of wives who feel trapped
may have chiefly themselves to blame. They won't or
can't accept the following realities of marriage: that it is
part of a wife's bargain to maintain her home, to care
for her children, and to be a helpmate in every way.

Further, many of her expectations in life are tied to
her husband's job. In a society that expects men to be
successful, and in which many wives base their status
on their husband's success, a man has little choice but
to invest his physical and emotional energy heavily
in his work. Naturally this leaves less time for his wife.
She translates this, through the inaccuracies of emotional
shorthand, into: "Your job is more important to you
than I am. You don't love me."

In the experience of family service counselors,
the trapped wife often makes the mistake of trying to solve
her problem in ways that increase the tensions. One is
"compulsive housekeeping." "If I have to be here
all the time, then I'm going to make it perfect!" she
rationalizes, placing undue importance on things she must
do anyway. And by nagging her husband about keeping
his feet off the sofa, she is unconsciously striking back
at him for having trapped her.

The "complete mother" is a variation of the compulsive
housekeeper. She throws herself 110 percent into
chauffeuring, PTA-ing, organizing parties, helping with
homework. Since she considers herself trapped in a
child's world, she overidentifies with it. The predictable

result: her husband is downgraded, often neglected, and the children are overwhelmed.

Some trapped wives fall into the habit of gossiping around the neighborhood. "The woman who spends much of her day visiting other trapped wives, to seek and offer consolation over endless cups of coffee, isn't solving anything," says one counselor. "She's indulging in self-pity."

Unless other unstable elements exist in the marriage, however, few wives fall into such completely destructive patterns as withdrawal into psychosomatic illness, drinking, or an extramarital affair. The majority simply wait for their husbands to come home, then release their frustrations with demands that seem perfectly legitimate to them, but which men consider nagging. "I'm tired when I get home," says a husband. "And right away she wants me to play with the children, or bathe the baby, or talk to her. Doesn't she realize that I need time to breathe?" "I'm tired, too," says his wife. "I've been with the kids all day, doing laundry and ironing. Why shouldn't he help me or pay attention to me? I haven't spoken to a grownup all day."

One counselor observes: "Neither man nor wife can have it all one way. There may be days when a husband comes home exhausted, depleted. A loving wife, sensing this, sees to it that he has time to calm down, to restore himself. A loving husband senses when his spouse has had a particularly trying day, and pitches in to lift the load."

For this to happen, spouses must be able to let each other know when they are upset, overtired, and in need of physical help or emotional support. Communication is vital. A woman has to feel sufficiently secure to talk openly to her husband about feeling trapped.

And there is much that a husband can do. Most important is to understand what his wife is really saying, to be interested in what she does each day for him, his home, his children. This automatically makes a wife's routine tasks and triumphs more interesting to her. One woman said: "You don't feel useful if the only time a man notices a housekeeping detail is when you forget to do it." Similarly, a husband can encourage his wife's individuality by learning enough about her interests and hobbies to discuss them with her.

Men are neither mind readers nor as emotionally intuitive as women. "If he loved me, he would know how I feel" is nonsense. The way out of the trap begins when a wife can clarify her feelings for her husband so that he can help her. Such reappraisal may free both wife and husband from a trap that neither quite realized was closing in on them.

Do you ever think, while in the midst of a pile of dirty dishes, with beds still to make, and children to dress, and ironing staring at you as well as a messy house, "Wasn't I made for better things than this?" And if we listen, the answer seems to echo and re-echo through the house: The routine work we do in our homes every day makes life secure and happy and orderly for those we love the most. The biggest hurdle we have to cross is our approach to our daily tasks.

Char J. Crawford

HAVE A MASTER PLAN

by Marguerite and Willard Beecher

When a carpenter starts to build a house he has a master plan. Parents, too, should have a master plan. Otherwise each member of the family operates according to his own blueprint. It is much the same as if a number of individuals decided to build a house and each had his own design in his head. Only a tower of Babel can be built in a family where there is no master-plan-for-all.

In homes where parents don't have control, a tower of Babel is essentially what happens. It's up to the parents to draw the plan by which they and the children shall live together. The children should make suggestions, to be sure, but it's for the parents to make the final decisions as to how the human situation is to be kept humanly straight.

We might illustrate by describing one such home where bedlam reigned. There were two adolescent daughters who were of an age to get telephone calls from boys. If one received a call, she would hang on to the telephone for three-quarters of an hour while the other made frantic cries that she would not get her calls. But when she did get on the telephone, she did exactly the same thing. Their parents had no chance whatever to use the phone during the evening. No matter that Father expected an important business call that would consummate a deal, or that Mother, as president of the PTA, had necessary calls to make. All they were supposed to do was pay the telephone bills.

There were two bathrooms in the apartment, one with more mirrors and better equipment. The girls insisted on using the well-mirrored bathroom. Occasionally the father managed to get into this bathroom to shave. Whenever he did, his daughters pounded on the door. Although he didn't surrender it each time they pounded, he had no peace, for his daughters kept pounding, sputtering, and scolding through the door as he remained in the bathroom.

Although each girl had her own room, the sisters constantly intruded on each other, uninvited. They raided each other's wardrobes without permission and even wore their mother's clothes. Each daughter behaved as though she owned everything in the house and as though the other members of the family were hostile bandits intent on stealing what belonged to her. Each felt damaged when she didn't get her own way or when she couldn't operate according to her own private blueprint. As for the parents, they were always treated as if they were interlopers or unwelcome guests in the home. These girls were so ill-mannered and argumentative at mealtimes that their parents not only couldn't digest their meals properly but had ceased, long since, to invite guests to share a meal with them.

It is obvious that no progress can be made in such a situation until some overall master plan is drawn that covers the mutual rights and mutual responsibilities of all. One master plan has to be substituted for four private plans. Until then, each member of the family will continue to feel hurt and damaged. No peace is possible while four separate and different blueprints exist.

These parents had wisdom enough, at breaking point, to seek help. They were instructed to tell their daughters that they had no right to regard the family telephone as private property and that all their calls would be stopped, both incoming and outgoing, unless they themselves worked out a way to handle the telephone problem without disrupting the peace of the home or depriving their parents of the use of the phone.

The parents had to make clear to their daughters that (1) the house, and everything in it, belonged to them and not to their daughters; (2) the girls owned nothing outright, in the legal sense of ownership; (3) they were in no position to enforce their arbitrary wills as if they were laws binding on those around them; and (4) they had no right to make warfare over property that didn't belong to them. As soon as the facts of true ownership were explained and the girls understood the idea of their parents' new master plan, they found a way to arrange their calls and their demands on the bathroom. Peace descended on this home. These two sisters, who had been bitter antagonists, learned to become friendly with each other and with their parents. The entire home situation became happier for everyone.

After a reasonable, practical master plan has been in operation for a period, it will be discovered that mutual tolerance and respect will become a natural way of living. The plan will then automatically lose whatever rigidity it originally had. A fluid, healthy plan will result.

The "insecurity" we so often see in children today exists because they don't know the limits of their authority and their responsibilities. They really don't know how to stop. They feel obliged to keep pushing and pushing until something stops them. They can't relax because they know no sure boundaries to sustain them. The child who has always ended up getting his own way has no choice but to be insecure, since he has found no limits anywhere. All that "security" means is knowing *protective limits.*

The search for protective limits starts at a very young age. Let us consider a child of three who is searching for such limits. Let's visit a crowded grocery store and watch what he does. This child's father and mother are in line waiting to be checked out. Their three-year-old is bent on snatching a bar of candy from the rack behind the cashier. The parents yell at him not to touch the candy, but if they happen to look in another direction for one moment, the child returns to the candy again and again. At each attempt the mother threatens punishment. But each time he repeats it, she does nothing other than to threaten him once again. His father proceeds no differently.

Here is a child who operates on his own blueprint. He can't relax in security because his blueprint has no limits. He searched to find one. But each time a limit is promised, his parents fail him, for they don't keep their promise. By their behavior they teach him that he can't depend on them. More than that, they teach him that they are liars. These parents would be horrified if they realized what their child learns from their mistaken efforts to control him. He learns that what they do is contrary to what they say. Realizing that he cannot depend on them, he is forced to keep on trying to find out if anything in them is honest and dependable.

If one attempts to explain to such parents that what they need most is a master plan that marks out definite limits, they grow frightened. They have been warned about not "frustrating" the child. Yet, these same parents wouldn't tear up the deed to their house, their insurance policy, their bonds, their work contracts, their tax receipts. These and countless other things are symbols of the limits by which all of us, as adults, are bound — the things that give us our feeling of security. Why should parents deny their children a secure place in the family configuration? Children need established limits as symbols of security. Without them, children are misguided and feel more frustrated in the end.

Many parents today imagine that they will "break a child's will" if they impose limits. These parents look dubious if the word "spanking" is mentioned. But it is for parents to draw up the master plan for interpersonal responsibilities so that the child will have an idea of how to express his will constructively. Then it won't need to be "broken." *The child must learn to use his will in socially useful directions.* If he insists on expressing it in ways that damage and limit others, then something must be done to show him that he may not, with impunity, hurt or burden others.

Parents should insist on keeping their own rights to privacy and property so their children won't be tempted to try to usurp parental privileges or time. If children know how much and how little belongs to each, then they are free to settle down, inside themselves, and develop within those limits. They won't feel defrauded and angry, as they always do whenever they have tried to grab and hold on to disputed territory. It is uncertainty that makes for discontent and fighting.

If parents refuse to submit to tricks and pressures, and cling firmly to what is their own, they don't need to worry about "breaking the spirit" of a child. Children have a keen sense of fair play. They are equipped with some kind of built-in "antenna" that senses fair play on an action level even though it may

not be expressed on a verbal level. They rarely object
to disagreeable things if they are fair. This is why
it's so necessary to have a master plan, so that fairness
of the total situation is apparent to all. Each can
endure privations, if necessary, if he knows they are fair.

Without a master plan, a child lives in a Netherland
of Pamperdom. He commands, and his parents do
his bidding, strewing sacrifices before him. Parents
wouldn't do this if they were aware that such sacrifices are
basically asocial because they mean that someone
does less than his fair share. The person for whom
sacrifices are made usually becomes more selfish
as a result. We appreciate only what we have helped
to create. The selfish child is headed for trouble
and unhappiness. He enslaves himself, his parents,
and others.

DOES ANYBODY LIKE HOUSEWORK?

by Wilda Fancher

You never catch up, you never get through, you can't keep everybody satisfied. So what's the point of housekeeping, anyway? At the risk of being elementary in defining such a monumental task, I'd say the point of housekeeping is to provide a house to keep a family in.

The young bride who looks at the mess she must spend the morning with after her loving husband goes to work is often brought to tears. Whoever told a bride how to go about cleaning up the mess that sleeping, bathing, dressing, cooking, and eating make in a place, small as it is?

One of her wedding presents was not a book called *Ten Easy Lessons in Becoming a Housekeeper.* That's good, because ten easy lessons wouldn't get the job done. Maybe ten hard lessons would be more believable.

Girls ought to be trained for housekeeping — and so should boys. Mothers ought not glibly say, "Oh, she'll learn when she has to." Learning ought to be done when its consequences might not be so devastating.

Maybe mothers don't teach their girls the arts of housekeeping because they themselves have never felt a sense of accomplishment in it. Maybe if they try to teach the girls, they do so with such boredom of spirit that girls reflect the knowledge. If every girl could have a few weeks with a really good housekeeper, one who really enjoyed keeping house and knew how to go about it, she would spend an invaluable apprenticeship.

Efficiency experts have found no way to peddle their wares to homemakers. Nobody punches a time clock or observes any of the other efficiency-producing techniques such experts recommend. Family members don't run on a strict schedule or go by a script.

Nor should they. Home ought to be a place of refuge, a haven, a storm shelter, a foxhole, an ivory tower, a place to go. It's up to you to achieve this sort of setup. But how, when your house is overrun by faulty human beings rushing in and out and up and down, pushing each other around, yelling at each other, and generally behaving like members of a family?

By hard, steady, disciplined work, that's how. By making up your mind to. That's how. By letting God's Spirit help you. That's how.

A favorite saying among our friends is, "He's nervous and thinks he's busy." Maybe that's how we women are about our housekeeping. We're nervous, and think we're busy. Thinking we just have to be doing something that will make us wear the badge "good housekeeper." Maybe we're afraid a neighbor will drop in and find us playing with a child instead of folding the pile of clothes in the middle of the bed. Afraid someone will think we're a poor housekeeper. Worse still, afraid to admit to ourselves that we're a little less than perfect.

Being busy is often a frame of mind. It isn't necessarily true that being busy all the time is the answer to the hectic schedule most of us keep. Just because our nearest neighbor or best friend feels that to be adequate in her housekeeping a woman must wax her floors once a week, we often accept her standards as ours even though we really don't feel that way at all about floors. Maybe our family doesn't either, but they have to accept the friend's standards, too, because we have.

This isn't the way to arrive at your plan for house-keeping. You and your family alone should be the ones to say what your standards of housekeeping are to be.

Sometimes even a mother has to bend a bit about the housekeeping. I started out entirely too clean. When the babies came along quickly and on schedule, I decided germs were not for them. It took me a while to accept the fact that boys and dirt go together. When I accepted it, I did so with reservations. Boys and dirt might go together but they didn't have to *stay* together.

Consequently, I separated them from their dirt and dirty clothes several times a day, proportionately increasing the number of rings to be washed out of the tub and the number of washers of clothes to be laundered, to say nothing of the proportionate drain on my energy and good nature.

I further decided that our house was not to be scattered

with playthings, which meant constant nagging. Finally, I decided that two daily pickup times would ease the tension between the boys and me. Thereafter, all of us pitched in right after lunch and put toys, books, and so forth in place. Then bath-time (only if really necessary) was followed by rest-time. We followed the same ritual after supper, and it worked. The boys didn't pull out as much junk as they had before, but they still got just as dirty.

It's vital for each woman at fairly regular intervals to take stock of the atmosphere and attitudes inside her house. A few questions might be answered in her inventory.

1/ Who lives here? The same people as at the last inventory, probably, but their ages, interests, activities, abilities, and responsibilities change as time goes by, so the function of the house does, too, along with the mother's role.

2/ What do the people who live in the house want from their physical surroundings? One of our boys told me one day when I had cleaned his room to a shine that he didn't like it because it didn't seem friendly when it was so neat and clean. A person's room really ought to make *him* feel good to be in it.

3/ Is there really any need to fret over everything about the house that I fret over? Is it worth the fretting?

4/ Are we relatively happy here? Don't forget to allow for normal fussing and grumpiness of each family member.

What is the object of your housekeeping? Is it simply to fulfill the desire you have to feel you are a good mother or wife? Is it to secure your own satisfaction? Or is it to maintain a refuge for everyone who lives there, a place where he knows he is loved, protected, and provided for?

Two questions are good to ask at the end of a day. What did I spend my time and energy on today that really wasn't important? What important thing did I leave undone that I could have done in the time I spent on the unimportant item? Chances are that some nights you'll be at odds with yourself over wasted time. But chances are, also, that some days you'll be

able to answer the first question smugly, "Not a thing."
And you'll feel good that night.

What to do about the exhaustion that drenches us?
Well, I've learned a lesson from our Siamese cat. A dozen
or so times a day that cat rests in a dozen or so different
places and positions. I have watched him wiggle, turn,
move, stretch, plop, and curl into a position exactly
right for resting.

I don't mean to sound irreverent, but I've learned
to take little catnap rests with God. It's scriptural.
Not the catnap part, but the resting part. Jesus said, "Come
to me when you are tired, and I'll help you rest."
I don't think he minds if my Siamese cat's example helps
me come to him easier.

Several times a day I momentarily position myself
into the presence of God. Maybe after I make up a bed
I sit down on it, considering the things that are important
to the boy who sleeps in that bed, and ask God to show
his will about those things.

Maybe after I hang clothes in a boy's closet I stand
there and thank God for the strong body that wears
those clothes, remembering anxious hours about his health.
Maybe after I've signed a boy's test paper I shiver
a little as I pray for the mind of that boy to be protected
from drugs and alcohol and faulty ideologies.

When my day seems impossible I may hear Jesus'
command, "Come here, and I'll help you rest," like this:
"Put your head down on your desk and think of me."
"Sit in your favorite chair for five minutes and consider
my strength. It becomes yours for the asking." "Curl
up on the couch and loll around in 'forever.' That's
how long I'm with you."

So, I obey. I rest. In him.

What physical needs does housekeeping provide
for a family? First, shelter — dry, warm, cool, reasonably
clean. Second, clothing — clean, mended, available
when needed. Third, food — cooked, served, expected to
be eaten.

The first week of school when we made the bedroom
rounds asking what each occupant would like for
breakfast, the percentage of answers something like "Ugh —
nothing" was roughly 95.6. We wheedled and pled

and got a few choking morsels down unwilling throats.

One of the first things I learned about boys —
and I expect it goes for girls, too — is that their ability
to be gotten along with is in almost direct proportion
to the fullness of their stomachs. Keep a boy's stomach
full and you're halfway there.

So early the second week, James and I declared war
on the breakfast ughs. The arms for our battle were
a conglomeration of favorite foods and drinks.

We announced that every member of the family
would be present for breakfast at 7:30 the next morning.
We got reactions like: "I can't hack getting up that early!"
"I just can't possibly be ready by 7:30." "Why so early?"

To the first two reactions we said, "Well, you'd better
give it a tussle," and "OK. We'll compromise — we'll get
you up at seven minutes until seven instead of fifteen
'til and have breakfast at 7:35 instead of 7:30."
To the third one we said, "So you can get to school
on time."

The next morning wasn't easy. It looked as if,
in spite of the cantaloupe, bacon, grits, eggs, catsup,
toast, jelly, coffee, milk, and Dr. Pepper on the table,
that the ughs would win. Finally every boy arrived at the
table, looked it over and sat down. They said not an
ugh and left very few crumbs.

The next morning was easier. Smelling blueberry
muffins baking didn't slow the boys down any. It got
easier every day. The ughs didn't win a single skirmish
in our war against them.

The point is, a child or a teen-ager doesn't always
know what he wants, and he may say he wants no food.
But its availability usually changes his mind. Good
food is vital for a teen-ager. A Christian woman in a
Christian home must provide the vital things for her
children.

When I was a little girl and I heard talk about
the abundant life, I really thought it meant Christians
were supposed to have big houses and cars and all
the trappings to go with them. I didn't put away that
childish thought as early as I should have, I fear. But I
did finally get it put away by a definite process of
deliberation upon how a Christian can exist in such a

world as this. And behave herself as she should. Especially a busy Christian woman in a Christian home.

A helpful part of God's Word in my Christian adolescence is the statement in Ecclesiastes 3:12 (RSV), ". . . it is God's gift to man that every one should eat and drink and take pleasure in all his toil."

And it has what seems to be a companion verse in 1 Corinthians 10:31: "So, whether you eat or drink, or whatever you do, do all to the glory of God." We're told what to do — eat, drink, work — and how to do it — to the glory of God.

To understand what "glory" means is necessary. The idea is that whatever we do ought to make the reputation and honor of God more secure in the world's eyes. It seems to me a Christian woman on a factory assembly line ought to do her best not just for her reputation, but for God's, to whom her fellowworkers know she belongs. So should a Christian mother about her work at home.

Someone said he'd be glad to work if he could find any pleasure in it. The Bible says for us to do just that. Pleasure is defined as an agreeable sensation. Maybe the agreeable sensation doesn't always come during the work but sometimes with the result of the work.

In our day home almost has to be a frame of mind as well as a locale. A member may dwell in the home a great deal more in mind than in body.

No time or energy has been better spent than that which causes a husband or child to carry away from home a subconscious looking forward to being back at home.

That's when housekeeping has succeeded.

"Work is love made visible."

God doesn't ask us to do more than we can do happily and without stress. Yes, there are times when we must go "full speed," but these should be the exception. When I want to feed my soul, I turn to the writings of people who did a few things well. I turn to people who took time to be still. The Lord says in the Psalms (46:10): "Be still, and know that I am God."

Ruth Brunk Stoltzfus

ENJOY YOUR FAMILY!

by Marion Leach Jacobsen

Lynne reached for another piece of ten o'clock coffee cake as she prepared to add the crowning touch to her account of the disorganized, outlandish, peppery performance her children had put on that morning getting off to school. "Then," she climaxed the recital dramatically, "right in the middle of Gregg's squabble with Kathy over the last doughnut, I heard him say, 'Now one of us ought to act like a Christian about this: how about you?' "

Sandy, Lynne's new and childless neighbor, chuckled audibly and then remarked almost enviously, "My, you must have a lot of fun at your house!"

"Fun!" exploded Lynne, "Wait till *you* have to live through it!" But even as the almost routine words came out, she caught a new glimpse of herself and her family through another woman's eyes. "Well," she hesitated, as color, excitement, sweetness, hilarity, and togetherness flashed past her reviewing eyes, "I guess maybe it is sort of fun. Perhaps the trouble is that we just don't realize it while it's happening. We're too busy and hurried and confused to enjoy having kids."

How much have *you* enjoyed your family lately? Are there times when the solemn responsibility of raising children and the endless work involved threaten to overshadow the joy of having a family? Perhaps at one point in your life you weren't sure you'd ever have children. You'd have paid any price, then, to have the family you now possess.

Do you sometimes think that your home would be transformed if your children would cooperate in even a minimum of the routine operations of living comfortably together? If only they'd remember to take off their boots before tramping into the house, hang up their coats, chew with their mouths shut, and brush their teeth. If only they could get off to school in the morning without a series of unnecessary frictions (if not battles) over what they will wear, finding a missing sheet of

homework, objecting to the tone of voice you used
when you called them the fourth time to come to breakfast
or asked them to drink their orange juice.

At their age you were probably more like them —
untidy and irresponsible — than you remember. Trust God
enough to believe that beyond these trying years
your children will come into their own maturity, hold
responsible positions, outgrow thinking only of themselves,
and actually serve others with delight. They will raise
their own families and come to appreciate then, if not
before, the hardships and sacrifices you're experiencing now.

Learn to take your present problems to God in specific,
believing prayer, and come away enabled to *accept* your
family as they are, and to *enjoy* them as they are,
confident about what they will someday become.

Some parents are so efficient ("responsible" and
"tidy") themselves that they have little time or heart
for what interests their children. They're so busy they miss
the fun of watching their youngsters grow up through
a series of trying but entertaining stages.

Learn to enjoy the sight of them in their moments
of loveliness — in the bathtub, or dressed in their
Sunday best, or relaxed in the touching defenselessness
of sleep. And don't miss their less lovely and often
ludicrous moments — bawling lustily, abnormally dirty,
wildly furious, or indecently gluttonous. Photograph
some of these "precious" experiences to enjoy *with them*
in later years.

I have discovered that recognition of my own
sometimes self-centered reactions often eases my indignation
against members of my family. I want them to appreciate
me, or do things my way. Try to see where you fail,
as clearly as you see where the rest of your family
falls short. Perhaps your child's lack of warmth and
affection toward you is rooted in his instinctive realization
that except in a perfunctory way he isn't really important, of vital personal interest, to you.

Cultivate a sense of humor at home if you want to have
fun with your family. Most young people can't stand
to be laughed at, but you can try with a straight face not
to miss the funny side of situations that at the time
may seem crucial. Like the moment, just before leaving

for Sunday school, when I found my kindergartner sitting on the kitchen table, spreading butter all over her patent leather shoes to make them shine!

Playing with a child creates closeness. Playing together breaks down walls that keep people apart. And the walls between parents and children are real — age difference; constant parental directing and discipline (which may seem to the little people much like bossing); the parents' so-much-greater size, strength, knowledge, authority. Playing together helps to break through these obstacles that separate one generation from the next.

Look at whatever it costs to have fun with your family not only as the price of present pleasure but as a vital investment in your future relationship. Ten or fifteen years from now it may not matter whether you beat someone else to a promotion, served a cheese sauce with your cauliflower, kept your living room perfectly dust-free, or attended every single gathering at your church or PTA. But it will matter tremendously whether or not you made the most of your opportunity, by family good times and whatever other means, to get close and stay close to your children.

Many parents don't have much fun with their children simply because they don't stay home long enough to have it. Sometimes outside involvements are so multiplied that it takes *planned staying at home* to get the family together.

Working mothers are not necessarily to be condemned for being away from home so much or for being so busy when they are home. They're often the salvation of a special family situation. But if, while her children are young, a mother works simply so that they'll have a better house in a finer neighborhood, more stylish clothes, more costly recreation, vacation, or education, she may discover — too late — that what they really needed was *more mother*.

It's a good idea to do some concrete thinking about family fun. Let Mother and Dad sit down together, with paper and pencil in hand, and examine what they've been doing in this area, what they can do, and then write out what they plan to do. As children grow up, such planning will be less formal or at least less outwardly organized.

At the beginning of the summer months, for example, we and our daughter have made a list of things we'd like to do together and places we'd like to visit during the long vacation from school. We have never accomplished all we hoped to, but we do more than we would if we hadn't talked and planned.

Remember that directing a child's play is no substitute for playing with him some of the time. When our daughter was in kindergarten, I remember reading a newspaper article about playing with one's children. I was a little embarrassed (I, a specialist in family recreation) when I was confronted with the question, "How long has it been since *you* sat down and colored pictures or played paper dolls with your children?" It had been quite a while.

I went into Lorraine's bedroom. There she sat at her little maple table with its two little chairs, neither of which was adequate for my ample proportions. She had a box of crayons and some coloring books. I shall never forget the expression on her face when I cleared my throat and self-consciously asked, "Would you like me to color pictures with you?" It was a look of startled amazement and delight.

I sat down in the other little chair, selected a picture, and set to work. I was embarrassed all over again when I realized how much, at my age, I could enjoy coloring a picture in a dime-store coloring book. The companionable performance elated my daughter and taught me a needed lesson. It isn't enough to supply play materials. We must sometimes join in and play with our children.

Look at it from the viewpoint of 1,500 school children who were asked the question, "What do you think makes a happy family?" The most frequent answer was "doing things together." It's not so much what we do *for* our children that makes fun at home as what we do *with* them.

Family fun requires not only time, effort, and planning, but also a philosophical acceptance of some degree of household disorder and mess. You may have to choose between fastidiousness and fun. If your home has to be kept so spic and span that your children don't feel free

to have a good time in it; if it's too "nice" to accommodate
the effects of having a pet; if your rules for the use
of the house are such that your children's friends don't
feel comfortable playing there; then you'll probably
soon find your children, as well as their friends, looking
for their good times somewhere else.

In the days when I was a professional church visitor,
I remember calling in a rather humble home that had that
generously-titled "lived-in" look. Rubbers and roller
skates were on the porch; blocks, paper dolls, comic
books, and ginger cookies were all over the living room.
The embarrassed mother spent most of the little time
we had apologizing for the disorder. To me, a woman
who at the time had neither husband nor children,
it looked beautiful.

My next call made me realize how doubly blessed
the embarrassed mother was. This second home
was large and elegant and in perfect order. But I sat
beside its handsome fireplace sharing the heartache
and tears of its owner, a woman who had a husband and
home but no children. They would gladly have traded
their "tidiness-unlimited" for even one of the untidy
children I had just left behind!

Show your children that you recognize the importance
of their playthings by providing adequate storage for toys.
Teach them as patiently as possible the business of being
neat, but remember that irresponsibility is usually an
integral part of being young. More mature performance
comes in due season.

The day will also come when your house will be in
perfect order all the time. Your children will be gone,
and you will yearn for the years when they were under
your roof, with all the disorder. Do the best you can
now to keep your home in respectable condition, but
don't let that goal rob you of the sheer fun of having
children, of watching them develop, and of enjoying them
through every stage, no matter how complicated.
The hardships and difficultes of raising them will soon be
forgotten in the vacuum of their absence. You will realize
then, if not now, how much delight and satisfaction
there is in having young people in your home. Out of
deep conviction, and perhaps with some regret, you'll say

to your children, as my mother said to me, *"Enjoy* your children while you have them!"

Parents should be aware of the importance of the memory-building process. In our adult preoccupation, we tend to think that the "important" experiences our children will have are still in the future. We forget that, to them, childhood is reality rather than merely a preparation for reality. We forget that childhood memories can form the adult personality. "What we describe as 'character,'" wrote Sigmund Freud, "is based on the memory-traces of our earliest youth."

Norman M. Lobsenz

THE SECRET OF HOSPITALITY

by Irene B. Harrell

Last summer I had to take my four-year-old, hard-of-hearing daughter to a faraway, big city hospital for three days of out-patient diagnostic tests. A widow I had never met, the mother of a friend of mine, invited us to stay with her. I accepted gratefully.

She met us at the huge airport, which would have been completely confusing to me if I had been there alone with my child.

The next morning, the three of us had breakfast together. My hostess had taken the day off from her work in order to take us to the hospital and to see that we found the right place to go.

She lived a long cross-town drive from the hospital. Since I didn't know what time the doctors would be finished with us, she suggested that we take a cab back to her apartment rather than call her to pick us up.

That morning, when the three of us were getting ready to leave, I was surprised that she came into the bedroom right along with us. I knew it was her room, but somehow I hadn't expected her to use it while we were there. She had slept on the pull-out couch in the living room. Momentarily startled by her action, I suddenly felt very much at ease, though I couldn't have explained why.

I liked it, too, that she went back to work as usual the next two days, expecting my daughter and me to rely on taxicabs for getting to and from the hospital now that we knew our way around. She always got home before we did and had a good hot supper ready when we came in tired and dirty from our day in the city.

Our meals were good — nourishing, but not elaborate. I had the feeling that she was preparing more helpings because we were there, but that we were eating substantially the same fare she might have had if we hadn't been there.

I liked that. It kept me from having to feel apologetic for causing her so much trouble. She didn't act as if

we were any trouble at all. The last night she and I sat
up late confiding in each other — woman talk.

The next day it was necessary for us to go directly
to the airport from the hospital. So my hostess and I said
our goodbyes before she left for work that morning.
I remember the look on her face as she stood beside
the chair where I was sitting.

"Promise you won't be offended if I tell you something?"
she asked. "Please *don't* get me a present," she said.
"I've *loved* having you here." She squeezed my hand
and was gone.

My eyes were suddenly wet. I knew why I'd felt
so comfortable in her home, so welcome living with her
those days. Because she hadn't been my hostess —
she had been my friend. She had simply shared her life
and her home with me. I felt thankful. And I was
richer for it.

The lesson I learned is one I hope to impart to people
who visit in *my* home. I'll not exhaust myself, or
them, with elaborate preparations for more food than
they can eat, or more special guests or entertainment
than they can enjoy. I won't make them apologetic
for interrupting my life. I won't attempt to be a perfect
hostess any more. I'll try to be a friend.

*No matter how crowded we were, there always seemed
to be room for guests in our house. Most of the time
Mother reserved a spare room for visitors, unless it was
already occupied by someone's extended residence.
Looking back, I realize now how much my life was
influenced by the many guests who experienced the
hospitality of our home.*

*My subsequent call to the ministry can partly be
credited to the godly succession of missionaries,
denominational leaders, and evangelists who shared
Mother's gracious hospitality while assisting Dad in the
aggressive activities of a growing church.*

*The Bible says, "Be not forgetful to entertain strangers:
for thereby some have entertained angels unawares"*

(Hebrews 13:2). The memories of Mother's guest room encourage me to wish that, even amid today's urban squeeze, more homes would provide a room where guests may share the abounding hospitality of gracious Christian love.

J. Kenneth Allaby

GET ALONG WITH YOUR IN-LAWS

by Edith M. Stern

When young couples have in-law troubles, the cause is often not so much in anything the older generation does as in the younger people themselves. Hard to believe? Probably, if you are coping with an "interfering" mother-in-law, "possessive" sister-in-law, or "dominating" father-in-law.

But research and experience have led marriage counselors, social workers and psychiatrists to believe that in-law friction tends to diminish when the younger set come to understand some of the emotions underlying their relationship with their new family, and when they learn to act toward parents-in-law with respect and common sense. "Rarely does the fault lie with the parents-in-law when there are difficulties," corroborates a senior caseworker at the Jewish Family and Children's Service in Miami, Florida. "Trouble more often comes from the way the sons-and-daughters-in-law treat them."

There are, of course, some in-laws with whom no young wife or husband could get along. Among them are the kinds of people who think everybody is against them, who make constant unfounded accusations, and are suspicious even of kindness and attention. There are mothers who keep a stranglehold on their grown sons. There are fathers who belittle their sons-in-law out of jealousy and competitiveness. Such parents may need professional counseling, and if they don't get it, the young people may need help to cope with them. But fortunately, family elders like these are rarities. The great majority of parents want their children to be married and to be happy in their marriages.

Whatever your in-laws may be as individuals, however, your attitudes toward them reflect your attitudes toward your own family, yourself, and your marriage partner. "The better you feel about your own parents," says a Washington, D.C., psychiatrist, "the less difficulty you are likely to have with your in-laws."

Elinor Jones Grant created in-law trouble for herself
by transferring her resentment of her own obstinate,
domineering, and self-righteous mother to the gentle mother
of her husband.

When Elinor was growing up in a small town,
her mother forcefully and unremittingly directed what
Elinor should think, do, and wear. Rebelling, Elinor
moved away and got a job in a city. There she fell in love
with and married Tom Grant, whose background was
similar to hers. So Elinor assumed that the elder
Mrs. Grant must be like her own mother. Before Elinor
had even met Tom's mother, the younger woman was
determined to show her that she wasn't going to live
by dull and limited standards.

With something of a chip on her shoulder Elinor
set out to shock Mrs. Grant. That lady's tradition
of restraint prevented her from criticizing Elinor directly.
But she confided to Tom that she couldn't help wishing
he had found a different kind of wife. When Tom
suggested to Elinor that she try not to offend his mother,
Elinor flared up and said that nobody's mother was
going to tell her what to do.

Hurt for his mother's hurts, Tom continued to remind
Elinor to curb herself. Quarrels resulted, which she blamed
unfairly on his mother "who's trying to set you against me."
It wasn't until Tom Junior was born that Elinor stopped
affronting her mother-in-law. For one thing, she became
too busy to bother. For another, she found that Grandma
was helpful and began to appreciate her as the kindly
woman she was.

More often than not, anger against one's own parent
is not as open as Elinor's. Bill Dawes was not even
aware of his suppressed, smoldering resentment against
his father when it burst out against his father-in-law.
His own father, though well-to-do, was stingy. Bill grew
up never having had the toys or bicycle he craved.

When he married, Bill unwittingly projected his
repressed indignation against his own father onto his wife's
father. "Your old man could certainly fork out a little
to make life easier for his only daughter," Bill would say
to Betty. He would point out to his father-in-law
how tired poor Betty was when she got home from work,

and when his in-laws bought a needed new car, he said, "It's wonderful to have rich relatives!" Naturally, his father-in-law reacted against these sarcastic hints and conveyed his annoyance to Betty, whereupon Bill complained that her family was "trying to make trouble between us." A defensive Betty cast aspersions on Bill's father, thus rubbing salt in a hidden wound.

When the situation eased up, it wasn't because of any change in Bill's father-in-law. He remained as he always had been, a good man, as generous as his income permitted. But when Bill began to make an excellent living as a junior executive, his new sense of financial independence lessened his resentments.

Financial independence, indeed, although no guarantee against in-law problems, can help avoid them; for there is an age-old universal tendency to bite the hand that feeds you. But more important than financial independence as a deterrent to in-law troubles is personal independence — that is, maturity.

Even though you're married, are you still your parents' child who depends on them for guidance and authority? Or are you on your own, an adult? Only if you are, will you be able to take suggestions, criticisms, even practical help from in-laws in your stride. If you're not, well-meant advice or plain affectionate interest may be misconstrued as interference. Gifts, recipes, even invitations to meals may touch off such thoughts as "They think I'm not able to manage by myself!"

Reactions like these are more common among young wives than young husbands, perhaps because women tend to be more deeply involved with personal and family relationships. Despite the stereotyped mother-in-law jokes and cartoons, trouble between young men and their wives' mothers is rare. A majority of complaints against mothers-in-law come from daughters-in-law.

"There is no doubt that the relationship between mother-in-law and daughter-in-law is potentially competitive," says one marriage counselor. "But if wives only realized how the cards are stacked in their favor, they would be less touchy. You don't have to love your mother-in-law, but do give her the chance to be liked!"

It can certainly be annoying when your mother-in-law
lifts the pot covers and tells you how much her son
loves homemade soup and how you should make it.
Irritating, too, to be informed that the baby needs
changing or that her children were never allowed to leave
their toys all over the floor. But remember that you're no
longer a little girl who has to do what Mama says
and that your husband is no longer your mother-in-law's
responsibility.

On the other hand, avoid feeling that just because
advice comes from your mother-in-law it's to be spurned.
Be glad for what helpful tips she may give you.
Not only is she a more experienced homemaker than you,
but also she's had more time to learn your husband's
likes and dislikes.

If a wife feels that her husband really has too strong a
tie to his mother, about the worst thing she can do is
give an ultimatum like "You'll have to choose between
me and your mother." It's much better to come to an
understanding by calmly talking things through. The
same goes for frankly but tactfully, making it known
to your in-laws when they do bothersome little things,
instead of letting these develop into major grievances.

In real life, communicating may take a while before it
has positive results, but in the long run it tends to be
effective. Grace Schmidt's mother-in-law, for instance,
habitually barged in with friends whenever she wished
to show off her son's house and babies. Grace liked
to show them off, too, but not when her hair was in curlers
and Junior was ready for his nap, wailing and cranky,
or when last night's dinner dishes hadn't been washed
and the unsorted laundry was piled on the bathroom floor.

When Grace decided that the intrusions had become
unbearable, she said, "Mother, I'm happy you're so fond
of the children and me that you want to bring your
friends over. But won't you please give me a little notice?"
Mrs. Schmidt burst into tears, remarked that it was
something new to her not to be always welcome in
her children's home, and flounced out. Mature and
secure in the conviction that she wasn't being an unreasonable daughter-in-law, Grace let her go without
comment. After the next time Mrs. Schmidt dropped

in with a friend, Grace asked her quietly, "Don't you remember, Mother, I asked you please to let me know beforehand?" There were no tears then, only a plaintive, "Am I on such formal terms with my children I have to announce myself?" This gave Grace a clue on which to work. "Not you," she answered, "but strangers." Mrs. Schmidt thought about this, and phoned the next time she wanted to bring a friend. When she found how much more pleasant it was to visit when the house was in order, Grace was unruffled, and the children weren't at their worst, she began to call before she herself visited.

Make up your mind, however, that some things you may not like about your in-laws are beyond your control. Their background may be different and, consequently, their manners, customs, and ways of expressing affection. As long as they don't interfere with your ways, you'll be happiest if you try to find the things you can like in them.

Some young couples think one solution to in-law problems is to move far away. Distance, to be sure, may eliminate minor friction, such as "To whose family do we go for Thanksgiving dinner?" But basic adjustment can't be achieved in terms of miles. The impact of a long-distance call from a demanding relative can be very upsetting to an immature wife who hasn't yet freed herself from her parents, or to a husband who has guilt feelings about not doing enough for the mother who did so much for him. Since the relative isn't near enough to engage in battle, the husband and wife may take up the dispute themselves.

But a caution here: Avoid attributing to your in-laws the things that go wrong between your partner and you. Marital conflicts may masquerade as in-law conflicts. It's easier to dislike your mother-in-law and blame her for bringing up a selfish child than directly to blame her son.

The situation can be particularly inflammable if, in defiant escape from your own family, you've married someone whose background is quite different from yours. You can never really escape from your family. It isn't true that you marry a girl or boy, not the family. Their values are an intrinsic part of your partner.

It isn't simple to have to adjust to another family,

especially when marriage itself requires so many changes and adjustments. But it can be rewarding. You have more relatives to care about you and whom to care about. In times of trouble or need, parents-in-law are often second or substitute parents; brothers-and-sisters-in-law supplement or replace your own, who perhaps live far away. If you don't set up an invisible wall against your second family, they may become a great asset.

A boy in the Swiss Alps went out on a rocky ledge one morning and seemed to become aware, for the first time, of someone else across the chasm.

"Hello! Hel-lo!"

"Hello! Hel-lo!" came back to him.

"Who - are - you?" he inquired.

"Who - are - you?" was the reply word for word.

Was there another boy across the chasm who was enjoying mocking him? After a few moments he became angry.

"Why don't you step out and let me see you?"

"Why don't you step out and let me see you?"

"I'm standing right here. Look at me."

The words came rushing back at him.

His blood boiling, the little fellow cried: "I'll fight you!"

And the other voice called for a fight.

Almost too angry for words, the boy rushed indoors and to his mother. He knew there was a boy on the next mountain who wanted to have a fight with him and threatened to do him bodily injury. The mother listened and smiled.

"Go outdoors again," she encouraged, "and shout, 'I like you,' and find out what happens."

The boy scampered out into the brisk, beautiful sunlight of the Alps.

"Hey, you, over there, I like you."

Another voice replied: "I like you."

The boy was surprised and rushed back to his mother with the wonderful word; he had made friends with the boy on the other side of the deep chasm.

Philip Jerome Cleveland

7 THE WOMAN AND HER GOD

HER
NEED
FOR
SECURITY
by Pat Hare

Charlie Brown of Peanuts fame was once confronted with the question, "What is security?" He paused and then his eyes lit up. "Security is knowing you won't be called on to recite."

Sally Brown, his younger sister, disagreed. She thought "Security is knowing who the baby sitter is." So Charlie asked Snoopy, his dog. Snoopy snuggled up to him and said, "Security is having someone to lean on." Still not completely satisfied, Charlie sought other opinions. He met Lucy at the mailbox and asked her what she thought security was. She replied, "Security is giving the mailbox lid an extra flip." Lucy's younger brother, Linus, said, "Real security is a thumb and a blanket."

Charlie Brown's conclusion about security was probably very similar to his conclusion for happiness: Security "is one thing to one person and another thing to another person."

What do we find security in?

1/ Do we long for the affection and approval of others? Are we easily hurt when someone rejects one of our ideas? Do we become frustrated when we cannot please people?

2/ Maybe dating and marriage is our source of security. Do we doubt our worth as women when we haven't dated lately?

3/ Are we happiest when we are in familiar surroundings with old friends? Do we avoid new situations and the unknown?

4/ Perhaps power and prestige give us a feeling of fulfillment. Do we find ourselves trying to outwit someone in order to convince ourselves that we're better than they are?

5/ We may be perfectionists, continually trying to correct weakness. This may show up both in personal appearance and in goals.

6/ Then we may find security in being self-sufficient

and independent. We may not be able to be independent at present, but this might be a dream for the future.

Dr. Karen Horney, a well-known psychoanalyst, gives the six areas just mentioned as some of the means through which we seek security.

Webster defines security as "the state or feeling of being free from fear, care, danger." There are really two definitions here. One is a *state* of being secure and the other is a *feeling* of being secure, and the two are different. One says that you *are* secure while the latter says you *feel as though you are*. For instance, when you walk across a frozen river, you may be cautious for fear of breaking through the ice. But then as you approach the center of the river, you notice a bulldozer cleaning off the ice. You then realize that you're secure and have no reason for being afraid. This would illustrate a state of security.

The following day you cross the river with confidence, not realizing that the weather has changed. Halfway across, you fall through the ice. This would be an example of feeling secure when confidence was misplaced. The object you place your faith in may or may not be truly secure.

Consider the six areas mentioned earlier. Do they represent actual security or just the feeling? Take the one women probably are most concerned about, dating and marriage. Why do we date? Here are some of the reasons: First, it shows that someone appreciates us and is willing to spend his time and money on us. Second, it relieves pressure from other girls. We'll be more readily accepted by them, because they realize men desire our company. Third, the thrill of being appreciated and treated as a woman builds our morale. Have you ever heard girls say, "When I'm with him, I feel like the woman I want to be"? Fourth, when we're dating occasionally, the fear of being an "old maid" is less of a problem.

Not only dating but also marriage seems to provide security. Marriage offers a home, children, and the companionship of a man. Plus this, you are given the opportunity of being an independent unit financially and socially. Yet obviously, dating and marriage offer a feeling of security but not a state of being secure.

The feeling of being secure can be removed at any minute through death, disease, or maybe divorce. Recent statistics reveal that one out of every three-and-a-half marriages ends in divorce. If you happen to be fortunate enough not to be that one, how successful will your marriage be? How many marriages do you know that meet the ideal you have set for marriage?

Since marriage can't give us absolute security, can any of the other means of gaining security meet our needs? Are affection and approval from others something we can depend on? What about seeking the familiar and avoiding the unknown? Do power and prestige give us a state of being secure? Is striving for perfection the answer? Can we depend on being self-sufficient and independent to fulfill our needs? You'll probably agree with me that the answer to these questions is no.

Can we ever find the state of being secure? Can we put our trust in anything or anyone and know that we can completely depend on them? Jesus Christ said yes. He said he could be completely depended on. He said he knows his children and they know him, he loves them, and will give them eternal life. He states further that no one can snatch them out of his hand. Doesn't that sound secure? No one will separate him from his children. Can anyone or anything else make this claim of never leaving you? Christ explains that he is different from a person who stays by you when everything is going well, but runs off when problems or difficulties come. Jesus Christ says he'll stay with his children. He even laid down his life for them.

Why is Christ different from all the other avenues of finding security? How can he say, "I will never fail you" when the other items of security fail us when we need them most? He can say this because of who he is. He existed before creation and all things were created through him. He is the promised Messiah who took on human form in order to reveal God's character and power to his children. Jesus Christ is the only Son of God. He describes himself as "the way, and the truth, and the life"; and says no one comes to the Father, but by him.

He came not only to reveal his Father to men, but also

to pay the penalty for man's disobedience to God. This penalty could be paid only by the shedding of blood by a sinless, infinite being. Christ sacrificed his life on the cross that those who believe in him and receive him might become children of God. Christ rose from the dead to show that he was God and lives today to draw his children to himself.

Therefore Jesus Christ can give absolute security to an individual because he is absolute and infinite. Other things that we put our faith and trust in will fail us, because they are finite and imperfect.

Where are you seeking security? How solid is your foundation of life? Christ explains how solid it is if it's in him. He tells of two houses. One was built on a rock by a wise man. The second was built on sand by a foolish man. Violent rainstorms came. The house on the rock stood, while the house built on the sand fell. No matter how skillfully the second house had been built, it couldn't withstand the forces of nature, because of its poor foundation.

What is your foundation? Will it stand when the forces of the world attack? Or will your life fall like the second house because the structure and existence of your life have been based on things that are finite and imperfect? Now is the time to evaluate your life. You may not be able to do anything about it later when you find that your foundation is sand.

How do you gain Christ as your rock and foundation? How do you become a child of God? Christ promises that to all who receive him, who believe in his name, he will give the power to become children of God (John 1:12).

It's a lot like getting married. Many steps need to be taken before the wedding and many things are changed afterward, but the actual act of getting married is simple. All you say is "I do." In becoming a Christian you first need to know who Jesus Christ is. This is similar to getting to know your husband before you get married. Then after you have discovered who Christ is, you need to receive him by accepting his death on the cross for your sins, repenting, and inviting him into your life as your Lord. This is like saying "I do." You have

received a person into your life. Since you have
acknowledged Jesus Christ as your Savior and Lord,
he will give you the privilege of being a child of God.

. . . through his death on the cross . . .
Christ has brought you into the very presence
of God, and you are standing there before him
with nothing left against you — nothing left that
he could even chide you for. Colossians 1:22, TLB

HER
NEED
FOR
LIBERATION

by Joyce Landorf

In the early '50s I was trying to survive the confining routine of being a working wife and new mother. I didn't need to work (my husband had a stable job), but I wanted to add to our income and *get out of the house.*

As it turned out, after I paid all kinds of new expenses and babysitting fees we had little or no "added income." I'd come home each night to work four times harder there than I had in my nonworking days. By the time I'd cleaned up the babies' and babysitter's mess from the day, made dinner, cleaned the kitchen, handled the dirty diapers, and had two disagreements with my husband, I was in no mood to jump into bed relaxed and romantic. Women's Liberation looked better all the time.

I had no opportunity to develop creative abilities and talents. I didn't have a clue to my identity. To say I felt inadequate, cheated of life, and sterile in my efforts to be a woman, wife, mother, and person was an understatement.

By 1955, with five years of being a working wife under my belt and two children under my feet, I was ready — no, hysterically ripe — to join all women fighting for their, to me, obvious rights.

Everything in me wanted to stand and scream to the world, "What do you think you're doing to me? Who do you think I am?" And most pathetically I wanted to cry softly, "Will I ever be loved?" The desperate needs in my life were so overwhelming that I never dreamed or even dared hope they would be met.

It was at that almost-beyond-hope moment that a fantastic miracle of God exploded in my little world. I have detailed the events of that incredible day in my book *His Stubborn Love,* and the contrasts between the "Before Christ" Joyce and the "Since Christ" Joyce are obvious. But now I'd like to be a little more personal and explicit.

From that day on, I was never able to be the same.
With God's rich, majestic forgiveness came inner peace.
I wasn't mad at God, at myself, or others. I didn't need
to seek liberation; I was *liberated*. I was no longer
gasping for air. I wasn't boxed or locked in. I was free.

Nothing changed in my husband, children, home, or job
that day. Yet everything was completely different. I
was free to breathe, move, and begin living.

It was as if I'd just been given my long-awaited
citizenship and was finally a person. It rang loud and clear
that I was now a child of God! I'd asked Christ to come
into my life and (as John put it) "If you believe that
Jesus is the Christ — that he is God's Son and your Savior
— then you are a child of God" (1 John 5:1, TLB).

Being no longer a nonperson but a child of God
meant not only that I was forgiven, my guilt gone,
but also, wonder of wonders, I was loved. Really *loved!*
My eyes blurred with joyous tears when I read, "See how
very much our heavenly Father loves us, for he allows
us to be called his children — think of it — and we really
are!" (1 John 3:1, TLB).

Now, in direct contrast to before, I adore living in today's
world. It's confusing, often disappointing, and sometimes
completely unjust, but then Jesus never said that life
in this world would be trouble-free. He only promised
to be with us to guide us, to love us, never to let us be
defenseless or without the wisdom to cope.

Not long ago a newspaper sent a woman reporter
to my home to interview me. She was a very unhappy,
cynical woman whose editor forced her to read my book
before the interview. She didn't like the book, its
views on being a woman, or me.

Very cynically she settled herself into my couch.
At that moment our 16-year-old beauty named Laurie
came bouncing in. I introduced her to the reporter,
and then Laurie turned to me and said, "Mother,
it's so hot today, can I make you both some iced tea?"

I said yes, thanked her, and then turned to the reporter
who said with some degree of awe in her voice, "How
did you get a daughter like that?"

I laughed, made some offhanded remark about beating
her twice a week whether she needed it or not,

and was about to get serious when our 18-year-old son Rick popped his head into the living room with his enthusiastic, "Hi, Mom."

After he'd chatted with the reporter and left the room, the woman looked very deeply into my eyes and said slowly but surely, "Your children are remarkable. What did you do to achieve that? They are so alive — really *alive*."

"I needed help to do it," I said. "It couldn't have been done by my efforts alone, or even my husband's and mine combined. It had to be done with God's help, and that's exactly how it was done."

She reached for her notebook and without any cynicism in her voice said, "Tell me all about yourself." (I thought she'd never ask!)

I told her for the next hour and a half how God had transformed me from a nonperson to a woman — like the transformation from a caterpillar to a butterfly. When I finished she sat still for a long time, then drew a cigarette out of her handbag, lit it, and after expelling a long puff of smoke shook her cigarette at me and said, *"You* have *got* to be the most *truly* liberated woman I've ever known!"

But I know scores of incredible, unique women, married and single, who have full lives, active homes and/or careers, and very productive, fulfilling life styles. Many are Christians and are at peace with their Maker, their world, and themselves, whether they are hard at work as a partner in their husband's business or at home reading aloud to their children. They don't stand on the sidelines watching the parade of life pass by. Even if they're in the "single woman" category, they jump in with both feet. Sometimes they not only march in the parade but end up leading it.

This is an exciting time for women. I've personally known some priceless examples of womanhood, and I know many others are like them all over the world.

At our New Year's Rose Parade in Pasadena, when her husband was Grand Marshall, Mrs. Billy Graham was surrounded by sign-carrying Women's Liberation protestors. One reporter asked about her feelings on women's liberation. She simply smiled and responded, "I'm liberated, thank you."

We can only know true freedom
when we are secure enough
to admit our failure
and call it sin, knowing
that the relationship
never changes
and
that immediate confession
restores the fellowship.

Rosalind Rinker

DARE
TO
TRUST
GOD

by Catherine Marshall

"Now don't push the term *faith* at me," a lawyer told me bluntly at a dinner party recently. "The word is like a red flag. I resent it. I see nothing wrong with 'Prove it to me first, then I'll believe.' "

As we talked, I realized that it had never occurred to this intelligent, well-educated man that in his everyday life he often follows the reverse order — belief and acceptance first, then action. Every day he lives, he acts on faith many times with little proof or none at all, and he doesn't feel that he is being impractical.

He demonstrates an act of faith each time he boards a plane.

Each time he eats a meal in a restaurant he trusts some unknown cook behind the scenes. He enters a hospital for an operation and signs a release giving permission for surgery. This is an act of faith in an anesthetist whose name he may not even know and a surgeon who holds in his hands the power of life or death.

He accepts a prescription from a doctor and takes it to a druggist, thus acting out his faith that the pharmacist will fill the prescription accurately. The use of the wrong drug might be deadly, but he isn't equipped to analyze the contents before swallowing the pill.

It's obvious that were we to insist on the "proof first, then faith" order in our daily lives, organized life as we know it would grind to a screeching halt. And since life together among men is possible only by faith, as we act out our trust in other people, it shouldn't seem odd that the same law applies to our life with God.

The New Testament makes it clear that in the spiritual realm, when for some reason or other we refuse to act by faith, all activity stops, just as completely as it does in the secular realm. There is no way for us even to take the first steps toward the Christian life except by faith, any more than a baby can get launched on his earthly life

For Women Only

without blind baby-trust in his parents and other adults. We have to accept the fact of a personal relationship with Jesus Christ by faith, even as our young children accept the fact of parental love. For the child, as for the new Christian, understanding and proof come later.

In the same way, every step in our Christian walk has to be by faith.

Much of my own problem with faith arose from an early misunderstanding of what faith was. First of all, I used to believe that faith had something to do with feeling. For example, when I had messed up some situation and had asked God for forgiveness, then I would peer inside myself to see if I *felt* forgiven. If I could locate such feelings, then I was sure that God had heard and had forgiven me. Now I know that this is a false test of faith.

We wouldn't be so foolish as to go to a railroad station, board the first car we saw, then sit down and try to feel whether or not this was the train that would take us where we wanted to go. Our feeling would obviously have no bearing on the facts. Yet I know now that at times my actions in the spiritual realm have been just that foolish.

Another misconception I once had was that faith is trying to believe something one is fairly certain is not true. But faith isn't hocus-pocus, opposed to knowledge and reality. In fact, faith doesn't go against experience at all; rather it appeals to experience, just as science does. The difference is that it appeals to experience in a realm where our five senses aren't supreme rulers.

Nor is faith a kind of spiritual coin which you and I can exchange for heaven's blessings. Nor is it simply believing doggedly in some particular doctrine. One can believe in the divinity of Jesus Christ and feel no personal loyalty to him at all; that is, pay no attention whatever to his commandments and his will for one's life. One can believe intellectually in the efficacy of prayer and never do any praying.

Perhaps one reason that the real meaning of faith eluded me personally for so many years was that it is so surprisingly simple, so practical. Faith in God is simply trusting him enough to step out on that trust.

My first lesson in stepping out on trust came in connection with the problem of financing a college education. We were then living in a little railroad town in the eastern panhandle of West Virginia. By the time I reached my senior year in high school, the town had for some years been struggling through the long aftermath of the 1929 crash. Its only industry, the Baltimore and Ohio railroad shops, were all but shut down. The church my father served as minister was suffering along with everything else. Father had voluntarily taken several cuts in his already meager salary. Even grocery money was scarce. It was fortunate that Mother knew how to prepare fried mush in a way that made it seem like a rare delicacy.

Something I had dreamed of as far back as I could remember, a college education, now seemed out of the question. The dream even included a particular college, Agnes Scott College in Decatur, Georgia.

Agnes Scott accepted me. Although the school was accustomed to ministers' and missionaries' daughters whose ambitions outstripped their pocketbooks, the financial burden nevertheless looked hopelessly heavy. Even with the promise of a small work scholarship and the $125 I had saved from high school essay and debating prizes, we were several hundred dollars short.

One evening Mother found me lying across my bed sobbing. She sat down beside me, put her cool hand on my forehead. No words were needed. She knew what the trouble was.

Presently she said quietly, "You and I are going to pray about this. Let's go into the guest room where we won't be disturbed." And she took me firmly by the hand.

"Let's talk about this a minute before we pray," Mother said slowly. "I believe that it is God's will for you to go to college, or else he wouldn't have given you the mental equipment. Further, all resources are at God's disposal. Do you believe that, Catherine?"

"Yes — yes — I think I do."

"All right, now here's another fact I want you to think about. Everybody has faith. We're born with it. Much of what happens to us in life depends on where we place our faith. If we deposit it in God, then we're on sure ground. If we place our trust in poverty or failure or fear, then we're investing it poorly. So keep that in mind while I read something to you." She opened a Moffatt Bible to 1 John 5:14, 15:

Now the confidence we have in him is this,
that he listens to us whenever we ask anything
in accordance with his will; and if we know that he
listens to whatever we ask, we know that we obtain
the requests we have made to him.

"Note how the thought goes in that promise, Catherine. Whenever we ask God for something that is his will, he hears us. If he hears us, then he grants the request we have made. So you and I can rest on that promise. Let's claim it right now for the resources for your college." And so we knelt by the bed and prayed about it.

I shall never forget that evening. During those quiet moments in the bedroom, I was learning what faith is and how it works. It is true that my faith was immature and weak, but the strength of Mother's was contagious. She had helped me take my first step in faith. The answer would come. We knew it would, though neither of us had any idea how.

When it came, it was the offer of a job for Mother with the Federal Writer's Project. Would she be willing to write the history of the country? Would she! Her salary would cover the amount needed for my college expenses with a little to spare. Since history has always been one of Mother's loves, no job could have been more to her liking. Moreover, she could work at home and, along with her writing, keep a hand on family projects.

That was the way I learned we must have faith *before* the fact, not after, if we are to function as human beings. The only question is, Faith in whom? Faith in what?

God challenges us to place faith in him rather than in fallible human beings: "Taste and see that the Lord is good." In my experience this is not an ivory-tower approach. It's the only effectual one.

Faith is only worthy of the name when it erupts into action. Were we to use the muscles of our legs as little as we do the muscles of our faith, most of us would be unable to stand. What can we do to strengthen them?

First, we can't trust God until we know something about him. The way to begin is by reading his Word and thinking about it. The Bible acquaints us with the nature and character of God: his power; his unselfish, unchangeable love; his infinite wisdom. We read instance after instance in which God exercised his power and wisdom in helping and delivering his people.

Second, faith is strengthened only as we ourselves exercise it. We have to apply it to our problems: poverty, bodily ills, bereavement, job troubles, tangled human relationships.

Third, faith has to be in the present tense. Now. A vague prospect that what we want will transpire in the future isn't faith, but hope.

Fourth, absolute honesty is necessary. We can't have faith and a guilty conscience at the same time. Faith will fade away every time.

Fifth, the strengthening of faith comes through staying with it in the hour of trial. We shouldn't shrink from tests of our faith. Only when we're depending on God alone are we in a position to see God's help and deliverance, and thus have our faith strengthened for the next time.

This means we must let him do the work. Almost always it takes longer than we think it should. When we grow impatient and try a deliverance of our own, through friends or circumstances, we are taking God's work out of his hands.

The Epistle of James declared that "faith, unless it has deeds, is dead in itself." And John added more bluntly still, "He who will not believe God, has made God a liar. . . ."

Believe what? Believe the consistent testimony in Scripture of the unfailing love and good will of God, of his ability to help us, and of his willingness, even eagerness, to do so.

The adventure of living hasn't really begun until we begin to stand on our faith-legs and claim — for ourselves, for our homes, for the rearing of our children, for our health problems, for our business affairs, and for our world — the resources of our God.

*If faith is not at work in life, then life is open territory.
And, usually, such an open invitation is welcomed
by fear. And where fear lays seize to a life, faith is
an unwelcomed stranger.*

*Faith is companion to all the ingredients that make
for the best things in life — hope, love, joy, to name a
few. Fear is stranger to all of these.*

*Faith keeps its options open for a brighter tomorrow.
Fear slams the door on tomorrow, by accepting today
as the best.*

C. Neil Strait

PRAYER IS CONVERSATION

by Rosalind Rinker

I have discovered that prayer's real purpose is to put God at the center of our attention, and forget ourselves and the impression we're making on others.

After all, it isn't the words we say nor how we say them, it's the open heart attitude which God looks for. He simply longs for us to speak person to person with him without any obstacles between.

He is there. He is there with you. He may slip your mind, but you never slip his mind.

Prayer is the expression of the human heart in conversation with God. The more natural the prayer, the more real he becomes. It has all been simplified for me to this extent: Prayer is a dialogue between two persons who love each other. We know to whom we're speaking. We're not talking with an unknown God, but to the God-man, Jesus Christ, who was in all points tempted as we are, so that we can feel freer to come to him with our temptations.

We need to learn to pray in his Presence, and to let him speak with us, to be in tune with him until we're willing to hear what he has to say to us.

We *need to learn to pray with one another*. We're all sheep of his pasture, and we need to be together.

"Again, I tell you, if only two of you on earth agree on what they pray for, they will get it from my Father in heaven. For wherever two or three have met as my disciples, I am right there with them."

Why pray together? Because Jesus promised that when two of his disciples (that means us today) meet to pray, he'll be there with them. Our risen, living Lord said and meant what he said: "I am there, right among them." In a particular way, in a particular promise, he is present. I've experienced it again and again, and so can you.

When we meet to pray with someone else, *the Lord is present* as a third person. Together we learn to talk, to him and with him, in openness and simplicity and

without self-consciousness. We leave our heavy burdens
at his feet by sharing and agreeing together. Our fears
and anxious worries melt away. He speaks and together
we learn to listen. He gives us guidance and direction and
spiritual healing. He makes us ready to receive all he has
to give us. We acquire new brothers and sisters. We
belong to a new family and we begin to learn to take
spiritual family responsibilities for one another. Even our
weaknesses become sources of strength when we are
consciously there in his presence, because *need* is the
door of opportunity through which our Savior meets us.

All this and more comes from just being there together.
All this and more comes from being there, consciously
in his presence. All this and more awaits those who
will answer his call to come apart with him — alone.

The Good Shepherd knows what his sheep need.
They need the pastures of being together with one
another, but they also need the quiet waters of intimate
security. Security comes from being alone with him
in the secret places. "My sheep hear my voice, and
they follow me." When have you heard his voice
and followed him into his secret place? When have
you found rest in just being with him?

None of us should say that due to our own
personality we are unable to be at ease in the presence
of other believers, or that we're unable to pray with
them. By the same token none of us should say that we
can't learn to be alone in a room for an hour or more
with God. In time and with willingness anyone can
learn to do both. To have one without the other is like
having day without night. They complement one another,
they help us become whole persons.

Several practical points may help you to make this
practice of secret prayer part of your daily life.
1/ Have a definite place to pray alone. Every time
you pass that place, whether it's a chair, your bedside,
an unused room, a little closet, your desk or your car,
you'll be reminded that both physical and spiritual
refreshment await you there.
2/ Anticipate meeting One who loves you in a personal
intimate way. Before you arrive at this special place,
let your mind constantly say, "I'm going to meet him,

I'm going to be consciously aware of him." After you're
there, say: "Here in this quiet place, he can show me
himself. I am his. I can put aside all else and worship
you, my Lord, and my God."

3/ Let your prayers be semi-audible. You *are* speaking
to a Person, and hearing your own voice will keep
your thoughts centered on him, although sometimes
there will be only deep unspoken torrents of love
and adoration welling up from within.

4/ Use a daily devotional book, and use some kind
of study book to give you needed direction in your daily
Bible reading.

In my not-too-long-ago-do-it-yourself approach to God,
I used to congratulate myself on the fact of my daily
faithfulness in having a Quiet Time. And when I
spoke to others, I gave the impression that I always
had a successful Quiet Time, and was, of course, always
"victorious." This was far from the truth.

Have you discovered that no matter what you're like,
he is always the same? His faithfulness is as sure as
the law of gravitation. This discovery will turn your
attention away from yourself to him.

Through all the years of my do-it-yourself period
I was still too often expressing my own selfish spirit,
not his spirit of holy love.

And then I discovered — worship.

True worship takes place within the quietness of the
individual. True worship is subjection to Jesus Christ.
True worship depends upon the kind of God you worship
and isn't conditioned by any religious atmosphere. It's
like a well of water springing up in the heart of the
lover for the Beloved.

It took a negative form of worship to open my eyes
to the meaning of true worship. I was visiting my first
Chinese temple in the city of Shanghai. It was dark
and shadowy inside and lined with double rows of dusty
idols on heavy pedestals. At the far end was a tall loft,
where a giant gilded idol was set among heavy draperies
that covered all but its feet. A Chinese woman came in
to worship. She burned incense, she waved it before
the dumb idol, she prostrated herself before the huge
fifty-foot god, and waited for an answer. Was there any?

There was none.

So that was "worshiping idols." Suddenly I knew
that the God I worshiped was alive, that he was a Person
who responded to me and to whom I could respond.

Suddenly I wanted to get out of that temple and go
home into my own room and close the door and lock it.
I wanted to worship the living God who created and
sustains all life, and who has revealed himself as he is
in the Person of Jesus Christ. I wanted to be quiet
and let all the love and adoration and worship of my heart
go out to him in a way I'd never done before.

My concept of worship has grown and deepened,
and this is now the most important part of my Quiet Time.
It is out of this personal worship that I find myself ready
to share and be a part of a group of God's children.

"But," you say, "I don't seem to be able to get answers
to my prayers the way other people do. I wish I had
that kind of faith." Did you ever make a study of the
prayer promises in the New Testament with the idea of
finding out what God is like?

After such a study, one word seemed to light up for me.
See if you can find it for yourself, in this next para-
graph, which blends several promises.

All are freely invited to ask and to receive. We are
told that we will receive what we ask for if we search
and knock and ask. We are told to ask in Christ's name
and he will do whatever we ask. We are told to abide
or to find our reason for living, in Christ, and then
we can have whatever we ask for. We are also told
not to doubt, and to believe that we are going to get
what we have asked for.

In all of these promises the word that gets our attention
is the little word *ask*. Think what that means. God
has told us to ask so that he may relieve the intolerable
burdens of fear, tragedy, and loneliness. The burdens
of illness, poverty, and injustice. God has told us
to ask so that he may pour his gifts into our hearts
and lives without measure.

What shall we ask for? The simple answer is, *ask
for what you need*. What are your deep personal needs?
Have you prayed about them? Have you asked the
Person who can take care of them to do it? Have you

had your prayers answered? Or do you just grumble
and rebel and blame other people?

Ask, says Jesus, ask largely, that your joy may be full
(John 16:24). How great is your need? How deep is your
desire? Will it bring you to his side? Will it carry you
past all that keeps you from him? Will you stop what
you are doing now and kneel at his feet, in his presence?
He is there. Ask, seek, knock. There *is* Someone
on the other side of the door, and he will open it
and give you all that he is. Christ and all his gifts are
yours.

". . . the proof of God's amazing love is this: that
it was while we were sinners that Christ died for us. If
God is for us, who can be against us? He that did not
hesitate to spare his own Son but gave him up for us all —
can we not trust such a God to give us, with him,
everything else that we need?" (Romans 5:8; 8:31, 32,
Phillips).

Do you believe in Jesus Christ? Then you have faith.
Faith to ask him for anything because you believe in him.
You will know what to ask and how and where, because
you believe in him and love him. Your greatest need
can be your greatest asset, for need is the door through
which he comes close to his loved ones. Christ promised,
"Lo, I am with you all the days — perpetually, uniformly
and on every occasion — to the close and consummation
of the age" (Matthew 28:20, Amplified).

Jesus Christ is our "point of contact," and as we touch
him, alone or with others, power is released and our
prayers are answered.

In our materialistic culture we know little of sacrifice.
We don't feel it when we give. A missionary, home
on furlough, was invited to a reception in his honor
in a wealthy home where there were many well-to-do
businessmen and finely-dressed wives. Later he wrote
home: "Dear wife, I've been entertained in a wonderful
home. Prominent people were present. The guests wore
two chapels, one school, an organ, and 1,000 books."

The missionary couldn't help translating silks, satins, furs, finery and diamonds into needs on the field. Loaded with luxuries, we suffer no sacrifice. What we need is to decrease expenses and increase our offerings.

Leslie B. Flynn

ME?
GROW UP?

by Mary Lou Lacy

Would it surprise you to be told that one of the most urgent requirements we women have is to grow up? "Oh, dear," we say, "I grew up so terribly long ago, I've almost forgotten what it's like to be young! I've had responsibilities, earned my living, raised a family. Grow up? I did that long ago."

No, we didn't. We didn't really grow up; we just grew older. In order to go farther along our way towards finding God completely, you and I, as women, must think seriously about this business of growing up — *up toward him.*

The Apostle Paul felt this need to grow up spiritually. He thought it through until he understood it and then, during his whole lifetime, he worked to meet it. He described himself in 1 Corinthians 13 by saying "When I was a child, I spake as a child, I understood as a child, I thought as a child: but when I became a man, I put away childish things." It took a lifetime for Paul to grow up. Much later he felt compelled to help the Corinthian Christians along with their growth, for he plainly told them that it was time for them to grow up and stop being babies. "I fed you with milk, not solid food; for you were not ready for it; and even yet you are not ready."

You cannot truthfully say you've never felt the need for someone stronger than yourself on whom to lean, for someone wiser than yourself from whom to learn, someone to comfort you in sorrow, to soothe you in sickness, and to make life itself worth while. You have felt this need as you have seen yourself wholly inadequate. You've reached out for the one unchanging hope that God's love presents. You accepted the gift; you became a Christian; you were born again. And there you were, a baby in the Kingdom of God. That's as it should be, a new life, a new creature, a new growth. Maybe.

Now look at yourself with eyes that are fair, eyes that are completely honest. Have you, have I, continued

to grow spiritually a little each day, a little each week,
or even a little each year? Have we grown any from
that first baby stage when we reach out and take and
accept and then hold and do nothing more? Admit it.
We have been living on milk when by this time we should
be eating meat.

In our family there were many times when we,
as children, had to go to our father and ask for extra
spending money. Now this was a thing we never enjoyed,
but soon we came to know that an unexpected approach
more often brought a hearty laugh and ready response
than did a trite, "Please give me some money, Daddy."
I remember one method that seemed never to fail,
although it was plainly ridiculous to all concerned.

"Oh, Daddy," we would say, with much, much overdone
devotion, "I love you so much. You are the nicest father
in all the world. I wouldn't trade you with anyone
anywhere. I love you, I love you. Please, Daddy,
give me a quarter."

This was quite a joke to all of us — such a shallow,
empty love. But it's not so funny when we admit
the very same approach to God.

On Sunday, Lord, I'll worship thee,
    I'll sing thy praises true.
I'll shift the burdens off of me
    And place them all on you.

I'll list my wants, and favors seek,
    But after that we're through.
So please don't bother me all week;
    If need be, I'll call you.

Yes, we women do need to grow up spiritually,
and the very first way is in our personal relationship
with God. We must put away childish, partial love
and grow a love that is whole, complete, unfailing.
It's no use to say that love can't grow, that it can't mature,
that love is love and there are no varying degrees.
That isn't true. Peter's love grew up. He loved Jesus
when he answered that call, "Follow me," but Peter's
love tasted denial and complete shame before it grew into
a mighty fortress, a rock. It became a complete love
that answered the Master's question: "Lord, you know
that I love you." Can we look Jesus straight in the eye

and say, "Lord, you know that we love you"? To become mature Christians we must grow up in our love for God.

Then there's another side to "putting away childish things" spiritually. We must put this love into practice, make it a powerful force that affects us. When Peter said three times to Christ, "Lord, you know that I love you," Jesus insisted, "Well then, Peter, do something about it. Feed my sheep, Peter; feed my lambs, feed my sheep." This kind of "feeding" requires a love for God that works on and for God's other children.

We have a spiritual experience and we see a hand stretched out to us. We feel the nail holes, we understand the Cross, we admit our inadequacy, and we say, "Oh, yes, Lord, we'll take your hand. We need it, we want it, we cannot live without it." And then suddenly we realize that clinging to the other hand of Jesus is all the rest of the world. Don't you see? If we take him, then we've got to take them. We've got to put this mature love for God, if we can get it, into mature, grown-up love for everyone else. Our hearts and souls become so full of love for God that it splashes over on his other children.

This growing-up process changes our attitudes toward other people until they *seem* completely different and until we *are* completely different. Things that Jesus said are no longer memory verses to be learned and taught. They are integral parts of our spiritually growing whole. "Love one another" becomes a part of you, and you love so "completely" that the color of skin, cultural background, and economic differences are unimportant. "Bear ye one another's burdens," and your own grow lighter as you reach out and help to carry someone else's. "Go and teach," and you go because you cannot stay away, and you teach because God's love so fills you that there is more than enough to pour out again and again for someone else.

Just as we learn through growth to reach up and say, "Father," so we naturally reach out and say, "Brother." We cannot grow upward unless at the same time we grow outward. That changes things a little, doesn't it? One without the other is impossible, and we aren't so sure we want to grow outward to the extent that we never

have to worry again about how to spend our money,
how to use our energies, how to invest our abilities.

A young friend of ours is working as a missionary
in Japan. For his first Christmas in the mission field
we wanted to send him something that would make his life
more pleasant in that faraway place. We talked it
over and finally decided that a gift of money would
solve our problem. "He needs so many things," we
said, "clothes, books, maybe a short sightseeing trip
to refresh his spirits. So let's send him a check with
the request that he use it for the thing he really wants
and needs the most."

A short time after Christmas we received this note
from Japan:

Dear Friends, Thank you for your very nice gift.
Since you gave me the choice I used it for something
I wanted and needed more than anything else. I bought
a secondhand tape recorder on which I can transcribe
good radio programs of organ music. Now I can add
this to the worship services that I hold in bombed-out
chapels. Thank you for making this vital aid to the glory
of God possible.

The thing he wanted most, needed most, was a way to
make the experience of worship meaningful to people
he had never seen before and might never see again,
but people he loved with splash-over love for God. That's
a grown-up, meat-eating, sheep-feeding Christian!

A marvelous thing about this growing-up process is
that we never finish. Each time we take a step closer
to God, our horizon seems to widen and we see new ways
in which to grow, new goals to try to reach, new sins
that we never before knew we had. Strangely enough
each step, each broader scope ahead, leaves us eager and
willing to attempt another stretching. We aren't discouraged
over what we see before us, only thrilled and thankful
over the newness of life brought about by the small progress
already made.

Sometimes we feel ashamed that we've slipped back
again, and are milk-fed Christians, babies in the Kingdom.
Even then, because we've once seen a broader vista,
joy and expectancy aren't completely lost. We're strangely
anxious and ready to try a little meat again. Just a little

at a time, a little more effort in studying his Word,
a little more time allotted to conversations with him,
a little more willingness to try his way, and a new step
is made. The meat begins to satisfy.

A crippled children's clinic in which I've worked
has taught me many things. I suppose patience is one of
the most important elements in any progress. The
patience of the parents, the patience of the physiotherapists
and doctors, and finally the hard-learned patience of the
little crippled child himself have all been essential
in whatever progress has been made. One child, born
with a pitifully twisted foot, was brought time after time.
His leg was put in a cast to stretch his foot just a frac-
tion of an inch toward normality. At regular intervals
he returned and the cast was torn off, a new one replacing
the old, each time forcing the crooked bones a little
nearer to being straight.

How like a woman growing spiritually! She begins with
a crippled soul that is turned completely away from God.
Just a little at a time she twists, she stretches,
she pulls, until gradually she turns toward him. Patiently
she seeks, and asks, and tries, until one day she knows
that she is turned toward the Light, away from the
darkness, with new growth always ahead.

"It is God's will that I should cast
  On him my care each day;
He also bids me not to cast
  My confidence away.
But, oh! I am so stupid, that
  When taken unawares,
I cast away my confidence,
  And carry all my cares."

Anonymous

UNFORGIVENESS IS UNFORGIVABLE

by David Augsburger

To forgive or not to forgive. That is the question. And when you think of it, why should anyone forgive? Why shouldn't the person who has wronged you be made to "make things right" to pay for his sins? Why shouldn't he be punished?

If any conviction about such things comes naturally to all men, it's the deep-seated universal belief that "somebody's got to pay." Forgiveness seems too easy. There should be blood for blood. Eye for eye.

Yes, you can knock out a tooth for a tooth in retaliation, but what repayment can you demand from the one who has broken your home, or betrayed your daughter, or ruined your reputation?

So few sins can be paid for, and so very seldom does the victim possess the power or the advantage to demand payment. In most cases, "making things right" is beyond possibility. Repayment is impossible. So, here's where revenge comes in. If you can't get equal payment or restitution out of the one who's wronged you, at least you can get revenge. Pay him back in kind, tit for tat. Serve him the same sauce.

"Get even" with him, if you insist. But remember, to get even you make yourself even with your enemy. You bring yourself down to his level, and below. There is a saying that goes, "Doing an injury puts you below your enemy; revenging an injury makes you but even with him; forgiving it sets you above him."

Revenge not only lowers you to your enemy's level; what's worse, it boomerangs. The man who seeks revenge is like the man who shoots himself in order to hit his enemy with the kick of the gun's recoil. Revenge is the most worthless weapon in the world. It ruins the avenger while more firmly confirming the enemy in his wrong. It initiates an endless flight down the bottomless stairway of rancor, reprisals, and ruthless retaliation. Just as repayment is impossible, revenge is impotent.

What? No repayment? No revenge? But I can

have the soul-satisfaction of hating the wretch! Well, yes, you can hate him. You can nurse a grudge until it grows into a full-blown hate, hooves, horns, tail, and all. But what do you gain? In hatred, everybody loses. Hidden hatred can sour a likable lady into a suspicious carper, a warm, understanding man into a caustic cynic.

What does it cost to incubate hatred? In addition to corroding a disposition, harbored hatred can elevate blood pressure, upset digestive works, ulcerate a stomach, or bring on a nervous breakdown. And ever hear of a coronary?

Why boil inside? It's a form of slow suicide. Get all steamed up with resentment and an explosion is inevitable. And just simmering a grudge or a grievance can have the same results. Do a long, slow burn and you hurt no one but yourself. The person who broods over a wrong poisons her soul.

Repayment? Impossible. Revenge? Impotent. Resentment? Impractical.

All right, but what about peaceful coexistence? I won't hate him, hit him, or hurt him. He's not worth it. I'll ignore him. Live and let live, but friendship? Forget it.

Now wait! Face it honestly. You can't afford the dubious luxury of an unforgiving heart. Only if you have no need for forgiveness yourself do you dare consider hesitating to forgive another.

We all need forgiveness constantly, don't we? The forgiveness of others, and far more seriously, the forgiveness of God. And those two go hand in hand. They interlock.

Jesus said, "If you forgive other people their failures, your Heavenly Father will also forgive you. But if you will not forgive . . . neither will your Heavenly Father forgive you your failures" (Matthew 6:14, 15, Phillips).

"I never forgive," Gen. James Oglethorpe said to John Wesley.

"Then I hope, sir," replied Wesley, "you never sin!"

George Herbert once wrote, "He that cannot forgive others breaks the bridge over which he himself must pass if he would ever reach heaven; for everyone has need to be forgiven."

Forgiving and being forgiven are all of one piece.

They cannot be separated.

An unforgiving heart is unforgivable. To be forgiven by God for our daily trespasses (and how desperately each of us needs his forgiveness), we must forgive, accept, and love. But true forgiveness is the hardest thing in the universe.

Forgiveness is hard because it is costly.
If I break a priceless heirloom that you treasure and you forgive me, you bear the loss and I go free. Suppose I ruin your reputation. To forgive me, you must freely accept the consequences of my sin and let me go free.

In forgiveness, you bear your own anger and wrath at the sin of another, voluntarily accepting responsibility for the hurt he has inflicted on you.

Forgiveness is costly because it is substitutional.
"All forgiveness, human and divine, is in the very nature of the case vicarious, substitutional," writes James Buswell, Jr., "and this is one of the most valuable views my mind has ever entertained. No one ever really forgives another, except he bears the penalty of the other's sin against him."

This substitution was perfectly expressed in Jesus Christ. Jesus Christ substituted himself for us, bearing his own wrath, his own indignation at our sin. That's what forgiveness costs. God took the total insult of our sin so seriously that he went all the way to Calvary to die. The cross shows how hard it was for God to forgive.

Hear Dorothy Sayers describe it.

Hard it is, very hard,
To travel up the slow and stony road
To calvary, to redeem mankind; far better
To make but one resplendent miracle,
Lean through the cloud, lift the right hand of power
And with a sudden lightning smite the world perfect.
Yet this was not God's way, Who had the power,
But set it by, choosing the cross, the thorn,
The sorrowful wounds. Something there is, perhaps,
That power destroys in passing, something supreme,
To whose great value in the eyes of God
That cross, that thorn, and those five wounds bear witness.

Why this talk about God on a cross? Because God

chose the cross as the only right way to right the wrongs of our world and our sin-loving selves, the only right way to make forgiveness!

If there is any justice in this universe, if God is a God of justice who loves what's right and fair, then we men really shouldn't get away with murder, rebellion, selfishness, and all the rest of the evil that we do and are.

If there is any justice, somebody's got to pay!

But who could? Who of us could ever live well enough to even up his own score? No, the debt we owe God for our insulting refusal to live right and for our rebellion against his love is beyond us all. Such an infinitely vast debt only God could pay. But God doesn't owe it. Man owes the debt he cannot pay. So God paid the debt he didn't owe.

"God was in Christ personally reconciling the world to himself" (2 Corinthians 5:19, Phillips).

Either the sinner bears his own guilt — that's cold justice — or the one sinned against, the first party, may absorb what the second party did — that's forgiveness! And that's what God did in Christ at Calvary. He tasted death for every man (Hebrews 2:9).

That's why God's forgiveness is the most costly thing in the universe. The price of forgiving is high. There are no cheap reductions. No bargain pardons.

The cost? Listen to the Apostle Paul. "Forgive as freely as the Lord has forgiven you" (Colossians 3:13, Phillips). "Be as ready to forgive others as God for Christ's sake has forgiven you" (Ephesians 4:32, Phillips).

You must forgive just as Christ forgave you. You must bear the cost of forgiving just as God did for you. God paid the immeasurable cost of your forgiveness. How can you hesitate to pay the infinitely smaller cost of forgiving your brother — or your enemy?

Yes, forgiveness is hard. If it weren't, it would be a farce, not forgiveness. The cost is high, but the value is higher.

What must I forgive? Not just the small things, the trivial irritations, the tactless, thoughtless mistakes others make. But everything. Even the hurts that cut and sear. There are no exemptions.

Seventy times seven.

*A great breakthrough in my life came when I had been
hurt and humiliated deeply by a friend. The experience
was so shattering that I was upset over it for weeks.
Finally I came to the place of desperation, because
I knew I had to be able to forgive freely in order to
have any peace in my own life. I prayed and prayed
every day — and the minute I got up from my knees,
the same old resentment rushed back. I kept on praying.*

*Finally one day she came to visit, and suddenly — the
moment I opened the door — the anger, hurt, resentment
had gone. I felt light and free. What had happened?
God had been busy. As I prayed to be able to forgive,
he brought to my mind some of the dark spots in my
own past — unkind words conveniently forgotten, petty
deceptions, neglected responsibilities, quite an apalling
list of misdeeds. These were things God hadn't "kept
account of" but had freely forgiven. As I remembered,
somehow my friend's offense against me kept shrinking
until at last it disappeared.*

*That's why nothing less than a constant remembering
of God's love toward us will do. Only against such
a vast portrait of love can our own little loves be seen
in proportion, and our forgiveness seen for what it is;
costly to us, but as nothing in light of the cost
of the Cross to God.*

Eileen Guder

THE WAY UP IS DOWN
by Mabel Francis

I have had many people in churches at home say to me, "Didn't you just feel like getting up and running away from Japan when it seemed that war was certain?"

In spite of the fact that I was an American, and treasured my own national citizenship, I had only one reason for being in Japan: God had called me when I was a young woman to be his ambassador in Japan. From the time I was a little child, I had the inward certainty that I'd be a missionary some day.

Memories of the living God at work in your own childhood can be a vital source of spiritual strength and encouragement when you've been separated from home and loved ones and country and comforts — in order to tell people about the love of Jesus.

I'm sure that almost daily in my childhood I had this feeling: "Our house is certainly a safe house, with Father praying, and with Mother trusting the Lord. How can there be any safety for people who don't pray?" (There were seven children in the family; I was the third.) I became a schoolteacher in my teens and then had opportunity as a girl preacher to explain the gospel in many communities in New Hampshire and Massachusetts. This was my youthful preparation for missionary work and service for Christ.

I struggled with the Japanese language, and though it was so difficult to learn, I had unusual joy in the process, for I would remind myself of the day that I could begin to use the language to communicate with these interesting people who were to become my adopted people.

That's why I didn't feel like running to safety when the dangers first became apparent in 1941. This is what the Lord said to me: "War cannot break out until I permit it, and when I do permit it, I will take care of you. There is no need to fear."

I remember the first sermon I tried to preach in the Japanese language. I told about the coming of Christ and about the ministry of Christ and about the ministry of John the Baptist. I said to them, "He lived on locusts and secrets." You see, the Japanese word for *secret* and the word for *honey* are very much alike. Well, I was close, anyway.

Even before I became fluent in Japanese, I could tell very quickly whether the hearers were really taking in the Christian message. Some, hearing it for the first time, understood and were saved, while with others it took a long time.

Very few have a consciousness of being sinners before they hear the gospel. I think most of the repentance, the true repentance, among the Japanese comes after they've accepted the being of the True God and have opened their hearts to him.

Then they must see the beauty of Christ on display in our lives. I look back now and remember many things that spoke to me of my need to know Christ in the crucified life, that I might not be a stumbling-block to the young Christians.

For instance, we had an elderly Japanese man in one of our groups. His salvation was indeed a miracle, and he would faithfully get up and give long testimonies, magnifying the Lord. But he had lost his teeth, and he couldn't talk plainly. No one could understand him very well. I used to sit there and pray, "O Lord, stop him. He's spoiling the meeting. Everything will go to pieces here."

One night the Lord spoke to me and said, "I can bless right over that old man. He is standing there trying to glorify me. But *you* do bother me," the Lord said, "by sitting here and fretting over it."

Then I was ashamed of the spirit I had. I saw it. And that's the way he took that fretting spirit out of my life. I just committed it to him.

During the time I was a student at Nyack Missionary Institute, I heard a guest missionary speaker make a statement in a chapel service that I couldn't believe at the time. She said, "While you're in school and while you're at home, you're busy praying for souls. When you get to the mission field, you'll find that you'll be often praying for yourself."

After I'd been in Japan for some time, I began to
realize what the speaker had meant. I'd had such
wonderful experiences with God at home, experiences
of seeing souls saved, and now — everything seemed
to shut down! The worst of it was that every little while
I saw this out-cropping of self — my own desires, my
own nature.

Now I had supposed that "self" had been properly dealt
with in my own earlier experiences. But on the field,
the Lord said to me, "My method of dealing with the
self-life is not cleansing. It is death!" And so God began
dealing with me about this. He spoke to me out of that
passage in Philippians, "He humbled himself, and became
a man, and then he went lower, and became a servant.
And then he went lower, and went to death. And
then he went lower and went to the death of the cross."

Through this the Spirit of God was saying to me,
"You will have to go lower yet, if you will follow me!"
I began searching and seeking the Lord with all my heart.
I thought he would surely come down upon me
with a wonderful anointing of the Spirit, and that would
be it. Then I'd be able to go out and win souls.
But, on the contrary, he let one terrible experience
after another come into my life, and each time I would
see some new form of the old life of self. When people
talked against me, I was upset and wanted to justify
myself. God dealt with me faithfully, step by step.
He spoke to me about Romans 7:4 — "Ye are dead . . .
that ye might be married to another." Married to him
"who is raised from the dead that we might bring forth
fruit to God."

I received glorious assurance that he was bringing me
into oneness with himself. That's what marriage means —
one with Christ, united with him, and that all
that he is, is mine.

I began to see that everything God allowed to come
into my life had a purpose. If he allowed someone
to be rude to me, the question was not about that person
but about how I would take it, how I would react.
God is always watching my reactions. From that time on,
no matter how painful the lesson, if it shed some
hitherto unknown light on the self-life, I could say,

"O Lord, I am thankful to you for showing me this."

I remember how God used Andrew Murray's book about humility in these steps down. "What is humility?" Andrew Murray asked. "Humility is never to be fretted, or vexed, or irritated, or sore, or disappointed." When I had read that far, I just threw the book down and wailed.

"Lord," I said, "I just don't know anything about humility. I do get vexed. I get irritated. I get sore."

And then I read on, "It is to wonder at nothing that is done to me. It is to feel no resentment against anybody or anything. It is to be at rest when nobody praises me, when I am blamed or suspected. It is to have a blessed home in the Lord, where we can go in and shut the door, and kneel to our Father in secret, and be at peace in the deep sea of calm when all around is in trouble."

I could only breathe a prayer, "Lord Jesus, make that a reality in me. I must have it!" And I thank him because he has. It's a reality and it is just glorious.

But he had to take me down step by step, until one morning, when I had been fasting and praying, his Word came to me, "If we are planted in the likeness of his death, we are in the likeness of his resurrection."

And it just seemed then as if death was over, and I was in the resurrection life. I knew what had taken place — God had brought me into oneness with his death. Not that there aren't other things to learn, but I knew that even at the core of my being, he had brought me into oneness with his death and that he had actually taken over control of my life. "It is no more I, but Christ!"

How I rejoiced in him, and from that time on, life and ministry have been so different. Troubles still come, but the fretting and the soreness are no longer there. At first, as I learned from him, I'd feel the little things. But God said, "I will hold you right there until you don't feel it any more, because I want you to be just as dead as Jesus was on the cross." You see, God doesn't want us to be living in struggling and trying to be like Christ, trying to do right, trying to be good. He wants us to let the Good One come and dwell within us. In order for that really to take place, we have to subside: "I must decrease but he must increase."

Another gracious experience came to me in Japan at a time when I had been trying to extend myself too far physically. I was sick and came to the point of what we call a nervous breakdown. Then the Lord reminded me, "The Lord thy God in the midst of thee." In faith and simplicity I said to the Lord, "You are what I need. I claim you as my 'inside' God. Lord, I'm going to trust you for your complete work in every nerve center in my body, because you have promised," I prayed earnestly.

God proved his faithfulness, and every nerve was healed and the condition was gone completely. For all these years, I haven't even known that I have any nerves, because his resurrection life has been flowing through me. I am stronger in my 90s than I was many years ago, before I found the secret of the Lord, my "inside" God!

Epilogue

The Japanese people in their darkest hours caught a realistic glimpse of the saving grace and compassionate love of Jesus Christ, the Savior of the world. They saw the gospel of Christ walking about in their ruined streets in the person of Miss Mabel Francis.

In 1962, when she had reached the age of 81 but had scarcely slowed down in her energetic career of preaching, teaching, and concern for the Japanese people, Miss Francis was asked to appear before the nation's highest officials. She was presented with a beautiful parchment scroll bearing the Emperor's seal and detailing her services to the Japanese people. Then she was given an unusual gold medal, conferring upon her the unique honor of membership in the highly exclusive Fifth Order of the Sacred Treasure.

Prior to this award ceremony in 1962, it had been the custom of the Emperor to bestow the medal as the highest civilian award upon Japanese who had served their country in some unusual way, but who had also passed on into eternity.

"Why have I been chosen?" Miss Francis asked herself.

After the war, she had helped feed the hungry, and she had visited those who were sick. She visited

others who were in prison. She took the children to
her heart and worked to better their conditions and their
opportunities.

Small wonder that there was always something more
for her to do in Japan. Small wonder that she took only
a brief furlough in the United States in 1962 and
returned to her life work in Japan at the age of 83!

She has continued her effective retirement ministry
from coast to coast, even though she reached her 92nd
birthday in August 1972. She continually urges Christian
young people to consider service in Japan, which
she has had to relinquish.

In a Life Investment Conference for young people
of The Christian and Missionary Alliance, a television
news reporter referred to Miss Francis as "a livin' doll."

"Bring that young man back," she said when she heard
about it. "Tell him that I'm an old war horse,
with still a lot to get done for the Lord!"

Make me Thy fuel

From prayer that asks that I may be
Sheltered from winds that beat on Thee,
From fearing when I should aspire,
From faltering when I should climb higher,
From silken self, O Captain, free
Thy soldier who would follow Thee.

From subtle love of softening things,
From easy choices, weakenings
(Not thus are spirits fortified,
Not this way went the Crucified),
From all that dims Thy Calvary,
O Lamb of God, deliver me.

Give me the love that leads the way,
The faith that nothing can dismay,
The hope no disappointments tire,
The passion that will burn like fire;
Let me not sink to be a clod;
Make me Thy fuel, Flame of God.

Amy Carmichael

FIND YOUR PLACE IN THE CHURCH
by Lois Bartel

The man in the Parable of the Talents who hid all his money wasn't praised for his caution. If Christ was referring only to money when he gave this illustration, many of us can forget about it, since we have little money to bury.

But the parable catches us too. Christ wasn't as concerned about money as he was about the servants. The talents he told about symbolize our abilities and and our natural gifts. Talents such as the ability to sing a solo or to paint a picture are included, but equally important are the small talents which, when added together and used properly, actually become the most dynamic. If we aren't stewards of these, their potential will be lost.

What does it mean to be a steward? It implies being included in the management of God's estate. We become God's stewards immediately after we become his children. As God's stewards it's inconsistent to believe we own anything, for he owns us. Do you think it selfish of God to claim ultimate ownership of all we possess?

God didn't institute stewardship for his own sake. Milo Kauffman writes: "Christian stewardship inevitably will result in enrichment of life. The greatest value of Christian stewardship is what it does for the individual. When Jesus told the rich young ruler to sell what he had and give to the poor, it wasn't the money that Jesus was especially interested in, it was the young man. It was the rich ruler that Jesus loved, not his possessions.

"Christian stewardship frees us from the tyranny of things, and helps us to a life of freedom and joy through the contribution of self, time, talents, and money to the advancement of the kingdom of Christ . . . Christian stewardship helps make God real to us. Thinking of God as the owner of our lives, our time, our talent, and our possessions helps us to think of him as a living personality."

To be God's stewards we must first know what we are

to be stewards of. Of course we are stewards of all God has given us: love, good health, good family, good friends, good home, good looks, education, talent, influence, social leadership, popularity, business ability, wages, income, material possessions.

And yet, isn't each of us responsible to find and use our special "talents"? This requires utmost honesty. Yet it's necessary. "What if I do with ardor what a thousand could, maybe/and leave undone forever what was only meant for me?"

Feelings of incompetence often keep us from venturing out in areas in which we don't feel secure. Why do we let feelings of incompetence limit us? Where would Helen Keller be if she had said, "I can't"?

Isn't it an insult to our Creator if we don't even recognize the gifts he gives us? If we sincerely believe we are made in God's image, we are bound to find strength and ability. Is our God too small, or can we let him use his creativity by letting it flow through us? If we become convinced that we must put ourselves to use, the results may surprise us.

E. Stanley Jones says, "It cannot be insisted too much that abundant living means abundant giving. . . . Just as you would smother yourself to death if you only breathed in and refused to breathe out, so if you are not outgoing, the whole process of incoming will stop, and you will die spiritually, mentally, and physically. If a cow isn't milked, it will go dry. If you aren't giving out to others, you, too, will go dry in spirit."

The visible church couldn't exist unless people were willing to contribute their talents and abilities. Such actions not only strengthen the church but also the individual involved. Working and praying together will bind Christ's church closer to him. Joseph Murray writes, "The more you do, the more you'll be asked to do. That is the blessed penalty for willingness. The more you do, the more you'll be able to do. That is the blessed law of effort. The more you do, the more it will mean to you. That is the blessed promise of reward in the Master's service. They know him best who serve him most."

Those serving in the church program should never do it

as a duty, but because they want to serve God. In a Sunday morning message, Victor Sawatsky referred to the Parable of the Talents. He compared the hiding of the talents to the individual who refuses to take any office in the church because he is afraid of becoming involved. The key word, he said, is "afraid." Some women won't teach a class because they're afraid of making mistakes and of having people laugh at them. They are afraid of saying the wrong thing and offending someone, afraid of opposition in any office. In other words, they are afraid to take upon themselves the self-discipline involved in holding any office in church.

Love for Christ, he continued, is the highest motive for service and the greatest force for faithfulness. He concluded, "We should give our best talent to the office, however small it may be. May we give of ourselves in living service to Christ and overcome our fear of becoming involved."

Since we've been made in the image of our Creator, we too should be creating — not only art and music, but also joy, understanding, and love. A mature steward will change privileges into responsibilities. May our prayer be that God will guide us to a life of greater stewardship of the abilities he has given us.

PUT ON YOUR COFFEE POT

by Helen Kooiman

What is a cup of coffee? To the coffee producer, it's aroma, tantalizing flavor, satisfaction, and money in the bank. To the man on the job, office worker, clerk, homemaker, the few moments spent over a cup of coffee are a refreshing pause in the day's work. But for the Christian it can be something more. It became something more for Mary Ann Mooney of Fullerton, California.

Mary Ann's hands ceased their busy activity. It was time for her mid-morning cup of coffee. But more important, it was her "quiet time." The thoughts she had been thinking came out in a fervent prayer, "Father, make me more useful."

Far across town, Irene glanced at the clock. Irene, who had ministered with her surgeon husband on the African mission field, bowed her head. The family had to leave Africa when their daughter contracted malaria. Irene could no longer contain a certain thought as she cried out, "Father, I feel so useless now. O Father, make me more useful."

That afternoon, Mary Ann put legs on her morning prayer as she went to the phone. "Irene, this is Mary Ann. I've asked God to make me more useful. We pray about our neighbors, but it's not enough. We've got to tell them about Christ. If I had a once-a-week get-together in our home, would you lead a Bible study?"

On the other end of the phone, Irene was speechless. She recognized this as an answer to prayer.

During a year and a half, more than eighty women walked through Mary Ann's door, sipped coffee out of "consecrated coffee cups" and heard the gospel. Many were introduced to Jesus Christ for the first time.

There was Naomi who came and listened, not only once but often. Each time she listened intently. Then the day came when Naomi said, "I am convinced that Jesus Christ was the Messiah."

Mary Ann and Irene saw women come who were anxious to discuss things in an informal atmosphere that they wouldn't discuss with pastors or others. Many came from a liberal church background, who believed that as long as you go to church now and then and live a good life you're on the road to heaven. The words "sin" and "salvation" were shunned and Jesus Christ was a stranger.

Another was DeeEtte, frustrated, unhappy, rebellious, constantly under a psychiatrist's care, so distraught that she had attempted suicide. She, too, heard the Word: "For all have sinned, and come short of the glory of God" (Romans 3:23).

That was two years ago. When Irene's husband began his surgical practice, Irene was needed. Mary Ann's "consecrated coffee cups" remained silent on the shelf. Once again she sought new direction in prayer. It was a time of waiting, a time of preparation. She longed to introduce others to Christ and his Word. She was restless, missing the weekly opportunity of sharing her home, hospitality, and love for her Savior with neighbors, their friends, and the strangers who came.

Then one day Margie, a Christian friend, phoned. Within a few days Mary Ann was surrounded by faces she had never seen, in Margie's home. God had answered prayer. This time Mary Ann was leading the Bible study. She'll never forget the morning when everyone's coffee cup poised surprised when four women came through Margie's front door carrying Leslie, who was paralyzed. Leslie, PTA president, was vivacious, lovely, charming, and intelligent, but she was in need of the Savior. Often Mary Ann thought, it takes several to bring just one to Jesus, and remembered the palsied man lowered through the roof by friends.

Soon Jane, another friend, requested that Mary Ann lead *her* neighbors in a weekly coffee-hour Bible study. I asked Jane how she invited them. "I phoned some, others I visited personally. I told them on Tuesday mornings I'd like them to come for coffee and to hear a friend lead a Bible study."

"Jane, were you concerned what they might think of you?"

"In a way, but the first few were so willing, even
anxious, I knew I was doing the right thing. It didn't
matter what they thought of me. The important thing
was introducing them to Christ and his Word."

There are many wonderful stories; I can share just a few.

Jane invited Olga, who brought another friend.
The study was in John 3 that morning. After the study
Olga invited her friend for lunch. She was troubled
and replied, "First I've got to go home, find my Bible,
and see if what we heard is the same in our Bible."
When she came back, they compared Bible translations.
When she saw that her Bible also said, "Except a man
be born again, he cannot see the kingdom of God"
(John 3:3), Olga's friend was convinced.

There was Midge, whose mother had been killed.
It left her bitter and she turned to the teaching of a cult.
Midge came to the Coffee-Bible Study more out of
curiosity than anything. Afterwards she approached
Mary Ann and wistfully said, "You know, I remember
being taught these things by my mother when I was
a little girl. . . ." Today Midge, her husband, and son
are attending an evangelical church faithfully.

Or consider Trudy, unable to accept love, according
to psychiatrists — just home from a sanitarium when
she first came. After six months she said, "This has done
more for me than anything else. For the first time in
my life I can now accept love, God's love through Christ."

Jerry was investigating a false "ism" in her search for
something to fill the aching void in her life. On her
first visit she openly received Christ. She was a leading
anti-Communist worker but sensed something lacking.
She knew what she was against — Communism —
but she didn't know what she was for.

When Joyce's car broke down in front of Jane's house
she used Jane's phone. Jane invited her to the Bible
study. She came. Today Joyce, her husband, and their
five children are Christians.

As the group grew, one neighbor telling another
neighbor or friend, the women's concern for their husbands
deepened. Two husband and wife evening get-togethers
were planned. Both Margie and Jane's homes were filled.
The Moody film *Red River of Life* was shown.

Women, practical creatures, are bound to have questions. What do you do with children? Enlist the help of a Christian friend and provide babysitting in your home. If you have a Christian neighbor, explain the idea and perhaps she would open her home for youngsters. Or hire a babysitter.

But what do you study? How do you begin? Mary Ann began with the Gospel of John. She emphasizes the need to avoid "hopscotching" through the Bible; but rather to use the verse-by-verse, one-book-at-a-time method. "Don't expect them to look up other portions of Scripture as you proceed. Remember, for the most part, these women are unfamiliar with the Bible. Nothing is more embarrassing than to sit fumbling." She also urges that you use only the Bible. She encourages reading Christian books and magazines, and lends her own and friends' reading materials, but in the study itself only the Bible is used.

She also stresses the need to avoid discussing what, in our Christian circles, we often refer to as "deeper things." "It's like teaching trigonometry to a first grader," she says.

Practically, she suggests that you offer a good cup of coffee and a roll, cookie, or doughnut when they arrive. Keep it simple and the coffee session brief. You'll find your neighbors offering to furnish the refreshments from time to time. Let them. It makes them feel an integral part of what's going on and encourages them to come back.

Follow the coffee-break with the Bible study. Procedure is simple. The leader asks someone to read a verse or a specified number of verses. She then gives a brief explanation and often uses illustrations. Questions and comments are invited. There is, at all times, free interchange of ideas. It's important that the leader not dominate the conversation though it's essential she be well prepared.

There will be those who make excuses. "But I'm not a qualified Bible teacher like Mary Ann, nor a returned missionary like Irene." God isn't asking for your qualifications. "It is required in stewards, that a man be found faithful" (1 Corinthians 4:2). Faithfulness. And

hasn't he promised to supply our every need?
"But my God shall supply all your need according to his riches in glory by Christ Jesus" (Philippians 4:19).

I'm convinced that this is practical New Testament Christianity. I've seen the Holy Spirit at work: I've witnessed changed lives. The Bible is liberally illustrated with evidence that the early Christians opened their homes and invited people to come in. Why should today's Christians do less?

Do you want to make this a more meaningful year for Christ? Are you really concerned for those neighbors up and down your street who don't know your Lord? Or is it just so much "talk" with you and your Christian friends? Are you satisfied with your exclusive little Christian clique, or does your heart yearn that others will know the peace and joy of being in Christ?

Open your home. Walk up and down your street, get on the phone. But invite them. Ask that Christian friend who's a good Sunday school teacher, or someone you know who really studies her Bible to lead, but do it! Present the idea in your church women's group. Help each other. The possibilities are tremendous. Jesus said, "Hurry out now into the streets and alleys of the town . . . go out to the roads . . . and make them come inside, so that my house may be full. . . . (Luke 14:21-23, Phillips).

DON'T LIMIT GOD

by Frances Gardner Hunter

I always get a kick out of people who give excuses for not witnessing and sharing the exciting news of Jesus Christ with their friends and relatives. And often I've been given statistics about the ages when people are most receptive to accepting Christ as their Savior. Statistics do bear out the fact that every Christian should concentrate on those in their early teens. This is when the ground is most fertile, when human beings are most receptive and most searching.

But whenever I hear this I wonder where I'd have been today if someone hadn't realized that age is no barrier to God. Becoming a Christian at the age of forty-eight or forty-nine, as I did, knocks a loop in most statistics and proves that *nothing* is impossible to God.

Recently I attended a Lay Institute for Evangelism put on by Campus Crusade for Christ. I listened to a dynamic Christian tell how he was obsessed with witnessing after he became a Christian. And yet the thing that meant most to him, the thing he loved most in life, he was unable to communicate to his own father.

I heard him tell how he as an individual had tried to persuade his dad to accept Christ. And how he finally realized he wasn't allowing God's love to show through him to communicate with his father. And how he was relying on himself and his desire to win another person to Christ instead of allowing the Holy Spirit to work through him. Suddenly the Holy Spirit convicted me about my own beloved mother-in-law.

I had discussed Christianity in a fainthearted sort of way with her. Because I have such great respect for her I didn't want to hurt her feelings by disagreeing with her. (Of course, I apparently didn't care whether she went to hell or not; I just didn't want to hurt her feelings while she was on this earth!)

Grandma had a traumatic experience with "church" when she was a very young girl. Her family always felt "you can be just as good outside a church as inside, because that's where the hypocrites are — inside," so there was just no need to attend church regularly.

When I talked with Grandma, I would always start off mildly with one or two little words, and then she would boom back at me, "Now, you let me tell you what's wrong with churches!" And then I would sit there for the next hour and listen to her tell me what was wrong with churches, because I didn't want to disagree with her or "hurt her feelings."

We always ended such discussion with her saying, "And you just watch out for those buzzards. All they're after is your money and they'll take every cent they can get."

Then she'd add, "And I'll tell you how I know. These friends of mine had a baby who died. They were destitute, and had no money to pay a preacher for a funeral service or anything. But they wanted their baby buried from a church, and the undertaker took the little casket there, and the church wouldn't let him bring the body in because the parents didn't have any money." And then she'd smile and say, "See, all they want is money out of people."

Finally, after a while, I just quit arguing with her at all, and finally my visits down there became further and further apart because I "knew" it was impossible to talk to her about the love of God and yet I couldn't stand to sit there and hear her say things I knew weren't the truth.

The tremendous tugging on my heart at the institute became a real pounding as the Holy Spirit spoke louder and louder to me about Grandma. And so I knew I could do only one thing.

I almost ran out to my car obsessed with one idea. I knew I had to let God's Holy Spirit use me that night as a channel for the words he wanted spoken. I was about thirty miles from where Grandma lives, and while I don't particularly enjoy night driving, *nothing* could have kept me from her home. And for the first time before going to visit her, I did what I should have done all along: I prayed! And I prayed! And I prayed!

I was so wound up from the exhilarating conversation

with God that when I got to Grandma's home, I felt
as if I'd been catapulted from my car as I opened the
door. By this time it was ten o'clock at night, but I
couldn't have cared less. All I knew was that God had
spoken and that *this was the night.*

Grandma was concerned when she saw who it was at
that hour, and naturally thought something was wrong
with my children. I assured her nothing was wrong with
my family, and that I was fine, and nothing was
wrong with me. But I also knew that God had sent me
down there for one purpose, and that wasn't for ordinary
chitchat, so I blurted out, "Grandma, do you know
why I came down here tonight?" I didn't even pause.
Since I'd relinquished myself to God's will, he took
over for me, and this is what happened:

I continued, "Grandma, you're eighty-six years old,
and you're as healthy as can be, but at your age you
could die tomorrow, and I *love you,* Grandma, and I
don't want you to go to hell!"

And then she said, "Now, let me tell you what's
wrong with churches!"

And do you know what I heard myself say? I said,
"Oh, no you don't. Now you listen to me, and I'll tell
you what's wrong with churches, and I ought to know
because I get in a lot more churches than you do."
Then I continued: "But I'm not here to tell you what's
wrong with churches tonight, Grandma, I'm only here
to tell you the plain truth about Jesus Christ. I want you
to know that God loves you, Grandma, and even
at your age, he has a plan for your life."

And so I shared with her the exciting story of how God
loved us so much that he sent "his only begotten Son,
that whosoever believeth in him should not perish, but
have everlasting life" (John 3:16b).

Sometimes it's impossible for us to believe that someone
could have lived a whole lifetime and never heard
the simple truth of the gospel. And yet it's true.

I reminded Grandma that God loved her so much
that he wanted her to spend eternity with him, and when
we realize how little time we actually spend on this earth
in comparison with eternity, we realize that eternal life
is far more important than temporal life.

I brought out the Four Spiritual Laws booklet, which is my favorite simplified way of soul winning, gave her a copy, and asked her to read along with me as I went through the various steps. When I got to the third law I very carefully went into the story of Nicodemus, and the necessity of being born again (or being born "from above"), the necessity for a spiritual birthday as well as a physical birthday. In other words, that time comes when you must make the decision to accept Christ, and this establishes your spiritual birthday.

Watching her rebelliousness and "let me tell you what's wrong with churches" attitude, I saw her shoulders stiffen, and I prayed even harder as I read the laws to her. And then I saw and felt the mighty power of God again as I saw this 86-year-old woman turn into a mass of jelly right in front of my eyes. I saw her shoulders drop. I saw a look in her eyes I'd never seen before. Then I saw her face light up, and I realized how we limit God many times.

Very simply I said, "Grandma, is there any reason why you don't want to accept Christ right now?"

And she looked at me with a perfectly beautiful, angelic look and said, "No, Honey, there isn't."

Then I said, "All right, Grandma, on the next page there's a prayer of repentance, and because the light isn't so good, and because the print is little, I'll read it to you, and you say it after me as you invite Christ into your life."

Grandma grabbed my copy of the Four Spiritual Laws out of my hand and said, "You'll do no such thing. I'll read them and pray *myself*." My cup of joy overflowed as I heard her ask God to forgive her and as she invited Christ into her life.

Then I said, "Grandma, where is Christ right now?"

She said, "In my heart, where do you think?"

The Holy Spirit had done the job again, and the angels in heaven must have rejoiced that night.

I'd like to reassure you of one fact: It's not a sin never to win someone to Christ, *but it's a sin not to try*.

Do you believe the Bible and what it says? Then you'll have to believe what the book of Acts has to say about the power to witness. It simply says all we have to do is appropriate the power of the Holy Spirit, because the Holy Spirit will give us boldness to witness. It doesn't say that only a few will be bold. It says the Holy Spirit will so empower your life that you'll be able to witness even to the ends of the earth. And it means *you* and *me,* every Christian. And I believe what the Bible says.

Is your Christianity alive? Is Christ such a compelling force in your life that you yourself have actually come alive? Does he really live his life through you? If he does, then I'm sure you're out on the battlefront witnessing. But if he doesn't, I'd like to suggest that witnessing starts at home!

The fate of Christianity is dependent not on the corporate, somewhat anonymous and amorphous body called the church as much as on individual Christians with a living faith.

Harry Hiller

FINDING PEACE IN DARK HOURS
by Elizabeth Strachan

George Bernard Shaw once commented that if the other planets are inhabited, they must be using this one as their insane asylum.

H. L. Mencken observed: "The cosmos is a gigantic flywheel making 10,000 revolutions a minute. Man is a sick fly taking a ride on it. Religion is the theory that the wheel was designed and set spinning to give him the ride."

But it isn't only cynics who find slings of outrageous fortune difficult to accept and to explain. There will be no one reading this article, even the most fortunate, who won't be carrying in his heart some pain, some unfilled longing, a burden. And no one reading this (unless he is a religious egotist like Job's friends) will know the full and final answer to his suffering. God doesn't seem eager to explain the why of our trials, but he asks us to believe that every one of them is necessary, an inevitable "thus it must be" for us, just as it was for our Lord in his life on earth. And he gives us light and help along the way.

I want to share a little formula that gives some of the light by which I try to steer in the darkness, practices I've found helpful in those times when it seems as though God has forsaken me. I didn't find the formula in a book, but it has been hammered out, as it were, in personal experience.

The first step is to get some strong word from Scripture and cling to it. To be honest, many passages in Scripture are difficult to understand, many assaults of the higher critics are difficult to refute, but there is one indisputable fact: unique power, comfort, and strength are found in the words of the Bible. I like the verse that says he sent his Word and healed them (Psalm 107:20).

A friend who suddenly lost her husband of forty-five years cried out, "O God, give me something. Give me something." As she knelt beside her husband's lifeless body, she thought she heard God saying to her over and over again, "My grace is sufficient for thee. My grace is sufficient for thee" (2 Corinthians 12:9). And she arose comforted and strengthened for the hard days ahead.

Step number two is to begin praising the Lord. Preposterous though it may appear, we are told, in everything give thanks (1 Thessalonians 5:18). Yet inexplicably, peace and joy follow the giving of thanks and the worship of God. This is especially true in those times when it seems as though God has let us down. If in the darkness we can say, "Lord, I don't understand any of this, but I do — by faith — love and praise and thank you," peace comes.

The third step: think about God. "Thou wilt keep him in perfect peace, whose mind is stayed on thee because he trusts in thee" (Isaiah 26:3). God is the x in the equation of life, without which there is no answer. In the midst of our troubles, by a deliberate act of the will, we can pause and think about God himself: "God is a Spirit, infinite, eternal and unchanging in his mercy, justice, goodness and holiness. And God loves me. He loves me just as I am. There will never be a time when he loves me more than he does right this minute. He is with me. He is for me. 'Say not, my soul, from whence can God relieve thy care? Remember that Omnipotence hath servants everywhere.' "

Phillip once said, "Lord, show us the Father and we will ask for nothing more" (John 14:8). I'm sure that if we could get even a faint glimpse of what the Father is really like, the purposes of his love toward us and toward all mankind, we would say with Paul that whatever we may have to go through now is less than nothing compared with the magnificent future God has planned for us (Romans 8:18). He who has God-and-everything-else has no more than he who has God only.

Number four is to pray — to tell God what we wish he would do about the problem. Let your requests be made known unto God (Phillipians 4:6). Prayer is not a magic button to press to get what we want. It's better than that. It's spreading out our needs and desires before the Father, knowing he will give us what we ask, or he will give us something better.

George MacDonald touches a deep truth when he says, "What if God knows prayer to be the thing we need first and most? What if the main object in God's idea of prayer is the supplying of our great, our endless need, the need of Himself? Hunger may drive the runaway child home, and he may or may not be fed at once, but he needs his mother more than his dinner. Communion with God is the one need of the soul beyond all other need. Prayer is the beginning of that communion, and some need is the motive of that prayer. So begins a communion, a talking with God a coming to one with Him, which is the sole end of prayer, yea, of existence itself in its infinite phases. We must ask that we may receive, but that we should receive what we ask in respect to our lower needs, is not God's end in making us pray. To bring His child to His knee, God withholds that man may ask."

The last step in the formula is an earthy one: get to work. After we have done the first four things, then it's time to go and do our next job. Paul tells us to work with our own hands (1 Thessalonians 4:11). To quote MacDonald again, "Bethink of something that thou oughtest to do, and go to do it, if it be but the sweeping of a room or the preparing of a meal, or a visit to a friend. Heed not thy feelings. Do thy work."

In Costa Rica there is a missionary of whom the nationals often speak. Only rarely do they mention something she has said. Usually it is something she has inconspicuously done: curtains she made for a young mother who is ill, a sick orphan she took into her home, an abandoned wife she befriended. This missionary makes it easier for everyone to believe the everlasting gospel — the incredible news that God loves us and has made complete provision for our redemption in the death of his Son — because they've seen that Divine Love shining in her.

The invisible God, who seldom explains his strange providences with us, asks us to serve our neighbor (Galatians 5:13). It can become a turning point in our lives (and incidentally a living answer to the cynics) when we choose not to be served, but to serve. No one needs to live in unmitigated loneliness or despair as long as there is one other human being to whom he can minister. And we will find as did St. Theresa that "though we do not have our Lord with us in bodily presence, we have our neighbor, who, for the ends of love and loving service, is as good as our Lord himself." And since none of us is ever far from some needy neighbor, the comfort of him who alone can lift burdens and in whose presence there is joy, can always be found close at hand.

God is in every tomorrow

God is in every tomorrow,
Therefore I live for today,
Certain of finding at sunrise,
Guidance and strength for the day;
Power for each moment of weakness;
Hope for each moment of pain,
Comfort for every sorrow,
Sunshine and joy after rain.

God is in every tomorrow,
Planning for you and for me;
E'en in the dark will I follow,
Trust where my eyes cannot see.
Stilled by His promise of blessing,
Soothed by the touch of His hand,
Confident in His protection,
Knowing my life-path is planned.

God is in every tomorrow,
Life with its changes may come,
He is behind and before me,
While in the distance shines Home!
Home where no thoughts of tomorrow
Ever can shadow my brow,
Home in the presence of Jesus,
Through all eternity now!

Anonymous